Wolf by the Ears

Witness to History

Peter Charles Hoffer and Williamjames Hull Hoffer, *Series Editors*

Williamjames Hull Hoffer, *The Caning of Charles Sumner: Honor, Idealism, and the Origins of the Civil War*

Tim Lehman, *Bloodshed at Little Bighorn: Sitting Bull, Custer, and the Destinies of Nations*

Daniel R. Mandell, *King Philip's War: Colonial Expansion, Native Resistance, and the End of Indian Sovereignty*

Erik R. Seeman, *The Huron-Wendat Feast of the Dead: Indian-European Encounters in Early North America*

Peter Charles Hoffer, *When Benjamin Franklin Met the Reverend Whitefield: Enlightenment, Revival, and the Power of the Printed Word*

William Thomas Allison, *My Lai: An American Atrocity in the Vietnam War*

Peter Charles Hoffer, *Prelude to Revolution: The Salem Gunpowder Raid of 1775*

Michael Dennis, *Blood on Steel: Chicago Steelworkers and the Strike of 1937*

Benjamin F. Alexander, *Coxey's Army: Popular Protest in the Gilded Age*

Donald R. Hickey, *Glorious Victory: Andrew Jackson and the Battle of New Orleans*

Wolf by the Ears

The Missouri Crisis, 1819–1821

JOHN R. VAN ATTA

Johns Hopkins University Press | Baltimore

© 2015 Johns Hopkins University Press
All rights reserved. Published 2015
Printed in the United States of America on acid-free paper
9 8 7 6 5 4 3 2 1

Johns Hopkins University Press
2715 North Charles Street
Baltimore, Maryland 21218-4363
www.press.jhu.edu

Library of Congress Cataloging-in-Publication Data

Van Atta, John Robert.
   Wolf by the ears : the Missouri crisis, 1819–1821 / John R. Van Atta.
      pages cm. — (Witness to history)
   Includes bibliographical references and index.
   ISBN 978-1-4214-1652-6 (hardcover : acid-free paper) —
ISBN 1-4214-1652-2 (hardcover : acid-free paper) — ISBN 978-1-4214-1653-3
(paperback : acid-free paper) — ISBN 1-4214-1653-0 (paperback : acid-
free paper) — ISBN 978-1-4214-1654-0 (electronic) — ISBN 1-4214-1654-9
(electronic) 1. Missouri compromise. 2. Slavery—Political aspects—United
States—History—19th century. 3. Slavery—United States—Extension to the
territories. 4. United States—Politics and government—1817–1825. 5. United
States—Territorial expansion—History—19th century. 6. Sectionalism
(United States)—History—19th century. 7. Missouri—Politics and
government—To 1865. I. Title.
   E373.V23 2015
   973.5'4—dc23   2014033402

A catalog record for this book is available from the British Library.

Special discounts are available for bulk purchases of this book.
For more information, please contact Special Sales at 410-516-6936 or
specialsales@press.jhu.edu.

Johns Hopkins University Press uses environmentally friendly book
materials, including recycled text paper that is composed of at least
30 percent post-consumer waste, whenever possible.

For the two Lucys, once again

Contents

Preface

THE SECTIONAL conflict that led to the Civil War supplied plenty of historical drama over the years, never more so than in the fight over Missouri statehood, which first surfaced in Congress in 1819 and did not grow seemingly quiet until early 1821. At the time, Thomas Jefferson said that dealing with the implacable issue of slavery in national politics resembled trying to hold a "wolf" by the ears. Focusing on whether federal lawmakers should, or even could, prevent slavery from spreading beyond the Mississippi River, the "Missouri crisis" provided the first full-blown sectional controversy in U.S. history. This fight held potential to end the fragile Union then and there. Angry exchanges during the Missouri debate proved as heated as any in the sectional disputes that followed and led to southern secession in 1860–1861, and while the Missouri confrontation *appeared* to finish amicably with a famous compromise, the passions it unleashed proved bitter in the extreme, widespread, and long lasting.

In North-versus-South struggles after 1820, the language that antagonists employed always seemed reminiscent of this earlier crisis, but why did pent-up feelings explode in 1819–1821—and not at earlier moments when the subject of slavery had arisen? The answer, in large part, is that the Missouri crisis revealed the power that slavery by then had gained over American *nation-building*, an impulse that fueled both anti- and pro-slavery convictions. Thus the need to focus on the larger historical processes at work in the years leading up to 1820, as revealed not only in Congress but also at the grassroots level—in towns, hotels, and taverns, churches, state houses, lecture halls, and the like, all around the country—a far broader "public sphere" than that of Washington, DC, alone.

It is now possible to tell a story of the Missouri question that is somewhat different from those told before. Recent insights have opened room in the literature for new angles of vision. In years past, historians have paid more attention to the *internal* political dynamics of the crisis—the strategies within the debate itself, the implications for party development, the mechanics of congressional deal making, and so on—than to the *external* social, cultural, and economic forces that gave the confrontation such urgency in the first place, informed the participants of the debate, and generated much of the reaction afterward. This book attempts, briefly, to unpack the crisis from that old box, examining the outside stimuli that gave the confrontation in Washington such resonance around the country.

The following discussion broadly tracks the slavery issue from the Revolution to the Civil War, with a primary goal of looking ahead to, concentrating on, and relating back to the events of 1819–1821. The analytical emphasis falls *less* on the insider politics detailed in other studies and *more* on beliefs, assumptions, fears, and reactions on both sides of the slavery argument. Some might fault this approach as "missing the trees for the forest." But that vast, tangled forest is where one finds the keys to changing sectional perceptions that distinguished the Missouri crisis from previous crises, animating not just the politicians in power but many other Americans at the time and later.

Acknowledgments

I ESPECIALLY wish to thank my editor and longtime friend, Robert J. Brugger, for encouraging me to undertake this volume. Thanks, also, to series editor Peter C. Hoffer of the University of Georgia and all at Johns Hopkins University Press for their scrupulous assistance. My appreciation extends furthermore to Glenn Perkins for his thorough and intelligent copyediting. My brother, Matthew E. Van Atta, took care of the indexing. Anonymous readers provided first-rate commentary and helpful suggestions. I owe a debt of gratitude, as well, to my good friends (and SHEAR poker buddies) John Belohlavek and John Ifkovic for reading earlier versions of the manuscript and for the improvements they recommended.

At the Brunswick School, thanks to the students, friends, and colleagues who expressed interest and gave support in various ways. Margot Gibson-Beattie applied her valuable talents once again by creating all of the maps, and technology genius Sunil Gupta converted them into publishable files.

Robert E. Kennedy, S.J., has been for many years my second father and the best of spiritual guides. My daughter, Lucy Rose Van Atta, mined some valuable nuggets of primary source material for me. As in previous efforts, I dedicate this book to *both* Lucys in my life, the greater and the lesser.

Wolf by the Ears

prologue

Knell of the Union?

ON FEBRUARY 13, 1820, Secretary of State John Quincy Adams and House Speaker Henry Clay walked home together from the newly reconstructed Capitol. The anxiety probably registered in their faces as well as in their words. For days, the city had been awash with rumors of disunion. The storm in Congress over the Missouri question—how, or whether, to admit the Missouri Territory to the Union as a new slave state—continued to rage without any certainty of breaking.

This crisis had begun exactly one year earlier, when New York congressman James Tallmadge had proposed an amendment to the bill to make Missouri the twenty-third member (after Alabama) of the United States. That amendment would have required the new state's constitution to ban any further entry of slaves within its borders and mandate that all human chattels born there after 1819 become free at age twenty-five. Antislavery northerners insisted that Congress had every right to deny Missouri's application if it would not accept these conditions and looked toward prohibition of slavery as a prerequisite for all further states west of the Mississippi River. Proslavery southerners replied that the Union consisted of equal states, with freedom to decide, each for itself, whether it be slave or free.

It was shocking to think of it, Clay told Adams, but he "had not a doubt that within five years from this time the Union would be divided into three distinct confederacies"—northern, southern, and western. Adams himself must have wondered whether his own moral obligation to oppose slavery mattered more than keeping together a Union that his father had helped to construct. Elsewhere in Washington, Secretary of War John C. Calhoun gloomily pondered that a collapse of the Union would force the South toward a defensive alliance with Great Britain, in effect returning it to a "colonial state." Was America's "great experiment" in republicanism about to prove pathetically short lived?[1]

A glimmer of hope appeared on February 16, when the Senate passed, 23 to 21, a proposition to admit Maine as a free state in return for Missouri's entrance without restriction on slaveholding, but in the House the anti-Missouri majority still refused. The following day, Senator Jesse B. Thomas of Illinois introduced the compromise amendment that a majority of senators saw as the only way to end the crisis: in return for admission of Missouri on its own terms, a line at 36°30' latitude, banning further introduction of slavery in the northern part of the Louisiana Purchase. The House majority remained obdurate, but bargain making behind the scenes, including President James Monroe's subtle efforts, opened the possibility of a breakthrough. Finally, on March 2, 1820, the Thomas Amendment succeeded by a paper-thin House margin of 90 to 87. Only a few northerners had defected, but these votes mattered critically. "The Constitution is a creature of compromise," as one, James Stevens of Connecticut, explained; "it originated in a compromise; and has existed ever since by a perpetual extension and exercise of that principle; and must continue to do so, as long as it lasts."[2]

The Missouri solution thus became national policy for the decades to come, an indisputable turning point in the history of the early republic. On the volatile matter of slavery, one crisis had been met and passed. Whether others, more frightening, lay still ahead remained anyone's guess.

From the time of the Continental Congress, American leaders had understood that an unpredictable time bomb—the question of slavery—lay at the heart of national politics. During the early decades of the republic, an implicit covenant between North and South helped to keep this slavery issue at bay. That agreement was that northern states, where slavery had been set on course for extinction via gradual emancipation, would respect the property rights of southern slaveholders. In return, southerners would view slaveholding as a practical, if not moral, evil and look for ways to get rid of it. Meanwhile, the Constitution of the United States in 1787 had promised to protect slaveholders' rights within a nationalist framework of compromises meant to keep the peace between sections, encourage prosperity, and promote common values despite extensive differences in politics, economy, and culture between the member states of that precarious union.[3]

By the post–War of 1812 period, however, this understanding had started to break down in several ways. Party competition between Federalists and Jeffersonian Republicans had pushed ideological issues to the forefront while keeping sectional ones suppressed, but the Federalist Party had declined precipitously by 1820, leaving the Jeffersonians to fragment internally for lack of a dangerous foe to unite them. Apart from politics, the populating of new lands west of the Appalachians, and beyond, had proceeded much faster and under less government control than policy makers in the 1780s and 1790s would have imagined—or desired. The Louisiana Purchase in 1803 had extended the territorial limits of the United States far beyond any before regarded as manageable for a republic. In the South, the lucrative expansion of cotton, the staple raw material of the industrial revolution, enhanced the appeal of slave labor and turned slavery into a dynamic, immensely prosperous, and forward-looking institution. Still, for plantation owners, insurrections and rumors of insurrection made the thought of living among *former* slaves potentially more chilling than that of keeping blacks in ever tighter bondage. Also for that reason, many slaveholders came to see a westward "diffusion" of slavery as making sense all around—not so much as a way of ending slavery, as the concept had once promised, but rather to mitigate the social side effects of the institution and to fuel the now-booming home market for chattels. Changing social and economic circumstances gave clearer definition to the slave states generally as a distinctive, self-conscious, and self-promoting part of the country. The Adams-Onís Treaty with Spain in 1819, meanwhile, caused southerners to ask why the western boundary of the Louisiana Territory had not provided more room for cotton expansion. The Supreme Court's *McCulloch v. Maryland* decision in 1819, along with nationalist stances on other issues—the tariff, internal improvements, public lands—also alarmed southern old-style Republicans and contributed to new fears of federal "consolidation."[4]

Market development and social change altered the North as well, giving rise to a sectional consciousness of its own that crystalized more and more in terms of basic economic, social, and cultural difference from the South. Within an extended northern public sphere, where "politics" had come to include a multitude of groups competing for agency in policy making, anti-slavery sentiment spread as part of this early-developing anti-southern disposition. In its broader implications, Tallmadge's February 1819 amendment calling for an end to slavery expansion, starting with Missouri, expressed this undercurrent of hostility toward the South in a more open and confrontational way than southerners had ever expected or thought they deserved. Ironically, however, as slavery gradually disappeared in the North, anti-black racism became more intense and advanced westward in the minds of thousands of settlers from the older states. Any kind of in-country diffusion of the black population could offer no logical remedy for that. In all, northern political economy and social beliefs, like those of the South, shifted bit by bit in response to new realities. The Panic (or recession) of 1819, worsening during the extended Missouri debate, worried investors in all sections and complicated perceptions all over.[5]

The controversy over Missouri, therefore, amounted to a *convergence* of political, economic, and social disturbances—West, South, and North—that brought an end to the old order of American life and suggested the broad outlines of a new one. Such events occur rarely, but one did in 1819–1821—the first in the history of the young republic.

None of this meant that rising sectional antipathy in these early years of American history made a violent outcome *inevitable* by the early 1860s. It did not. Many people read the history of this period backward from the Civil War, as if all points of conflict between North and South somehow anticipated that tragic result, rather than forward in time: future undermined, options open for decision-makers. We sometimes forget to interpret those leaders on their own terms, in context, perceiving events in frames of reference different from ours. True, the Missouri crisis prefigured the intersectional conflicts that ultimately brought down the old Union, but the 1820 dispute also ended with a compromise making sense at *that* time. Each section received a vital concession: the North, ample room in the West above 36°30' for free-labor expansion; the South and West, the right of new states to determine their own economic future with very limited congressional interference. Upon this foundation of compromise, and a second party system pitting Jacksonian Democrats against Whigs in the 1830s and 40s, rival sections could coexist. They might have coexisted indefinitely were it not for later developments, many of those also contingent on political choices.[6]

A few clarifications may be required before the reader goes further. As for expressions like "North," "South," "northerners," and "southerners," rarely in the pre–Civil War era did political leaders in such broad geographical areas unite as a block on any major principle or policy. The same goes for "Missourians," "Illinoisans," "New Yorkers," "Virginians," and so on. Wherever possible, of course, the narrative specifies *which* groups of people within these states and regions are being referred to. More broadly, however, "northerners" refers to the politically attuned population of the free states; "southerners," the similarly aware types in the white population of the slave states; and "westerners," normally subdivided by "Northwest" and "Southwest" (and further subdivisions within those), means those living in the newer free states or slave states, respectively. Looking at the antebellum South politically, one must try to distinguish lower, middle, and border divisions within the slaveholding region. The "lower" part, synonymous with "Deep South," included the seven southernmost states, from South Carolina southward and westward to Texas—the first seven to secede from the Union in 1860–1861 (slave population about 46 percent at that time). The "middle," or "Upper South," refers to Virginia, North Carolina, Tennessee, and Arkansas (29 percent slaves in 1860). The "border" section means Missouri, Maryland, Kentucky, and Delaware (14 percent slaves at Lincoln's election). Third, any use of the word "nation" for this period must be understood as referring more properly to the early republic constitutional union of states that, for various reasons, seldom operated "nationally" except in foreign policy and perhaps war.[7]

1 Origins

THE SINS of the fathers, it is said, are visited on succeeding generations. And yet, few whites in early America would have considered owning
slaves to be "sinful." The practice had existed in one form or another since
ancient times, but in the European-settled New World it rested on racial assumptions, especially the unconscious predilection of whites that people of
color stood inferior to them by nature—an "unthinking decision," according to historian Winthrop Jordan. By the time of the Missouri crisis, white
racism in the American South had evolved into what another historian,
George Frederickson, called a "*herrenvolk* democracy" that automatically distinguished—and elevated—all whites from all blacks. For well over a century before 1819, white Americans had traded in human flesh as casually as
they traded tobacco, indigo, sugar, and rice. Slaves became legally part of the
owner's estate, salable and inheritable like any other form of property and
utterly subject to white control. Enslaved African American men and women
could not enjoy the simple rights to refuse work, defy unjust authority, testify
in court, avoid humiliation and arbitrary punishment, repel the advances of
lustful masters, or even keep their own children. In almost every way, white
masters constituted a law unto themselves, unconditionally.[1]

Over the decades before American independence, all thirteen British colonies on the Atlantic seaboard had slavery, but southern planters especially came to recognize their social status, sense of honor, and even their self-esteem, along with political freedom and economic security for whites, to be intertwined with slaveholding. In the early 1700s, the master of Westover plantation in Virginia, William Byrd II, boasted that, "[l]ike one of the Patriarchs, I have my Flocks and my Herds, my Bond-men and Bond-women, and every Soart of Trade among my own Servants; so that I live in a kind of independence on everyone but Providence." Living among the honor-sensitive Chesapeake gentry in the mid-eighteenth century, the skeptical Scottish tutor James Reid once scoffed: "If a [man] . . . has Money, Negroes and Land enough he is a compleat Gentleman. These . . . hide all his defects, usher him into (what they call) the best of company, and draw upon him the smiles of the fair Sex. His madness then passes for wit, his extravagance for flow of spirit, his insolence for bravery, and his cowardice for wisdom." Thus, an overarching irony of slavery came to characterize the American South: Plantation masters not only dictated every facet of life for their slaves, but slaveholding also came to dominate the economic world, culture, and psyches of the slave owners themselves.[2]

The Revolution of 1776, still a living memory for older Americans in 1819, would dramatize the supreme irony of slaveholding in the new United States, as the principles of liberty and equality for white men seemed increasingly difficult to square with the practice of keeping blacks in bondage. All of the main threads in Revolutionary belief—Protestant Christianity, Lockean natural rights theory, Scottish "Common Sense" philosophy, radical "country" ideology, and the rest—could, if so interpreted, undercut the institution of slavery. Whenever whites wrote and spoke of British "tyranny" threatening to reduce *them* to a condition of "slavery," as revolutionary pamphlet writers often did, how could black men and women not marvel at such overt hypocrisy? And yet, the worry that Parliament might someday try to outlaw slavery had contributed to decisions in the plantation colonies to seek independence. Lord Mansfield's *Somerset v. Stewart* decision in 1772 had declared that slavery claimed no justification under the law of England, and although the ruling did not address slaveholding in the colonies or the Atlantic slave trade, southern slaveholders feared the legal trend in Britain might eventually threaten them. In that case, even the wealthiest planters, whose assets lay primarily in land and slaves, would have been wiped out. The Treaty of

Paris of 1783, which ended the Revolutionary War and established the independence of the former colonies, included a clause that defined slaves unequivocally as a form of property, nothing more.[3]

Apart from the promise of liberty and equality, however, the Revolution
also asserted the right of self-government, of newly independent states to
control their own internal affairs and defend property rights, including those
of slaveholders. When southerners in years to come would speak of state
sovereignty, states' rights, self-government, and the self-determination entitled to them and to the new western states alike, they drew on hard-fought
tradition and believed what they said. The political language they employed
with regard to slavery did not simply mask their material interest in keeping
slaves.[4]

The most significant progress toward restricting, and eventually ending, slavery in the post-Revolutionary period took place at the state level—
gradually, except in one case (Vermont), and only in the North. Pennsylvania
led the way, even though its statute, adopted on March 1, 1780, freed no one
at that time, only the future offspring of slaves when they reached the age
of twenty-eight. Connecticut and Rhode Island, following the Pennsylvania
model, pledged for gradual abolition in 1784. Slavery in Massachusetts ended
not with legislative action but as the result of a court decision: *Commonwealth v. Jennison*, 1783. In that ruling, Bay State chief justice William Cush-
ing declared slavery to be irreconcilable with the Massachusetts Constitution
of 1780. The number of bondsmen there had already declined precipitously
and by the census of 1790 would fall to zero. In New York and New Jersey,
where by far the most northern slaves lived, post-Revolutionary efforts to
phase out slavery stalled in favor of "property rights" arguments and the view
that blacks in the North, if humanely treated, had fared better enslaved than
as freemen. Emancipation initiatives in those states would have to wait until
1799 and 1804, respectively.[5]

Only after the states began ceding their western land claims to the United
States, beginning with Virginia's in 1784, could the Confederation Congress
for the first time address whether slavery would expand into the distant territories. Even then, American leaders believed that the land and government
policies they adopted for the West might determine the social and economic
destiny of the United States. And so, the question of whether to allow the westward expansion of slavery stood at the very heart of Congressional decision
making from the start of the republic—not suddenly in 1819 over Missouri.

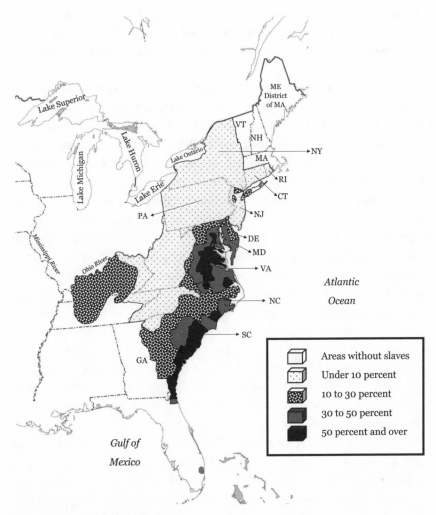

Slavery in the United States, 1790.
Drawn by Margot Gibson-Beattie.

In 1784, a committee chaired by Thomas Jefferson, a slaveholder himself, proposed an ordinance that would have prohibited slavery and all other forms of involuntary servitude throughout the West after the year 1800, but southern congressmen, including the other two members of Virginia's delegation, combined to defeat the prohibition by a single vote. Had Jefferson's ordinance passed, and the Confederation been capable of enforcing the provision, it might have discouraged the spread of slaveholding already under way, confining the institution mostly to the original states. In that event, there would have been no Missouri crisis in 1819 and, indeed, no Civil War in 1861.[6]

And yet, some progress toward a limiting of slavery west of the Appalachians did occur before the end of the Confederation period of 1777–1789. One of the most forward-looking policies ever launched, the Northwest Ordinance of July 13, 1787, departed from the British strategy of empire. Instead of colonies stuck in unending dependence on a metropolitan center, frontier provinces of the new United States were to evolve into full, equal members of the Confederation—or, later, the Union. But the policy required tight governmental control over the West, mandating the expansion of republicanism, freedom of worship, trial by jury, and public support for education, while in its Article VI nominally prohibiting slavery north of the Ohio River. To check the anticipated excesses of democracy, the ordinance required dictatorial leadership in the early stages of territorial development—an appointed governor with the advice of an executive council, to be joined by an elected legislature (based on strictly limited suffrage) only when the free adult male population reached 5,000. It would have to be a "strong toned government," said Richard Henry Lee, to safeguard property against the "uninformed" and "perhaps licentious people"—meaning lawless types—who coveted western lands without the intention, or the means, to pay for them. Statehood would come eventually to the various parts of the Northwest, but only when the population of free white inhabitants reached 60,000. When new states did enter, it was to be "on an equal footing with the original states."[7]

All of this, of course, would bear heavily on territorial politics and the admission of other new states in decades to come, including the trans-Mississippi ones like Missouri. But two things, the "equal footing" requirement and, more immediately, the prohibition on slavery in the Northwest Territory, would carry both the heaviest weight of precedent and the greatest potential for controversy. The ordinance provided no definition of terms or policy guidance for either. Those vital parts would have to emerge instrumentally at all levels of government—national, territorial, state, and local. Political, economic, and cultural forces in the West itself would drive that process far more than federal officials ever could—and for a simple reason: the territories lay far too distant from the center of power for such a nationalist frontier vision to work in a two-mile-an-hour world.[8]

Meanwhile, when the delegates to the Philadelphia Convention gathered, also in mid-1787, to hammer out a new constitution for the nation, they produced an edifice of compromises that provided only further vagueness on the sovereignty of states and the powers of Congress over the territories. Perhaps most framers of the Constitution harbored no intention to favor *either* side of the slavery divide, assuming that question would remain a state matter. By 1787, as northern states embarked on gradualist abolition programs, a host of antislavery societies already existed in the fledgling United States. Upper southern states of Maryland and Virginia had acted to make private manumissions easier legally for masters who wished to take advantage. During the war and after, every state except Georgia had at least temporarily stopped importing new slaves. These actions had occurred under private or state authority; the Confederation government had only proscribed slavery in the Northwest Ordinance for a region beyond the scope of individual states. Some delegates still wished to see the institution ended altogether, but they assumed this most likely to occur state by state. To condemn the Constitution's framers, as some modern writers have, for not providing a more explicitly antislavery charter for United States is to mischaracterize their assumptions and disregard the context in which they operated. But also, to downplay the provisions clearly meant to enhance the political influence of the slave states and protect the property rights of slave-owning Americans, as antislavery advocates later would, is to coat the work in Philadelphia with an abolitionist gloss contrary to historical fact.[9]

The Constitutional Convention did adopt formidable assurances on property rights, understood to include slaves, and the distribution of political power along lines that satisfied southern states. As a North-South sectional issue, slavery first arose at the convention in relation to the question of proportional representation in the new federal republic. Would the Constitution in some fashion permit slaves to be counted in determining representation on the basis of population? On this consideration depended the number of slave-state seats in the House of Representatives, as well as their influence in presidential elections via the Electoral College. Southern patricians argued that civic virtue in an elitist republic required that propertied groups enjoy protection against the threat of a restless, nonpropertied white majority, and since slaveholders represented extra property—slaves as well as land—they should receive extra political power to guard that interest. South Carolina's Pierce Butler, owner of nearly 500 enslaved African-Americans who labored on his Sea Island rice and cotton plantations, wanted the *entire* population of slaves included in this calculation. Charles C. Pinckney of South Carolina said he would agree to nothing less than a three-fifths agreement, counting three of every five slaves, along with the state's white population, for apportionment purposes. The vehemently antislavery New York merchant Gouverneur Morris, who represented Pennsylvania at the convention, answered that slave labor was "a nefarious institution," the "curse of heaven on the states where it prevailed," responsible for the "misery and poverty which overspread the barren wastes of Virginia, Maryland, and the other states having slaves." If they are men, then "make them citizens, and let them vote," Morris demanded. "Are they property? Why, then, is no other property included?" In his denouncing of slaveholders' influence at the convention, Morris probably came closer than anyone to anticipating the later northern "Slave Power" fear of an ultra-aggressive, expansionist South, bent on undercutting fundamental republican liberty in favor of aristocratic planter-class interests.[10]

Most of the delegates, more open to conciliation, expected the arbitrary three-fifths ratio of the slave population to become the basis for a settlement. James Wilson of Pennsylvania, as opposed to slavery as Morris but anxious to secure sectional harmony, had earlier proposed a compromise exactly on that line. The overarching goal of achieving union sufficed to extinguish this flare-up over slavery, a battle that most framers cared not and saw no reason to fight in the first place. Some southern delegates still viewed the compromise as giving up the principle that *all* slaves should be counted, but for years to come, the convention's acceptance of the three-fifths rule looked to many northerners like a submission to southern political blackmail. Grant us this concession, slaveholding interests seemed to have demanded, or the whole deal is off.[11]

The second dispute involving slavery developed over the empowering of Congress to regulate commerce between the states. Southerners, again led by a South Carolinian, John Rutledge, feared that a northern majority might employ a broad grant of regulatory power to ban the African slave trade. At first, proslavery delegates insisted on a specific clause forbidding Congress from ever prohibiting the importation of slaves or taxing that trade—again, much to the horror of antislavery delegates like Morris and Rufus King. Unlike the quarrel over the three-fifths clause, however, southerners divided on the desirability of continued slave imports. Virginia and Maryland had recognized their economic interest in discontinuing the trade. To settle the issue temporarily, Connecticut's Roger Sherman and Oliver Ellsworth, betting that slavery in America could somehow end without federal interference, proposed to let the Deep South have its way. A committee, under New Jersey governor William Livingston, recommended that Congress be held back from touching the slave trade until the year 1800. Unwilling to back down completely, South Carolina offered to accept a twenty-year ban on federal intervention—until the year 1808—and the convention agreed. Like the three-fifths compromise, this slave-trade arrangement represented a middle ground between early abolitionist impulses and plantation-labor interests.[12]

The final concession to slavery in the Constitution, approved late in the Philadelphia Convention, came in response to South Carolina's desire to include a clause requiring the return to their masters of slaves who escaped across state lines. Only Sherman of Connecticut and Wilson of Pennsylvania questioned the wisdom of such a provision; the other delegates, perhaps weary of their task and eager to get home, agreed without argument. Thus, a policy that in later decades would generate so much acrimony between North and South passed without much excitement and, in the end, with no states opposed. It helped the slave masters' cause that the Northwest Ordinance also contained a fugitive slave clause. Strongly racist white settlers in the Northwest had no intention of welcoming free black inhabitants in any case.[13]

Like Sherman, most northerners over the next three decades would tend more often to regard slavery as the South's "problem," one that the "good sense of the several States" eventually would resolve. Others in later years recognized the North's complicity in the perpetuation of slavery in the southern states. While it implied no direct defense of slavery, textile mill operators in New England and the Middle States would need cotton for their manufacturing in years to come, and slaveholders would produce that cotton. Meanwhile, tobacco, rice, and sugar contributed heavily to the vitality not just of certain regions but the economy as a whole. Southerners would revel in these economic truths and find security in them. Besides, the racism present all along in the North differed only by degree from the more practical version of southerners. The antislavery commitment in northern states sprang not from a radical belief in the equality of races but rather the idea that no man held a right to enslave another. Politically, southerners stuck to—and most northerners, until the time of the Missouri crisis, accepted—the view that the Constitution had created a federal system of strictly limited central power, where the protection of property rights implicitly included that of slaveholders to their bondsmen. In the eyes of slave-state leaders, therefore, Congress could claim no power to interfere with slavery where it existed or keep the institution from spreading to new states that wanted it.[14]

Slavery related marginally to major issues that divided the Federalist and Jeffersonian Republican parties in the years after 1789: federal government finance, a national bank, taxation, foreign policy, and a quasi-war with France. A few squabbles during the 1790s occurred, predictably, over the continuing slave import trade. Quaker groups in New York City and Philadelphia, along with the Pennsylvania Society for the Abolition of Slavery, urged Congress to take any action it could to curtail American involvement in the trade. South Carolina and Georgia congressmen protested that Congress held no authority to consider the question until 1808 or, for that matter, even to address antislavery petitions until that time. The Senate went along with southern wishes, but when a House committee in 1790 reported that Congress might regulate some parts of the slave trade during the twenty-year buffer period, South Carolina's William L. Smith answered as if abolitionists had attacked slavery generally. The institution "was so engrafted into the policy of the Southern States," Smith protested, "that it could not be eradicated without tearing up by the roots their happiness, tranquility, and prosperity." The subtext here needed no clarifying: The Deep South could not stay in a Union that endangered such crucial elements of its welfare. Getting the message, Congress in 1793 enacted a perfunctory policy to enforce the fugitive slave clause of the Constitution. After that, foreign concerns had pulled attention away from potential sectional quarrels. But in 1800, Thomas Jefferson would owe his election as president to the South—and the three-fifths clause—winning 48 of the 52 electoral votes from Virginia and states farther south.[15]

At the time of the Louisiana Purchase in 1803, no one could yet say what kind of society would develop west of the Mississippi River, but the question of how far to let slavery expand *did* occur—and not just in Washington. Slavery already existed in pockets of the Louisiana Territory north of what would become the new state of Louisiana, and the purchase treaty had guaranteed the property-holding rights of French slave owners. Even so, in January 1804, Federalist senator James Hillhouse proposed measures to forestall the expansion of slavery into the newly acquired region. Hillhouse, of New Haven, Connecticut, had opposed ratification of the Louisiana Treaty, causing some to suspect his motives. His 1804 plan included the prohibiting of imported slaves from entering the territory directly, limiting service of slaves brought in to just one year of their adulthood, barring entirely slaves of recent import into the country, and permitting only actual settlers (as opposed to slave traders) to bring any slaves into Louisiana.[16]

In answer to all this, the brash, rice-growing, pistol-wielding James Jackson of Georgia anticipated the expansionist interests of the Deep South. "You cannot prevent slavery," he avowed, "neither laws moral or human can do it—Men will be governed by their interest, not the law." As for the Louisiana Territory, he declared, "Slavery must be established in that country or it [the territory] must be abandoned." Other southern senators voiced far more ambivalence, however, showing that strict sectional lines on the issue of slavery expansion did not yet exist. While Samuel Smith of Maryland opposed Hillhouse's propositions, he supported the general intention: "let it be remembered," he insisted, "that although I am a slave holder, I declare I disapprove of slavery." North Carolina's Jesse Franklin spoke against the slave trade in terms as ardent as any New Englander: "My wish is to prohibit slaves altogether from that country [Louisiana], except those carried thither by actual settlers from the United States—but I despair of obtaining such a vote in [the] Senate. I will vote for such a prohibition as I can obtain."[17]

Hillhouse's three proposals involving the slave trade passed the Senate easily, but the most radically antislavery one—the restricting of a slave's obligation to just one year after he or she reached maturity—went down 11 to 17. Here was another pivotal moment. Had both houses adopted that provision, President Jefferson affixed his signature, and the federal government been committed (and able) to enforce it, there might have been no Tallmadge Amendment in 1819 and no talk of secession or civil war thereafter. As it turned out, Jefferson, owing his political wherewithal to a South that remained heavily invested in slavery and states' rights, refrained from entering the debate on either side. Many of his fellow Virginians still nursed the dream of new plantations on richer lands in the far West. Beyond that, slaveholders and slave-traders in lower Louisiana did refuse, as James Jackson said they would, to abide by the restrictions on slave imports. Any other outcome would have required a constant, extensive, and possibly brutal military presence in the region that Jeffersonian Republicans, and many Federalists too, would have shuddered to imagine—worse than British rule after 1763. When, in 1805, Congress split the Louisiana Territory into two separate parts, it said nothing about restricting slavery or disturbing slaveholders already present.

And so, the entire trans-Mississippi West remained open to any American who wished to settle there, no matter what kind of property he or she chose to own.[18]

Tallmadge

At the time of the Missouri crisis, Jabez D. Hammond, a lawyer from Cherry Valley, New York, and member of the state senate from 1817 to 1821, declared James Tallmadge to be "politically eccentric and wrongheaded." Several years later, Thiron Rudd, of Tallmadge's Poughkeepsie, thought he, too, understood the man whose controversial amendment had placed the Union at risk, adding that "in regard to political operations, Tallmadge is one of nature's *bad bargains*." In a state like New York, where fidelity to political faction had become de rigueur, a maverick who thought and acted independently, sometimes even as his conscience dictated, could expect little approval from his peers.[19]

Tallmadge had become this sort of nonconformist. Although a New York Republican, he did as he pleased often enough to lose favor with just about every party kingpin in the state. If one assumes that politics primarily motivated him, then Tallmadge could not rely on much organizational support and had to find ways to drum up his own following at home. But principle apparently guided him, too. The *New-York Columbian* reported that he had "on more than one occasion shown himself as the able and liberal advocate of humanity"—advocating a grant of land for the Irish Emigrant Society, for example. He more or less gravitated to the anti-southern Clintonian faction of the Jeffersonian Republican Party in New York, as opposed to the southern-leaning Tammany group known as the "Bucktails." Governor De Witt Clinton's coterie of nationalist Republicans, known to ally sometimes with the Federalists, especially resented the aristocratic southern domination not only of Congress and the White House but also of their Republican Party generally since its inception. The governor, however, had no prior knowledge of the Tallmadge Amendment and apparently supported it only when he realized how popular it was in New York.[20]

Apart from issues of party control, however, ample reasons justified New York abolitionists' concern about the course of events prior to the Missouri confrontation. Despite gradual emancipation programs in the North, and the federal government's ending of the legal slave import trade in 1808, slavery had expanded more rapidly in the United States than anyone had expected. According to the 1820 census, the slave population of 1,538,038 had increased some 30 percent over the previous decade. Slave importing had continued in defiance of federal law, while the domestic reproduction of slaves boomed. Even in the "free" states, more than 19,000 bondsmen and bondswomen still resided there, awaiting the day of their mandated release or that of their children. Of those, some 10,000 lived in Tallmadge's New York.[21]

Commitment to emancipation had not come easily in the Empire State. The antislavery campaign there dated to the early years of the American Revolution. In 1777, John Jay, one of the state's most ardent antislavery men, had drafted legislation calling for immediate abolition, but the bill failed, as did a similar one in 1785. Still, Jay's commitment remained firm over the years. As he would write in December 1819, referring to the Missouri question: "The obvious dictates both of morality and policy teach us, that our free nation cannot encourage the extension of slavery, nor the multiplication of slaves, without doing violence to their principles, and without depressing their power and prosperity." Signs of mounting support for *gradual* emancipation in some form, even among New York slaveholders, had started to appear, however. In 1785, a group of prominent New York politicians, including Alexander Hamilton, Aaron Burr, Robert Troup, and Melancton Smith, formed the New-York Society for Promoting the Manumission of Slaves, with Jay as its first president. The society grew quickly to thirty-one members, more than half, ironically, owners of household servants. They launched a petition campaign in favor of the gradualist approach, sponsored boycotts against merchants and newspaper owners involved in the slave trade, and urged printers to refuse advertisements for the sale or purchase of blacks. Later that year, the New York assembly passed a law prohibiting the sale of slaves brought into the state and facilitating manumission of others either by a registered certificate or at the owner's death. Three years later, under continuing manumission society pressure, lawmakers forbade the purchase of slaves for removal to another state and extended to blacks trial by jury in capital cases.[22]

By this time, all other northern states except New Jersey had adopted plans to end slavery, but in New York opposition persisted in the upstate Dutch areas and in New York City, where during the 1790s the number of slaves actually had increased 23 percent and the number of slaveholders 33 percent. The possibility of black citizenship was a large stumbling block to emancipation. Media exchanges in New York all through the 1780s and 1790s reflected disparate views on the fitness of liberated blacks for such a role in society. Further, the number of potential freedmen, if allowed to vote, could transform state politics and benefit any leaders, like Tallmadge, who might try to harness that support. In 1798, about 33,000 slaves still remained throughout New York—far more than any other northern state. Racial bondage, rooted as it was in racist assumptions, had to be delegitimized before it could be ended. Defenders of slavery often mimicked the black "voice" in print, appealed to the memory of African American loyalty to the British during the Revolutionary War, and cited the West Indian slave uprisings of the 1790s to persuade readers that blacks lacked intelligence and political trustworthiness. The contest over abolition thus became an argument whether blacks came anywhere close to being natural equals with whites. Another part of white anxiety was the realization that newly freed blacks would have to fend for themselves economically, whether accorded political rights or not. If they could not, then white taxpayers faced a grim future of providing for ever-growing numbers on public assistance. One New York City Presbyterian minister, Samuel Miller, speaking in 1797 for the manumission society, admitted that emancipation required a racial leap of faith on the part of doubting whites: "Say not that they [blacks] . . . can never be made honest and industrious members of the community. . . . Make them freemen; and they will soon be found to have the manners, the character, and the virtues of freemen."[23]

Finally, in 1799, the New York legislature agreed on a bill to end slavery gradually. Jay, now the state's governor, hastily signed the measure into law despite his misgivings about gradualism. Beginning July 4 of that year, all children born to slave parents would be "free" but required to undergo a period of apprenticeship to their mothers' owners until age twenty-eight for males and twenty-five for females. This law imposed no specific limitations on the political rights of free blacks, but African American citizenship and voting rights in New York would be seriously curtailed in decades to come despite further emancipationist efforts to hasten full realization of their cause.[24]

Meanwhile, the manumission society concentrated on getting this law, a mere half-measure, amended. On the society's behalf, Governor Daniel D. Tompkins forced slavery back to the attention of New York lawmakers in 1812 and, five years later, again pleaded for "slavery to be expunged from our statute book." On March 31, 1817, less than two years before Tallmadge's amendment to the Missouri bill, a coalition of antislavery New Yorkers from both the Federalist and Republican camps succeeded in passing a new law promising freedom to *all* 11,000 New York slaves remaining at that time. Reflecting the ongoing antislavery discontent in the state, Federalist Theodore Dwight's *Albany Advertiser* had condemned the 1799 statute for drawing "the great line of slavery and freedom between members of the same family—between parents and children, brothers and sisters." Further, Dwight warned, any slave whose condition the law had refused to remedy would "have every possible inducement to relieve himself from its calamities." This danger loomed especially in New York City, where slave uprisings had occurred before. One unsuccessful plot in 1741 had threatened to send the entire city up in flames.[25]

The reformed emancipation law of 1817 promised "the final and total abolition" of slavery in New York as of July 4, 1827, applying equally to the enslaved born after and before 1799. Recently elected to Congress, Tallmadge had used his influence back home to help secure the measure's passage. Missouri by early 1819 had about the same number of enslaved blacks, roughly 10,000, as slave owners in the Empire State still held—a point that Tallmadge hardly could have missed—and the slave percentage of Missouri's population closely compared to that of New York in its colonial days. Missouri must have seemed to him as ripe for gradual emancipation as his own state, which had now proceeded further and faster than the Tallmadge Amendment asked Missouri to go. Besides, if viewed cynically, the amendment would have allowed Missouri slave owners, like those in New York, to sell their slaves "down river" before they reached emancipation age. Still, this New York statute marked the first *total* emancipation adopted by any state except for Vermont. Around the same time, state courts in Pennsylvania, in 1815, and Ohio, in 1817, defied the federal Constitution by trying to free individual slaves that southern owners had brought within their borders.[26]

Along with these events, antislavery New York editors highlighted with dismay the cotton boom in the South and its implications for the future of slavery. The recent surge of "kidnappings" from New York and New Jersey, where slaves had been promised eventual emancipation but remained vulnerable to illegal sale or theft, largely accounted for this growing anti-southern feeling. In February 1817, the Federalist-supporting *Commercial Advertiser*, under Zachariah Lewis, addressed the abducting of blacks for transport to

Georgia: "The extent to which this has been carried on from this, and the other Middle States, exceeds the belief of many." No one could doubt the reason. "Prime negros," Lewis reported, "have been sold for eight hundred dollars, and upwards." Barely restraining the contempt he felt for southern culture, Lewis quoted from the journal of a "young gentleman" who had visited the southern states the previous winter, where he had witnessed the stalls of human chattels to be exposed for sale. That young visitor encountered a hypocritical "land that boasts its freedom: a land of high toned democracy, where human beings, like dumb brutes are driven to market, and, instead of dying by the hand of the butcher, die a lingering death of slavery and bondage!"[27]

Recent developments in New York surely influenced the way its delegation in Congress viewed the Missouri question, even though Tallmadge's February 1819 amendment stopped short of his own state's 1817 reform. Still, Tallmadge and others could now curry favor among New York's antislavery constituency, including free blacks, who voted in New York until after 1821. "The *people of color*, are not to be ridiculed out of their rights by the low and despicable wit" of certain publications, declared the *Columbian*. "They view JAMES TALLMADGE, *jun.* as the enlightened and humane advocate of their oppressed race, and we presume will support him at the polls." The Clintonians, however, did little to encourage his political fortunes. They had already decided that he would not be a candidate for reelection to the House, nominating him instead for state senator (an election he would lose) in a district heavily populated with Quakers, manumission society members, and free blacks. Those groups comprised the constituency that Tallmadge respected most and courted most heavily with his amendment to the Missouri bill.[28]

Barbour

The two brothers could hardly have been more different. Both proud Virginia men, they were sons of Thomas Barbour, Orange County planter, member of the House of Burgesses, and leader in the Revolutionary movement. Their mother, Mary Pendleton Thomas, hailed from a prestigious Spotsylvania County family and boasted a family connection to the prominent Virginia statesmen Edmund Pendleton and John Taylor of Caroline. James Barbour and Philip P. Barbour both became lawyers, planters, politicians, and slaveholders in their own right. But everybody noted the stark divergence of their personalities and political views.[29]

James, the elder, born in 1775, came across as gregarious, easy in man-ner, good-humored, and loquacious in conversation, well-suited for a career in politics. Philip, born in 1783, struck people as reserved and socially taci-turn, a brilliant logician and eloquent speaker but never comfortable in the public glare. Even in appearance, the two seemed unrelated. James, ruggedly handsome, strong in physique with piercing eyes and long flowing hair, im-pressed one who knew him as evocative of the "grandeur of a Roman citizen in the best days" of that ancient republic. Another observer described the more slightly framed Philip as far less imposing, a "decidedly ugly man." In their political outlooks, too, the siblings seemed to offer little in common. James became a nationalist, embracing the "implied powers" view of the Constitution, while Philip turned in the direction of strict construction and states' rights. They represented archetypal opposites within same post-1815 Republican Party that embraced them both. In 1820, James as a member of the Senate would support the Missouri Compromise; Philip, in the House of Representatives, staunchly opposed it.[30]

The Barbour brothers, though born into the Virginia plantation elite, lived in a time when the famed power and prestige of those once-proud planters had started to ebb. To begin, it could only seem that the great men of Wash-ington's and Jefferson's time overshadowed the second generation of post-1776 Virginia leaders. Those born during or after the war of independence had inherited glory, as opposed to winning it themselves. Virginians like John Randolph, Spencer Roane, Taylor of Caroline, and, indeed, Philip P. Barbour, more often "looked backwards" as historian Susan Dunn has written, "cling-ing to the aristocratic idyll of a leisurely, gracious life of family, hospitality, books, and slaves." Meanwhile, the more energetic, commercially ambitious, and faster-growing population of the northern states made much of the Old South look all the more like a place of the past.[31]

Virginia's economy, moreover, wallowed in stagnation. Soil exhaustion and market dislocation after the Revolution, especially in Tidewater areas, had undercut the tobacco economy, driving more and more planters to try their luck with grain crops. The value of their farmland sank to less than a third that of fertile Pennsylvania soil. In 1800, the aggregate exports of Mas-sachusetts totaled $11 million, compared to Virginia's $4.5 million. The clos-ing of European markets during the War of 1812 sank tobacco prices to just two cents a pound before a brief period of postwar prosperity revived them. But then, the Panic of 1819 inflicted another disaster on southeastern agriculture, depressing the prices of the wheat and corn upon which former tobacco growers increasingly depended, along with the cotton trade so vital to South Carolinians and Georgians.[32]

The malaise in the Chesapeake region even affected political behavior, as fewer and fewer eligible voters bothered to visit the polls on election days. Literacy among whites lagged farther and farther behind the New England and Middle Atlantic states. Wealthier Virginia taxpayers refused to finance public schooling. By 1820, not just ordinary Virginians but also discouraged scions of the elite, whose talents might have served the Old Dominion, migrated westward to places like Kentucky, Alabama, or Missouri Territory. Whereas about half the population of the United States resided south of Pennsylvania in 1790, only 46.7 percent did so in 1820, and subtracting slaves from that calculation, the percentage falls to 35.8 percent. Virginia's rate of population growth fell by 1820 to the lowest of all the southern states. Meanwhile, the population of blacks in Virginia edged ever closer to that of whites—about 423,000 to 551,000, the census of 1810 reported. As land values dropped, the demand for human chattels outside the state made slave property the planters' most valuable asset, rendering emancipation less practical than ever, despite the worrisome overpopulation of blacks in eastern counties like Orange and frequent rumors of insurrection in the state.[33]

Even the Barbours' famous Orange County neighbors, James and Dolly Madison, had to reckon with pecuniary ruin. Crop failures, sour investments, and mounting debt weighed on them in post-1817 retirement years at Montpelier, their now crumbling 5,000-acre estate. The "times are hard indeed, . . . the more so, as an early change is so little within the reach of any fair calculation," the former president groaned to Francis Corbin in November 1820, as he pondered more than just the Missouri crisis. Many Virginians, he continued, "had no resource but in the sale of property, which none are able to purchase." For the nation's future, James Madison at times found solace in the agricultural "safety valve" of westward expansion, yet he despaired over Virginia's plight as the lure of new lands drained away its most promising citizens. Thomas Barbour, his finances also distressed and Fredericksburg creditors clamoring at his door, had resorted to selling over a thousand acres of his land between 1787 and 1792, only to encounter continuing reverses so devastating that he could not pay for his sons' educations. Young James Barbour had to forgo college, apprenticing himself to a Richmond lawyer before starting his own practice at home. In the au-

tumn of 1800, his brother Philip, despite similar deficiencies of legal training, sought more promising opportunities in Bardstown, Kentucky, before
returning a year later and borrowing money to attend the College of William and Mary and read law, briefly, under the celebrated jurist St. George
Tucker.[34]

Partly because of these economic troubles and the psychological disillu-
sionment that accompanied them, more and more southern politicians before 1820, especially in Virginia, took protective refuge in the old-fashioned,
anti-federal ethos of early Jeffersonianism. Indeed, some of the most strident
voices opposing the War of 1812 had been the "Old Republicans" in Madison's own political ranks. The war itself and the thorny economic issues it
would generate—the need for a second national bank, protective tariff
legislation, and federal aid for internal improvements—widened major philosophical differences within the party. One group, the "War Hawks," con-
sisting of nationalists mostly from new states in the West and parts of the
South, most ardently advocated war against Britain to vindicate American
rights at sea, end the British presence in the Northwest, and win much of
Canada for the new Republic. They included, among others, Henry Clay and
Richard M. Johnson of Kentucky, Tennessee's Felix Grundy, John C. Calhoun
and William Lowndes of South Carolina, and George M. Troup of Georgia.
Even the Federalists, while disagreeing on war issues, tended to regard the
War Hawks as the "best informed," most promising Republicans because of
their nationalist perspective. Another group gravitated to the Clinton family
in New York. These "Clintonians," representing primarily northeastern commercial areas, lamented the economic restrictions the war brought on and
favored greater federal support for trade. Also favoring those things, northeastern Federalists had thrown their support behind De Witt Clinton against
Madison in the presidential election of 1812, narrowing the latter's margin of
victory.[35]

And then, Philip P. Barbour's group, a third key faction of the Republican
Party, called the "Old Republicans" or "Quids," included some who deprecated the War of 1812 as much as the Federalists—for reasons that would
echo loudly in the Missouri debate of 1819–21. These southern agrarians, led
by Virginia's John Randolph and North Carolina's Nathaniel Macon, among
others, fancied themselves as keepers of the true flame—the antigovernment
"spirit of 98," hostile to federal authority and suspicious of "implied powers."
More than just strict constructionists and defenders of states' rights, mem-

bers of this contingent saw both the Federalists and nationalist Jeffersonians as threatening the very core of republicanism: the limited governance, social order based on agriculture, and the individual and state self-determination without which liberty, they thought, could not survive. By 1820, Old Republicans would hold intellectual sway beyond their actual numbers, especially in the South. Right after the war, when the Madison administration advanced a host of proposals meant to strengthen the fiscal-military infrastructure of the country, and to appeal to both War Hawk and Clintonian nationalists, this so-called Madison Platform of 1815–1816 triggered Old Republican fears of internal corruption and the kind of government "consolidation" they believed to threaten fundamental liberties. Internal taxes retained from wartime, federal subsidies for road and canal building, increased expenditures for a peacetime army—the program "*out-Hamiltons* Alexander Hamilton," Randolph cried.[36]

Clay

For one who in 1819 would denounce the Tallmadge Amendment, it might seem odd to find Henry Clay among the founders of the American Colonization Society. Filling in for Supreme Court justice Bushrod Washington, Clay presided over the initial meeting of the ACS on December 21, 1816, at the Davis Hotel in Washington. The purpose of the new organization was to encourage the manumitting of slaves and their repatriation to Africa, thus addressing the "problem" of an increasing free black population in the United States.[37]

Thirty-nine years old, a bit over six feet tall and slender, charming but roguish in reputation, a devotee of late-night card games, snuff, and whiskey, Clay already sat as Speaker of the House of Representatives. His impulsive, mercurial nature would seem to make him an unlikely candidate for the reputation he would later enjoy as "the great compromiser." Perhaps more than anyone else of his time, political ambition consumed him, but he had intellectual ability along with that thirst for power. In the style of a classical conservative, Clay feared the effects of social disorder. "From their condition," and whites' "unconquerable prejudices resulting from their color," he told the 1816 meeting, these African Americans "never could amalgamate" with the white population of the country. No one in that audience, which included prominent Virginians such as James Madison, John Marshall, and

James Monroe, would have disagreed. Better, then, to "drain them off . . . to the land of their fathers," Clay continued, and by doing so "hope that America will extinguish a great portion of that moral debt which she has contracted to that unfortunate continent." There could be no "nobler cause than that which, whilst it proposes to rid our own country of a useless and pernicious, if not dangerous portion of its population, contemplates the spreading of the arts of civilized life, and the possible redemption from ignorance and barbarism of a benighted quarter of the globe!" Translation: the specter of a potential race war in America haunted Clay just as it did many other whites, whether slaveholders or not.[38]

Clay had known slavery all his life, owning human chattels since the age of five, when he inherited two from his recently deceased father. The population of African American slaves in Hanover County, Virginia, where he was born in 1777, outnumbered that of whites. Well over a third of households in Kentucky, where he had settled in 1797, owned slaves. As he gained land and wealth over the course of his life, including a 600-acre hemp- and tobacco-growing plantation outside of Lexington, he purchased more and more slaves to make his farms productive. At the start of his career, he had expressed contempt for the institution and had advocated gradual emancipation in Kentucky, but further experience in state and, soon enough, national politics showed him that electoral success demanded a revised position. In a republic of sections divided against one another, slavery threatened political disunity no less than a growing underclass of free blacks seemed to augur a social crisis. Thereafter, he made sure to say that slave property was as inviolable as any other kind of material possession. The ACS fit the political needs of one who aspired to national prominence, as Clay did. It furnished a middle ground by appealing to "enlightened" southerners without offending the rest, while placating northerners on the gradualist fringes of the antislavery movement. And it preserved his nationalist hope for a cross-sectional support of protective tariffs and federally funded internal improvements.[39]

Apart from practicing the politics of moderation, Clay also understood and acted according to the vernacular of southern honor. Never far removed from the cultural exigencies of slave owning, the dictates of that complicated code of white behavior had evolved from colonial times. Britain's belligerent and condescending disregard for American sovereignty had made him a War Hawk in the months leading up to the War of 1812. To him, the insulting actions of a foreign power demanded a forceful, self-vindicating response. Any

Henry Clay, circa 1820s.
Courtesy of the Library of Congress.

affront by a disrespectful peer would be no different. A running antipathy in the House of Representatives between Clay and the irascible John Randolph, starting in 1812, would culminate in a duel fourteen years later. At that point, while Clay served as President John Quincy Adams's secretary of state, Randolph publically called the Kentuckian a "blackleg," that is, a "swindler," or in Clay's case perhaps, an alleged "card sharp," one who cheated at cards. Here was the kind of deliberate slur and dueling offense that could not go unanswered accordingly. At an agreed upon location, on April 8, 1826, the two antagonists measured out a distance of ten paces and carried out the violent gentlemen's ritual of firing flintlock pistol shots at each other, luckily with no damage inflicted on either side.[40]

Some southerners, of course, embraced possible ways of slowly ending slavery other than colonization, even if those alternatives did not also promise ridding the country of blacks. The Missouri crisis notwithstanding, several manumission and emancipation societies would form in the Upper South after 1815, aiming for the same result that the young, inexperienced

Clay had once explored in Kentucky. One of those, the Manumission Society of Tennessee, reflected some of the broad influence of the Second Great Awakening. A meeting in Green County, Tennessee, in November 1817, implored the "religious denominations of Christians, throughout the Union" to note the "degraded state of servitude" experienced by their people of color—"the privations they suffer, . . . their offspring doomed to drink the same cup, unless the friends of philanthropy . . . should step forward and plead their cause." Its proposed remedy, though harder to apply in a region of cotton plantations, seemed little different from the Tallmadge Amendment for Missouri: "to abolish slavery gradually, by having laws passed, declaring all those born after a fixed period, to be free at some reasonable age."[41]

Despite its mixed motives, however, the greatest boost to antislavery prior to the Missouri crisis came with the formation of the ACS. Apart from Clay and its more active organizers, Robert Finley of New Jersey and Virginia's Charles Fenton Mercer, the society's ordinary supporters spanned the sections and could be found even in the deeper South. One reader of the *Charleston City Gazette* in South Carolina, with its troubling black majority over the white population, responded: "Would it not be better to colonize them, either by sending them off the State, or by giving them [Indian] lands for settlement"—or even to pass a law "declaring that every negro introduced into this state, should be immediately free and liable to be sent to the intended New Colony[?]" The major obstacle for any colonization scheme would be the massive expense it would entail, but a writer in Milledgeville, Georgia, proposed one solution: a tax of one or two dollars annually on each slave throughout the United States, with free persons of color subject to the same. From that fund, the society's commissioner might purchase the slaves of those owners who were disposed to sell and convey them to the new colony within thirty to fifty years, with "due compensation" to their masters. None would oppose this plan, the idealistic Georgia writer continued, "except those destitute of equity, humanity, and republicanism."[42]

The ACS appealed across religious lines, attracting Presbyterian, Baptist, Methodist, and even some of the Anglican clergy, as well as across political lines, Republicans and one-time Federalists alike. With pockets of support in the Lower South, it appealed more widely in the upper plantation states, where, as Maryland's Robert Goodloe Harper contended in 1818, free blacks constituted a destabilizing, if not threatening, element in the community—the basic view that Clay had expressed. Colonization, Harper wrote in a widely noted pamphlet, offered the best way to relocate "a population for the most part idle and useless, and too often vicious and mischievous." Harper also worried that the presence of blacks, both free and slave, discouraged the emergence of a free-laboring class, as landless whites too often "saw labour as a badge of slavery."[43]

Most members of the ACS assumed, as Clay did, that whites and blacks could not coexist freely in the same nation, especially not as social and political equals with benefits of citizenship. Racism and fear of social disorder underlay this belief, of course, but not only those things. In historical experience going back to antiquity, no example existed of a culturally heterogeneous republic, let alone a successful multiracial one, except for those that had transformed into empires ruled by tyrants. At the same time, colonization offered the perceived merit of being a noncoercive way for slaveholders themselves to eliminate the black population without impairing the supposed legal privileges of slaveholders. In years to come, Clay continued to emphasize, as he would in 1829, that the approach involved "no project of emancipation, no new chains for those who unhappily are now in bondage, no scheme that is impracticable. It has no power, and it seeks none. It employs no compulsion, and it desires to employ none." It relied on persuasion. "Abolition" polarized northerners and southerners into rival camps; "colonization" offered to unite them. Much of the funding would flow from "spontaneous grants," its means, agents, and objects strictly voluntary. But in truth, Clay knew that federal administrative power also would be necessary, including expansion of the navy and a probable earmarking of tariff or land-sales revenue to support the cost.[44]

James Monroe, becoming the sixth president of the United States in March 1817, came prepared to advocate colonization with a degree of commitment that no previous chief executive had brought to the slavery problem. Jefferson, too, had once endorsed colonization as the best alternative to an exploding slave population and to sexual mixing of the races. Monroe, in a December 17, 1819, addendum to his Annual Message to Congress, unveiled a plan to send two agents to the African coast to find an overseas refuge for American blacks. By 1821, the ACS had acquired a large tract of land in West Africa, the future republic of Liberia, where it expected freed slaves to emigrate.[45]

Radical abolitionists like William Lloyd Garrison, of course, would later deplore the gradualism of the colonizationists. The majority of the free black community, in both North and South, never saw colonization as an attractive possibility at all; to most of them, and others still in bondage, America was now home. A generation of free blacks in the North already looked forward to receiving someday the full rights of citizenship, political participation, education, and a chance for economic security—all this, despite white incredulity and new laws, even in the "free states," that would restrict blacks' citizenship and deny their right to vote.[46]

James Tallmadge, the Barbour brothers, Henry Clay, and many others dealt, of course, with the same vexing problem. When the Missouri crisis unfolded, slavery remained the glaring hypocrisy of the early United States, a source of shame but in the southern states also a key to prosperity. In those first decades of the republic, many in the North and some in the South viewed slavery as wrong, though not necessarily a moral "evil." The root of the problem, regardless of proslavery constitutional provisions, was this: slaveholding threatened to undercut the republican creed as the Revolutionary generation had fashioned it, contradicting Enlightenment-inspired promises that white Americans had made to themselves and the world. Within three decades after 1776, northerners had put their slavery on course for extinction via gradual emancipation. Tragically, the South did not. New lands opened for plantation agriculture. Eli Whitney's cotton gin in 1793 enabled southerners to intensify their commitment to cotton growing and slave labor. With that, they accepted a heightened risk of slave insurrections. And in the end, both sides knew deep down that the real destiny of the republic—and the fate of millions, black and white—hinged on what kind of society would take shape on the remote borderlands of the new nation.

2 The West

LOOKING BACK from 1820 to early European settlement in the American West, the more curious fact is not that slavery became well established there but that so many nationalist policy makers in Washington *still* thought they could end it by legislation. Like the antislavery nation builders of that time, historians have sometimes underestimated how well entrenched slavery west of the Mississippi River already was in the decades before U.S. expansion into that long-contested region.

Notwithstanding the ban on slavery in the Northwest Territory, it would have taken great ingenuity for Congress to reverse the French, Spanish, and British processes that long had shaped the practices of labor, settlement, and trade in the Ohio, Mississippi, and Missouri Valleys. The Southwest Territory in 1790, Kentucky in 1792, Mississippi Territory in 1798, the Louisiana Territory in 1804–1805, and the Missouri region prior to 1820 all featured thriving slavery-based societies before federal governance came into the picture. In effect, the United States had little choice but to accept, and even protect, the rights of southwestern slaveholders as a condition of extending its sovereignty between 1783 and the early 1800s. In that respect, slavery actually helped to bind many white westerners to the early United States. In the 1790s, Kentucky and Tennessee would enter the Union without a peep from Congress about new state constitutions that safeguarded the practice of unfree labor.

As recent scholarship has emphasized, the United States did not so much *create* an empire for slavery as it *acquired* one. Prior to 1760, slaveholding in the trans-Mississippi West had spread throughout the environs of New Orleans and lodged in scattered European outposts inland. Then, beginning with the expansion of Caribbean plantation-style agriculture in the following decade and with the reshuffling of imperial possessions after the French and Indian War, the institution proliferated quickly from the Mississippi Delta, that is, the whole area between the Mississippi and Yazoo Rivers, northward into the Ohio and Missouri River regions. Eager to strengthen their hold on North America after 1763, Spain and Great Britain both gave generous land grants to settlers, urged production of staples and other goods to supply their more precious Caribbean island holdings, and fostered the further importation of slave labor. Pursuing the market, British merchants went to work purchasing human chattels in the Caribbean to be sold in Spanish New Orleans, about 8,500 enslaved men, women, and children in the 1770s and 1780s. In the 1790s, as slave revolts rocked the West Indies, the Spanish encouraged full-scale plantation development of the lower Mississippi Valley, expanding the Gulf trade beyond the Caribbean to the wider Atlantic commercial world and feeding further the demand for slaves to work the rich bottomlands. Saint-Domingue planters, unsettled by the 1791 slave revolution there, increasingly sought refuge in Louisiana, bringing coffles of blacks and a wealth of sugar-growing knowledge with them.[1]

And so, the great plantation boom of the deep Southwest had accelerated long before Americans first dreamed of gaining control of the Louisiana Territory. Between 1763 and 1800, the population of the lower Mississippi Valley had skyrocketed from roughly 10,000 to nearly 50,000, with the slave population constituting about half of that total. Full-blown "slave societies" rooted deeply. As it had for the new states south of the Ohio River, Congress would admit the new states of the lower Mississippi region—Louisiana in 1812, Mississippi in 1817, Alabama in 1819—not so much allowing slavery there as accommodating the system already well established. As planters in the southeastern United States now looked westward to a lucrative future beyond their wildest imaginings—a mainland replication of West Indian riches—they expected, too, a Mississippi Valley and a Gulf Coast relatively secure from the contagion of slave rebellion that had so disheartened Caribbean whites.[2]

Three Empires

Far from "virgin territory" when the United States received it, the trans-Mississippi region, which included what would become Missouri, has been called a "child of three empires": French, Spanish, and American. When President Thomas Jefferson in summer 1803 received the stunning news of the Louisiana Purchase, he little grasped how much the vast area west of the Mississippi featured a rich past, as well as a bright future.[3]

Jefferson undertook plans right away to impose governmental control over this new prize while tightening the nation's grip on the older frontiers. New Orleans and its environs were already well known; the far more extensive area to the north was not. The Virginia president's first impulse was to remove Indian tribes from east of the Mississippi, where they interfered with advancing white settlement, to the Missouri country. Once there, America's native inhabitants would be weaned from their traditional ways and turned toward the more "civilized" practices of farmers and herdsmen. Their presence would also constitute an effective buffer between white American settlements and the Spanish possessions farther west. Meanwhile, the Spanish and French inhabitants west of the river, now required to become American citizens, were to be coaxed eastward. Jefferson imagined all this would engineer a slow, systematic expansion of white Americans, advancing compactly as they multiplied.[4]

The initial strategy, however, did not mesh with the ground-level facts of upper Louisiana. For one thing, the white population long present in the new territory already had multiplied, scattered, and planned to stay put. In 1804, the Missouri country already hosted a small but vibrant—and profitable—slave society, with French, British, and even Native American inhabitants using human chattels in their agricultural and fur-trading operations. The federal ban on slavery in the Northwest Territory had chased additional French slaveholders living east of the Mississippi to the other side. River towns of St. Louis, St. Genevieve, and Cape Girardeau (founded respectively in 1764, 1735, and 1793) teemed with boatmen, merchants, and trappers with no intention of sacrificing their livelihoods in favor of Jefferson's dubious ideal of Indian philanthropy. Nor did they care to relinquish their slave property, which then constituted up to one-third of the population, for anyone's moralistic vision of a free-labor West. Eager to push the Louisiana Purchase through Congress before Napoleon changed his mind, Jefferson finally laid aside a proposed constitutional amendment that, first, would have blocked further white settlement of Missouri and, second, postponed indefinitely Missouri's chances for statehood.[5]

The 1820 Thomas Amendment line at 36°30' would change the whole way of American thinking about the trans-Mississippi frontier by deliberately sectionalizing it. Before that, the "West" seemed like an unbroken expanse of territory from the Great Lakes to the Gulf of Mexico and, after the Adams-Onís Treaty of 1819, stretching as far westward as the Rockies. The 36°30' line would create a more defined "Southwest"—the place beyond the Mississippi, including Arkansas Territory, the yet-unorganized area of Oklahoma, and the recently admitted state of Louisiana—all open to slavery. Few knew much of this expanse except that much of it was arid and supposedly unfit for traditional agriculture.[6]

The 36°30' line also gave political definition to the northwest part of the purchase, but many assumed that region, too, held little promise agriculturally. New York's Rufus King, never very keen on westward expansion anyway, would gripe that the Thomas Amendment had given the North only "a prairie, without wood or water, excepting the great River [the Missouri] and its branches," whereas the area south of the line, especially with the anticipation of Texas, provided room "for at least five slave states" in the fullness of time. The Lewis and Clark expedition of 1804–1806, and subsequent explorations, had been insufficient to dispel the widespread notion that the new "Northwest," lying above the future Thomas line and designated as closed to slavery after 1820, provided little more than a vast "American desert." Given this, southerners had reason to believe they had sacrificed little by accepting the prohibition of slavery in such a remote and presumably unappealing place.[7]

In any case, American settlement of most of the trans-Mississippi expanse looked far off indeed in the two-mile-an-hour world of 1820. The first transportation revolution of the nineteenth century—the proliferation of roads and canals, along with the earliest dreams of railroad travel—had scarcely begun. Back when Spain and France held imperial control over the trans-Mississippi West, the area that would become Missouri promised riches in the form of valuable minerals—especially lead—and fur pelts. For the French in the 1700s, the prospect of trade via the great river and trading depots at locations like the future site of St. Louis, a continental crossroads, interested settlers more than the richness of the farmland. Still more intriguing, however, were the mysteries of the great watercourse that emptied into the Mississippi just north of the fur-trading settlement that would become St. Louis: the Missouri River.[8]

After France lost all its North American territory in the 1763 Treaty of Paris, which ended the French and Indian War, Spain took over the vast trans-Mississippi region. But Spanish policy vacillated in the three decades that followed. At times, the Spanish welcomed immigrants looking to escape tobacco-exhausted Virginia or the fast-filling areas of Kentucky, Ohio, and Tennessee, but the idea of closing the Missouri region to settlement and keeping it as a secure buffer zone also appealed in Madrid. As of 1795, most of the Missouri area's inhabitants were French settlers from Canada or the eastern side of the Mississippi. In that year, however, the Treaty of San Lorenzo between Spain and the fledgling United States, which provided Americans trading rights on the great river, encouraged an influx of immigrants from the new republic—men and women (including frontier icon Daniel Boone) who went farther westward for not only fresh land but also freedom from taxation.[9]

Settlers west of the Mississippi already had learned to regard with considerable suspicion the faraway presence of centralized power, whatever its location. Being subject to long-delayed, poorly informed, and sometimes even hostile decision making in Washington would prove most exasperating. The fur trade, vital but undependable, required more definitive government support than traders usually received. Beyond that, after 1803, remained the issue of land titles that the Spanish had bestowed so lavishly but the United States refrained from honoring. Eastern private interests coveted those lands, while others in government calculated the federal revenue potential of their future sale. Related land disputes in Missouri would continue in one form or another until after the Civil War. Sharp disagreements over Indian policy also complicated the relationship, as did suspicions in the Missouri Territory well before 1819 that Congress planned to free all the slaves in the region included in the Louisiana Purchase. No wonder the separatist machinations of land speculators like William Blount in Tennessee, or the alleged "Burr Conspiracy" in 1807 to detach the trans-Mississippi states and territories from the United States, fell upon sympathetic western ears.[10]

The vast majority of settlers who streamed in, often with their slaves, came from south of the Potomac and Ohio Rivers. To them, slavery was anything but a fading institution. Unlike the Northwest, upper Louisiana beckoned as a region where the halting efforts of Congress to restrict the further expansion of slavery had failed. Almost as soon as news of the Louisiana Purchase hit the Missouri country, slaveholders there began to announce stiff opposition to any idea of extending Article VI of the Northwest Ordinance west of the Mississippi. Lawmakers in Washington, prompted by James Hillhouse's resolutions in 1804, had prohibited the domestic slave trade and tried to attach Missouri to the Indiana Territory, where the Northwest Ordinance had banned slavery. But in 1805, resistance from white Missourians, opposition from some southerners, and northern indifference led Congress to rescind the restrictions, and all later provisions for territorial government of upper Louisiana left slavery not only untouched but unmentioned. Thus, the first efforts toward gradual abolition west of the Mississippi collapsed almost as soon as they began. Afterward, slaveholding in Missouri Territory continued apace, limited, if at all, by local law but not federal ordinance.[11]

Diffusion

Meanwhile, an alternative to colonization for deconcentrating the population of blacks, and thus "whitening" southern society, gained currency in the older southern states: a "diffusion" of the problem westward. Assuming slavery weakened as it spread across space, diffusionists figured that finding a way to end the institution—or perhaps just mitigate its danger to whites— came down to simple demographics playing out over time. The argument sounded almost Madisonian: Extend the sphere of slaveholding and you reduce both the character-damaging effects on whites and the brutality of the institution for the slaves, assuming that masters treated smaller groups of slaves with more tenderness. Lessening the pressure on slaveholders to control their slaves by force, the nostrum of diffusion might also heighten the likelihood of voluntary manumissions and, eventually, gradual emancipation in the slave states. Madison himself endorsed the theory, as did Jefferson in his later years. Clay would do so as well during the Missouri crisis, finding in the concept no contradiction with the colonization scheme he had already embraced. In economic terms, scattering the slave population would diminish the supply of slave workers and raise their value, thus their sale price, making cheaper, free-white labor more attractive in the long run.[12]

Another major assumption behind diffusion really amounted to a confession: that slavery was a destructive, though not necessarily "evil," institution that southerners needed to reform, if not eradicate, for the good of all. Jefferson had given the classic statement of this admission in his 1785 *Notes on the State of Virginia,* his concern focusing less on what slavery did to blacks than on its negative impact on the behavior of white southerners. For Chesapeake slave owners living on depleted soil and eager to unload excess bondsmen, however, the argument held the attraction of profitable sales of experienced slaves to planters in the new states where virgin soil beckoned. Ultimately, the logic of diffusion appealed plenty to Upper South planters more animated by their pocketbooks than by their consciences. That consideration also accounts for their ardent defense of the interstate slave trade. Between 1790 and 1820, Maryland sold roughly 75,000 slaves to other parts of the South; Virginia, nearly 140,000—totals amounting to between half to three-quarters of the entire 1790 slave population in those states.[13]

But to put too fine a point on slaveholders' material interest is to miss the appeal of diffusion by half. Slaveholders in the Southeast lived in a world haunted by high black-to-white ratios. The slave population in the South Atlantic states would grow by leaps and bounds in the early decades of the nineteenth century, from roughly 684,000 in 1800, to 863,000 in 1810, to 1,038,000 in 1820. A similar percentage increase would manifest in the southwestern states— from 17,000 to 97,000 to 229,000 within that same twenty-year span—but the aggregate numbers of enslaved men and women in the West seemed less daunting than in the older South. Whether they owned slaves or not, southeastern white southern families lived in constant fear of slave insurrection, a threat that would worsen after the Missouri debate. *That* was the real "wolf" they held by the ears. Slaveholders in New York and New Jersey, with low black-to-white ratios, could end the institution and still cope with issues of race adjustment. By contrast, no Virginian or South Carolinian or Georgian could seriously consider ending slavery without a more promising way of getting rid of both slaves and resentful free blacks than colonization offered. Diffusion, as they imagined it, would drain away the troublesome population and "whiten" the South enough to make it safe for the whites themselves.[14]

Thus concerned with the political economy, the social sustainability, and, to a much lesser degree, the morality of slavery, diffusionist arguments appeared almost as soon as the first new territories adaptable to plantation-style agriculture opened in the West. Kentucky and Tennessee featured intriguing possibilities, but the 1798 debate in Congress on the expansion of slavery into Mississippi Territory, occurring at the same time that short-staple cotton promised a cash-crop windfall in the Lower South, provided an opportune moment for proponents of diffusion to tighten their case. Virginia's John Nicholas argued that encouraging slaveholders to settle the "Western country" would "be doing a service" not only to the slaves but "to the whole Union," as to "spread blacks over a large space" might eventually make it "safe" to "effect the plan which certain philanthropists [emancipationists] have so much at heart." Another Virginian, William Branch Giles, though less interested in gradual emancipation, agreed that diffusion meant the "amelioration" of vile conditions and harsh discipline resulting from slaves being "crowded together" in the Atlantic seaboard states. When Federalist George Thatcher from the Maine district of Massachusetts had the audacity to propose that Congress extend Article VI of the Northwest Ordinance to the Mississippi Territory, South Carolinians answered persuasively that doing so would only drive the Natchez country into the hands of the Spanish. Thatcher's initiative collapsed for lack of any serious support—only twelve House votes in favor. Even prominent antislavery congressmen such as Philadelphia's Thomas Hartley saw no sense in the measure if it would mean the loss of the Southwest.[15]

A few years later, former Virginian John Breckinridge, now of Kentucky, resumed the argument when Congress debated the expansion of slavery into the Louisiana Territory, telling fellow senators that he wished "our negroes were scattered more equally not only through the United States, but through our territories"—again, not to hasten their freedom but "so that their power might be lost." The "power" he meant was the threat of insurrection, a worry filling the minds of planters more and more after news of the Saint-Domingue revolution arrived. The ongoing plantation boom in lower Louisiana would have stopped dead without a steady influx of slave labor, and the sugar barons there, like the original Natchez elite, indicated determination to have their bonanza whether as part of the United States or not.[16]

To antislavery people, of course, any diffusion of the institution sounded crazy. As John Adams famously told Jefferson, when a cancer spreads, it kills the patient rather than curing him; so, too, with slave labor. "Miserable as the wretches are in the Carolinas," said one critic of the theory in the *Alexandria*

Gazette, "their condition with the good *old gentry* of those states is comparatively enviable when placed by that of the unfortunates in Louisiana." If what he had heard of the treatment of slaves in New Orleans contained even half-truth, the writer went on, it would be more humane to "send the wretches . . . in ships, and sink them in the sea."[17]

Northwest

The wording of Article VI of the Northwest Ordinance seemed more definitive than it actually was: "There shall be neither slavery nor involuntary servitude in the said territory, otherwise than in the punishment of crimes, whereof the party shall have been duly convicted: provided always, that any person escaping into the same, from whom labour or service is lawfully claimed in any one of the original states, such fugitive may be lawfully reclaimed." This ban did less about slavery in the Northwest than it might appear today. The unfolding reality on the ground would have a more critical bearing, not only on the settling of the Northwest but also Missouri Territory and, eventually, on the 1819–1821 controversy over Missouri's admission to the Union.[18]

Why did the ordinance exclude slavery in the first place? One key reason stands out: the main private party offering to purchase lands in Ohio, and thus deliver badly needed revenue for Confederation coffers, was the antislavery Massachusetts clergyman and former army chaplain Manassah Cutler. A congregation of wealthy Ohio Land Company associates stood behind him, a group that included several Revolutionary War veterans from New England. A ban on slavery in the Northwest Ordinance, pleasing to the land customers at hand, thus helped to lubricate the sale of several million acres. Most Confederation congressmen probably cared much less whether the ban would actually prevent an expansion of slaveholding, although some, like Rufus King, hoped it would. The original title of the legislation—"an Ordinance for establishing a temporary Government beyond the Ohio as preparatory to the sale of that Country"—implies in itself the influence of the impending land deal. Virginia's Richard Henry Lee, for one, stressed the importance of completing the land sale as soon as possible, before squatters seized it, thereby reducing the attractiveness to buyers and legitimate settlers. "We owe much money, the pressure of Taxes is very great & much complained of," he vented to Francis Lightfoot Lee a day after the ordinance passed, but at least they now had "something to sell that will pay the debt & discharge the greatest part of the Taxes."[19]

Others closely involved pointed to the imperative of selling the land and securing the proceeds, none more so than the delegate most credited for authoring the ordinance, Nathan Dane of Massachusetts. "We found ourselves rather pressed," Dane told King on July 16, 1787, as "the Ohio Company appeared to purchase a large tract of the federal lands, about 6 or 7 millions of acres." Dane, like other northeasterners, wanted a replication of New England settlement, culture, and values in the Northwest. But he also assumed that the easternmost state of the first three to be carved from the territory—soon to be Ohio, "and more important than the rest"—would "no doubt be settled chiefly by Eastern people." With this, he expected a "full and equal chance" of its "adopting Eastern politics," which by Massachusetts standards included a constitutional outlawing of slavery beyond a certain point in time.[20]

Even so, why did the southern delegates assent so easily to a provision clearly against slavery and potentially far-reaching in implications? The New England towns model in no way furnished *their* vision for society. The most likely answer was that Upper southerners saw the prohibition as an implicit protection of the right to hold slaves *south* of the Ohio River, which mattered to them more. This way, staple crop growers in Virginia and Kentucky would not, in years to come, have to compete with the similar product of slave labor from north of the river. Virginia delegate William Grayson, who sat on the committee that drew up the ordinance, told James Monroe in August 1787 that the prohibition of slavery had been "agreed to by the Southern members for the purpose of preventing Tobacco and Indigo from being made on the N.W. side of the Ohio, as well as for sevl. other political reasons," including the Ohio Company influence. In addition, a rapid, thick settlement of the Ohio Company purchase would, as Grayson also observed, elevate the value of surrounding lands, "valuable from their contiguity to these settlements," and excite land speculators (like Grayson himself), many of whom lived in Virginia. Meanwhile, planters living in the deeper South, eyeing the rich lands that would eventually become Tennessee, Alabama, and Mississippi, had even less reason at the time to care what happened north of the Ohio. Still another factor was the recent memory of the ever-so-narrow defeat of Jefferson's antislavery initiative in 1784—a close call that southern members wished not to revisit. For plantation interests, to gain a foothold in the southern half of the West, along with a fugitive slave clause in the ordinance that guarded against successful escape north of the river, appeared much more as gain than loss.[21]

If the 1787 ordinance signaled to slaveholders not yet living in the Northwest that they had best settle elsewhere, it did nothing to end the slavery that already existed north of the Ohio River. Even there, slave owners would not quickly bow to the will, vaguely expressed, of some far-distant lawmaking authority. For them, like their southern counterparts—and also for the large number of slaveholders still in New York and New Jersey—bondsmen and bondswomen registered as economic assets, and it would take more than the liberating implications of Revolutionary ideology to trump their property rights. Moreover, the free states emerging from the Northwest Territory in the early years of the republic all shared borders with slave states. The rules of comity among states after 1789 could not allow suspension of the right of transit or temporary residence, meaning that the frequent presence of slaves and their owners in the Northwest, along with every kind of practice that upheld the institution, would have to be honored in state law.[22]

The First Congress in 1789 repassed the Northwest Ordinance and its Article VI prohibition of slavery while also voting to protect slavery already established in the Southwest Territory. The migration of settlers from New England onto the lands north of the Ohio did heighten the likelihood of maintaining the exclusion of slavery, but Article VI of the 1787 ordinance still went only so far to enforce itself. Neither the federal government nor local magistrates in territories within the Northwest, especially Indiana and Illinois, paid much attention to the prohibition in years prior to the admission of these as new states. Early on, some government officials—and many more private voices in the Northwest—who claimed a desire to end slavery subscribed to the "diffusion" theory as an eventual answer and, in the interim, a benefit for both blacks and whites. In places where blacks did not outnumber whites, including those in the West that would allow slavery, emancipation might finally be embraced without an economic collapse or the paralyzing fear of retribution.[23]

If the bar against slavery had little short-term legal force in the Northwest, its *psychological* impact would prove more significant. National authority held the greatest sway at ground level by planting a troublesome uncertainty in the minds of slave owners and those who might wish to be. The same would have been true in Missouri had the Tallmadge Amendment been applied to it in 1820. The 1763 Treaty of Paris between France and Great Britain had safeguarded the property, including slaves, of French settlers who lived in the Northwest. When Virginia ceded its claim to the region to the Confederation government in 1784, its act of transfer also required that existing property rights be honored subsequently. Article II of the Northwest Ordinance also called for "the just preservation of rights and property" and guarded "private contracts or engagements" from infringement by law. But no one could be sure what future legislation might bring. Unable to predict antislavery actions that Congress might attempt later, concerned inhabitants of the "Illinois country" in 1788 sent an agent, Barthelemi Tardiveau, to lobby on their behalf. He argued that Article VI of the ordinance threatened a kind of ex post facto tyranny—just what the American Revolution, had been fought to prevent. That argument would come in handy for Missourians in 1819–1820, when proposed antislavery stipulations again threatened holders of slave property. After the government in Philadelphia ignored Tardiveau, along with a litany of petitions from proslavery settlers, many slaveholders moved to Spanish territory west of the Mississippi—the region that later was the Missouri Territory. Lamenting the departure of some of the wealthiest inhabitants, Tardiveau told territorial governor Arthur St. Clair that "panic" had "seized upon their minds," impelling them to avert "their utter ruin" before it might be too late.[24]

Dozens of additional petitions to Congress asking for clarification or modification of Article VI of the ordinance would continue to receive a cautious no-response in the first decade of the nineteenth century. Interestingly, *none* of those petitions argued that slavery was a "positive good," as southerners would in the decades preceding the Civil War, or that slaveholding conformed to republicanism. Instead, they emphasized political necessity, economic benefits, and the doubtful logic of diffusion. In the absence of federal policy, territorial governments in Indiana and Illinois protected slavery on their own, always careful to avoid de jure violations of the Northwest Ordinance. These de facto subterfuges included rental contracts, a system of long-term indentures amounting to slavery in everything but name, and a variety of enforcement measures that fixed the status of slaves present before 1787. Slavery would continue in Indiana beyond its admission to statehood in December 1816. The Indiana Supreme Court then declared the practice irreconcilable with the state constitution in the 1820 case of *State v. Lasselle*, when the federal census reported 190 slaves still in bondage there. In Illinois, admitted two years after Indiana, there would be no judicial ruling like that of its sister state, and slaveholding lasted in various forms until 1848, when the state's second constitution finally would put an end to the practice.[25]

In some respects, the unfolding of late-frontier politics in Ohio, Indiana, and especially Illinois also foreshadowed the drama that would play out full-blown over Missouri. Two of Ohio's most prominent founding fathers, Edward Tiffin and Thomas Worthington, both of Chillicothe, had emancipated their slaves before moving west from Virginia and remained devoutly antislavery thereafter. Many other antislavery Ohioans who migrated from Virginia had first settled in Kentucky, only to be disappointed that Kentuckians chose against a plan for gradual emancipation at their 1799 constitutional convention. In the 1802 election of delegates for the Ohio state constitutional convention, voters unequivocally chose Republican candidates pledged to uphold the Northwest Ordinance and oppose the establishment of slavery in any form, including the quasi-slavery that more resembled lasting indentured servitude. A group of Ohioans in 1806, styling themselves the "Freeborn Sons" of their state, gladly remained "true to the rights of humanity, and the principles of liberty," while preventing the "foul form of slavery to tread on their sacred soil." While both the Jeffersonian Republican and Federalist camps in the territory claimed contempt for slavery, the Republican side succeeded in capturing the dominant narrative as the ones most determined to preserve the "principles of genuine republicanism," which meant advocating for small-scale producers (farmers and laborers) against abstract forces of hierarchy, aristocracy, and inequality—regarded as conflicting with the American Revolution. Under the Ohio Enabling Act, which Congress approved in 1802, voters still could have left a door open to slavery in years to come, but Ohioans persistently refused to do so.[26]

By contrast with the Buckeye example, the future states of Indiana and Illinois during their territorial phases developed into more of a cultural middle ground between South and North, slavery and freedom. Among the few American military successes during the War of 1812, the Battle of Lake Erie in September 1813 and the Battle of the Thames four weeks later secured the Northwest from British occupation and Native American power. The large influx of settlers into the region after the war included men and women of southern heritage who brought slaveholding practices with them. The Ohio River had not yet become the dividing line between bondage and freedom that 1780s lawmakers had tried to establish. Oftentimes, slave catchers, acting legally, pursued fugitive slaves across the river, returning frequently enough with other blacks they had, quite illegally, kidnapped instead. Indiana territorial governor William Henry Harrison, Virginia-born and proslavery, argued repeatedly that Congress should repeal the ban on slavery as a matter of fostering maximum economic growth of the region. He and other slaveholders living there tried to avoid the Ohio example of letting the slavery issue become the substance of hot public debate. Only after antislavery Hoosiers managed to win control of the territorial legislature, by championing the interests of yeoman farmers against the "Virginia aristocrats," did Indiana lawmakers agree on a state constitution in 1816 that prohibited slavery.[27]

Illinois

The population of the Illinois region, like that of Indiana, grew dramatically in the years after the War of 1812, jumping by roughly 160 percent, the increase reflecting dislocations in both the East and the South. Multiple crop failures in 1816, "the year without summer" because of the 1815 volcanic eruption of Mount Tambora in Indonesia, chased thousands of easterners to the northwestern frontier. Farmers from the old states, their pockets empty, their lands fruitless, their patience shattered, found hope in the rich soils north of the Ohio River. Although Illinois settlers had proved to be a diverse lot, most who lived in the southern part by 1818 came from the slave states, like many also arriving on Missouri lands across the Mississippi. In the southernmost regions of the old Northwest, daily life would take on much of the character of the Upper South: family connections, settlement patterns, architectural styles, economic relations, figures of speech, even the food people ate. Of about 35,000 white inhabitants in Illinois at that time, roughly 38 percent came from the southeastern states, mostly Virginia and North Carolina. Another 37 percent had migrated from the Southwest, primarily Kentucky and Tennessee. Ravaging speculators and endless litigation over unclear land titles sent a large number of embittered migrants from western Kentucky. Others from the Bluegrass state, like Abraham Lincoln's father, simply preferred to move to the less-settled regions northwest of the Ohio River, where they believed slaveholders unlikely to follow. The Middle Atlantic states, Pennsylvania in particular, contributed only about 13 percent of the territorial population—and New England, primarily Massachusetts and Vermont, less than a quarter of that. Immigrants from Europe made up the rest.[28]

Temporary climate change in 1815 little affected the postwar boom in cotton production farther south. It did, however, pressure southern yeomen, who grew little cotton, to leave the South in droves, headed for the fertile regions north of the Ohio River. Sometimes they went with the aspiration of replicating the planter world they had left behind, sometimes not. Southern origins did not always equate with proslavery feelings. Plantations expanded wildly, as the price of upland cotton more than doubled between 1814 and 1818, from 15 to 34 cents a pound in the New York market. But smaller southern farmers—the yeoman class—experienced this shift often more as loss than gain. Some disliked the expansion of slavery, others the advance of greedy nouveau riche planters and growing social stratification, still others the prospect of living near large numbers of blacks, whether enslaved or free. For some of these yeomen, like the Kentucky-born future governor Richard Yates and Methodist minister Peter Cartwright, who both had moved from Tennessee, Illinois loomed in imagination as a potential refuge from a southern society that more and more rewarded the slaveholding elite, degraded free labor, and undercut the sacrifices and the values of ordinary nonslaveholding farmers. Those, by contrast, who carried westward the hope of becoming slaveholding planters themselves usually thought in smaller, more egalitarian terms than the cotton barons of the Old South. Some did bring small numbers of slaves with them to Illinois, taking their chances that Congress might not admit Illinois to the Union except as a free state.[29]

Well-connected former southerners and slaveholders, including Daniel Pope Cook, Ninian Edwards, Jesse B. Thomas, and Elias Kane, would lead the push for Illinois statehood in 1818. For a while, it looked as if Illinois, not Missouri, might become the test case on further slavery expansion. The issue clouded the selection of delegates to the Illinois constitutional convention, where an article in favor of slavery went down by a vote of only 14 to 17. Finally conceding that Congress would reject an unequivocally proslavery constitution, Kane put forward a compromise. In essence, it proposed that no new slaves would be introduced in Illinois, but it did not free those already living there. "French-owned slaves," whose owners had been protected under Virginia's act of cession in 1784, would remain as they were. An indentured servant system, in which blacks "contracted" to work for white owners—a system of quasi-slavery—could continue in Illinois, but the servants' male children would gain freedom at age twenty-one, their female offspring at age

eighteen. Slaves could still be brought to work the salt deposits near Shaw-
neetown but only until 1825. Slave owners, trusting that their human property would not be stricken from them immediately, had plenty of time to "sell
south" the bondsmen they already owned. In all, it appeared that slavery in
Illinois, including that masquerading as indentured servitude, had been sched-
uled for termination—at least until after Congress granted statehood.[30]

Even so, the constitution that Illinoisans submitted to Congress in 1818
prohibited slaves from being "introduced" in years to come but without providing a speedy liberation of any in bondage there already. That ambiguity
troubled antislavery political observers in the North who hoped the third
state to be carved from the Northwest would make a much more decisive
leap toward abolition. In Salem, Massachusetts, the *Essex Resister* rightly
noted a lingering uncertainty in Illinois as to outlawing slavery. "The doubt
is disgraceful," said the editor. "After Slavery has been established, it is a serious evil, which claims some indulgence in the manner of treating it. But to
begin wrong, has no excuse"; any remaining ambivalence was "shameful."
For others, the decision in Illinois to apply as a free state represented "an
auspicious commencement." So declared New York City's *National Advocate*,
adding, "however important and serviceable a portion of black population
may be in that quarter, the only method to prevent the extension of slavery in
the west and depress it in the south is constitutional provisions against such
measures in the new states—thus giving to the population all the benefits of
equal rights."[31]

In autumn 1818, the House took up Speaker Clay's resolution to admit
Illinois into the Union under a proposed state constitution more unclear on
slavery than those of Ohio and Indiana before it. The speeches and votes
against the admission of Illinois represented only a small minority, but they
anticipated the sectional crisis over Missouri in early 1819. No one objected
more vociferously to the Illinois constitution than James Tallmadge, who
claimed (rightly) that the Illinois Territory contained fewer than the number
of inhabitants the Northwest Ordinance required for statehood. Further, he
contended, the sixth article in its constitution could be interpreted as justifying slave trading in the former Northwest Territory. The Virginia Cession
of 1784, Tallmadge insisted (erroneously), had required the same antislavery stipulation that had been written into the 1787 ordinance. Therefore,
Congress had an obligation to strictly enforce Virginia's original intent.[32]

George Poindexter of Natchez, Mississippi, rose to the defense. He retorted that Illinois had "virtually" complied with its contract under the Northwest Ordinance, following the example of the two states already formed from the same territory, Ohio and Indiana. As for the Illinois provision regarding "persons" (quasi-slaves) held by indenture, he expressed only the "hope" that slavery might as far as possible be expelled from the country. Kentucky's Richard Clough Anderson added that the census-taking in Illinois had been done in the same manner as in the Ohio and Indiana territories prior to their admission and should be regarded as satisfactory. As for the Virginia Cession, he correctly noted that no such provision as Tallmadge claimed had been included in its stipulations. In any case, fairness demanded that Illinois be admitted with as much "a sense of expediency" as any previous new state.[33]

Tallmadge stubbornly answered that he considered Congress obligated to prohibit slavery by "a tie not to be broken." If he had been mistaken in his understanding of Virginia's requirements, and if the issue was to be governed under "a sense of expediency," then he thought "that tie ten thousand times stronger." The "interest, honour, and faith of the nation" demanded that Congress guard scrupulously against the passing of slavery into a territory where Confederation lawmakers in 1787 had exercised the nation-building power to prevent it. Even so, that prompted an impatient William Henry Harrison, now of Ohio, to insist that no earlier provision whatsoever had shorn the people of Illinois of their "sovereign authority." He considered the supposed pre-1789 pledge of the Confederation Congress to prohibit slavery in the Northwest Territory a "dead letter" and believed others, including Alexander Hamilton in the *Federalist Papers*, had considered it so because it antedated ratification of the Constitution. Congress, he said (incorrectly), had not "renewed" the prohibition.[34]

It was Tallmadge who won media praise not only in New York but in other parts of the Northeast as well. The *Hartford Times* reported an "unexpected" and "spirited" debate on the resolution to admit Illinois into the "confederacy," referring to Tallmadge as "a liberal republican, and a gentleman of fine talents." The *Times* writer also maintained that Virginia had ceded its claim above the Ohio River "under an express stipulation, that neither slavery, nor involuntary servitude, otherwise than as a punishment for a crime, should ever be allowed within that territory." Distorted history, yes, but it made good copy for antislavery readers and anyone else who liked political controversy. Indiana, he more accurately noted, had not only banned slavery but also added a special clause in its constitution prohibiting any amendment ever being made to sanction human chattels. Illinois had not. Tallmadge, though speaking for a distinct minority in 1818, "was anxious that our government should wipe away the unjust imputation, that while in one hand we hold the torch of freedom, we in the other are brandishing the whip of the slave driver."[35]

Some congressmen from New England and other northeastern states joined the protest against continued slaveholding in Illinois, 34 voting against its admission for that reason. But the 117 votes in favor carried the day, and the Senate followed suit without a single dissent. President James Monroe signed Illinois into statehood, the twenty-first member of the Union, on December 3, 1818—a mere two and a half months before the Tallmadge Amendment shook the capital. Meanwhile, the two Illinois senators-elect, Ninian Edwards and Jesse B. Thomas—both Maryland born, both proslavery, both slaveholders themselves—arrived in Washington, found their lodgings, and prepared to assume the full duties of office.[36]

Southwest

Even though the Panic of 1819 hit southern agriculture with fury, southerners with slaves to sell could by that time look forward to westward expansion much more than they did a few decades earlier. In the 1790s, white settlers in the Southwest had grown more and more frustrated with the inability of the United States to protect their interests. Rumors swirled in Tennessee and elsewhere of plots to deliver borderland regions into rival Spanish hands. Early northern population growth foretold that free-state representatives in the House of Representatives would increasingly outnumber those of the slave states. Prior to the War of 1812, much of the Southwest, the Mississippi Delta, and lower Louisiana stood vulnerable to foreign conquest, Indian unrest, and slave rebellion, as well as separatist agitation. Despite Pinckney's 1795 Treaty with Spain, which had secured navigation rights to the Mississippi, and the Louisiana Purchase, which technically brought that watercourse under U.S. sovereignty, failure to secure the southwestern borderlands region had contradicted the early belief of Madison and other southerners that internal migration would naturally flow southwest instead of northwest. For reasons both geographical and commercial, Britain, Spain, and the United States all coveted the city of New Orleans, and many residents there would have been as happy to swear allegiance to a foreign monarch as to an American republic. While lower Louisiana had become a refuge for planters fleeing the revolution in Saint-Domingue, some of their slaves surreptitiously embraced the "contagion of liberty" they had witnessed in the Caribbean.[37]

But for many southerners, the War of 1812 amounted to a huge victory, thanks largely to Andrew Jackson and his ragtag army of Tennessee militiamen and volunteers. At the March 1814 Battle of Horseshoe Bend in the Alabama half of the Mississippi Territory, Jackson's forces brutally routed the "Red Stick" Creeks, massacring women and children along with some 900 warriors. That outcome wrecked any possibility of a pan-Indian alliance between hostile southern tribes and Native American groups on the northern frontier who identified with Chief Tecumseh, the inspirational Shawnee leader (who had died at the Battle of the Thames). The ensuing treaty victimized friendly Creeks as well as the troublesome "Red Stick" faction, establishing American control over all Indian lands—some 23 million acres—in Alabama and western Georgia.[38]

Then, in summer 1814, came the alert that a sixty-ship British battle fleet, carrying 8,000 hardened redcoat veterans of the Napoleonic Wars, was headed straight for New Orleans. A successful British conquest would have not only blasted the cherished dream of southern expansionists but also, just as likely, galvanized slaves in the region to rebel en masse. Dispatched to repel this invasion, Jackson arrived in New Orleans with his Tennessee men in early December, added a disparate contingent of locals that included everyone from free black militia to opportunistic French pirates under Jean Lafitte, and engaged British regulars several times prior to the decisive showdown on January 8, 1815. On that day, line after line of redcoat infantry marched right into a withering rifle and artillery barrage from the fortified but heavily outnumbered Americans. The result was momentous, a major turning point for the South: Jackson's men, unflinching, shot down roughly a quarter of the invading force—300 British killed, 1,700 wounded—while suffering only about 50 casualties of their own. Jackson's victory tightened the U.S. grip on the entire region and proved that the lower Mississippi borderlands belonged in fact, as well as in law, to the new republic. The war that had seemed so disastrous for Americans in the Northeast had given slaveholding southern expansionists not only a hero in Jackson but also, it seemed, a bright future in the West.[39]

And that was not all. Early in 1818, only a year before the Missouri crisis exploded, the War Department sent Jackson, now a major general in command of the southern division of the U.S. Army, to Fort Scott in Georgia, where he readied another force to march into Spanish-owned Florida, the only remaining European possession on the Gulf Coast. Not only had Spanish power over Florida weakened, but its wilderness attracted runaway slaves who made allies with Indian tribes there, much to the chagrin of Georgia planters. Jackson and his men mounted a three-week campaign, hunting down fugitive blacks, incinerating Indian villages, murdering native chieftains, and executing a pair of "meddling" British agents they captured, named Arbuthnot and Armbrister. They pushed on to Pensacola, where Spanish authorities handed over the city along with effective control of the Florida Panhandle. "I have no doubt but in a few years, the Banks of the allabama will present a beautiful view of elegant mansions, and extensive rich & productive farms," Jackson effused prophetically. Building on this further success, Secretary of State John Quincy Adams pursued negotiations that ended in the Adams-Onís Treaty. In part of this pact, signed in Washington on February 22, 1819, Spain ceded East Florida to the United States and gave up its claims to West Florida. Pending Senate ratification, the United States would command the entire Gulf Coast. Still, southerners, their territorial ambition refueled, wondered why the treaty also renounced American claims to Texas, leaving slaveholder incursions into Mexican territory to be arranged in years to come. To them, the Tallmadge Amendment would supply a clear answer: Antislavery northeasterners, including Secretary Adams himself, thought slavery had spread far enough.[40]

Meanwhile, a dynamic new political economy of slavery advanced westward. This shift reflected southern capitalistic forces at work since the 1790s, as well as wartime gains. While slaveholding slowly ended in the northeastern states, it now burst into the Southwest. Eli Whitney's cotton gin had arrived in the lower Mississippi region by 1795, transforming both the production of cotton and the demand for slaves. The global market for manufactured textiles guaranteed that southwestern short-staple cotton would replace tobacco, rice, and indigo as the plantation crop of the future. Cotton production tripled in the five years before the Missouri crisis, from 54,000 bales (a bale equaling about 500 pounds) in 1814–1815 to 159,500 in 1819–1820. Federal land sales skyrocketed in the Deep South to nearly 5 million acres by October 1819. So did cotton prices: from 17 cents a pound in 1814 to 27 cents the following year to nearly 30 cents in 1817, before first signs of the Panic of 1819 drove them back down.[41]

Racism aside, the unforgiving climate of the Deep South along with the shortage of white workers seemed to make forced labor a foregone conclusion. Major cotton growers often insisted that free labor could not answer their needs. To them, naked economic truths reinforced that judgment: landless whites could demand high wages, would not stand harsh supervision, resented working other men's fields, often left to squat on claims farther west, and would not tolerate a hot climate and its diseases as African men and women forcibly did. Fabulous riches, material luxury, and political domination rewarded the cotton entrepreneurs who spearheaded the westward onslaught of "slave society" in the Deep South. Although it proved far from a yeoman's paradise, poorer whites still aspired to a piece of the bonanza even if they often resented their haughty, quasi-aristocratic "social betters." The internal slave trade took care of the voracious demand for new plantation labor, while driving higher and higher the value of prime field hands from the slave-glutted Upper South. After the closing of the legal slave import trade, Virginia owners far more often opted to sell rather than manumit their surplus slaves, never mind scattered pangs of conscience or an occasional chiding from evangelical clergymen.[42]

At the same time, sugar planters in Louisiana vied for hemispheric domination over the insurrection-tormented cane moguls of the Caribbean, further spurring the internal demand for slave labor along with the now-illegal foreign trade. Refugee planters from Saint-Domingue contributed their experience and technical knowledge of sugar cultivation. While black population growth vastly outstripped that of whites, the *Louisiana Gazette* nonetheless embraced and reiterated the increasingly bogus case for diffusion: Sugar plantations offered the eastern slave states "an outlet for the superabundance of their black population, and an extravagant price for what will shortly be to them, an incumbrance instead of an advantage."[43]

It jarred northern ears after 1815 to hear slave owners, including new southwesterners, speaking about slavery in positive terms overall, if not yet as a "positive good." The "diffusionist" argument of just a few years before had accepted the premise that slavery was undesirable, that spreading it westward offered a means to dilute its ill effects and eventually prepare the way for gradual emancipation on the northern model. In the Missouri debate, however, southern congressmen and senators, emboldened by southwestern success, would rally behind the rhetorical barricades of paternalism, transforming slavery into a benign "domestic" institution, philosophically defensible in the language of sympathy, humanitarianism, and family values. As addressed to northerners, this paternalism argued that slaveholders were not bad people; to fellow southerners, the doctrine became a set of instructions for avoiding the potentially ill consequences of holding slaves—and perhaps a way to convince themselves on the vaunted "merits" of an immoral labor system. Far from being the brutalizing "tyrants" that antislavery northerners increasingly said they were, slaveholders more and more regarded themselves as benevolent "patriarchs," responsible for the welfare of three interlocking dependencies: their own families, the members of their slave communities, and the larger society of whites and blacks living together, unequal but bound in an unending, precarious balance. This shift evidenced an entirely revised perspective on slavery, a new rationalization of the institution, based on a slaveholders' warping of evangelical Christian messages of the early Second Great Awakening. The end of the slave import trade in 1808 aided indirectly in their rationalizing: Limiting the slave population to natural increase left slave masters with acculturated native-born chattels who might prove loyal, compliant, and less rebellious.[44]

Missouri Territory

Spring 1817 brought fabulous news for War of 1812 veterans entitled to bounty lands. A Tennessee newspaper reported 5 million acres in the Missouri and Illinois territories to be in a "rapid state of preparation" and soon to be allotted among the former soldiers. Eighty companies of surveyors—more than 400 men—had two months to finish their ordering of the land, carefully measuring out the federally mandated township grids. That process of land organization conformed to the Congressional Land Ordinance of 1785, the other great legislative accomplishment of the old Confederation, along with the Northwest Ordinance of 1787. The soil promised to be "superior in fertility" to the richest lands in Kentucky. The military tract in Illinois covered one of the most desirable locations in the Northwest: washed by the Mississippi River on the west and the Illinois River on the east, with "an easy communication" to New Orleans, or to Lake Michigan through frontier Chicago, or to New York when "the canal of that state is finished." The tract on the Missouri side allured equally well: "watered by the Mississippi, the Missouri, and its tributaries the Great Osage and the Gasgonade"— promising for wheat, hemp, and tobacco, scattered with lead and salt deposits, and abundant in fur. Perhaps the only real area of difference came down to a basic choice the former soldiers had to make, one soon to prove historic: Illinois territory remained nominally off limits to slavery. That had never been so in Missouri.[45]

The good news did little to allay the resentment that many settlers living in Missouri Territory still felt toward the federal government. Between the end of Jefferson's presidency and its application for statehood, Missouri had changed dramatically—and in ways that radicalized many of its inhabitants. Territorial census returns for Louisiana showed only about 20,000 non-Indians residing in the region between the Missouri and Arkansas rivers in 1810, a total only slightly exceeding the numbers of Osage, Shawnee, Delaware, Cherokee, and Choctaw inhabitants. White pioneers who lived in sparsely settled districts any distance away from the Mississippi River lay dangerously vulnerable to Indian attack—all the more so after Congress declared war on Great Britain in June 1812. Both sides in the war scrambled for Indian allies in the West. Only three days after President James Madison issued his war message, he also signed legislation carving out the Missouri Territory with "second-stage" privileges of electing a territorial assembly and sending a delegate to represent it in the House of Representatives. Now, federal officials thought, Missourians might more happily prepare their defense against the British and their Indian allies. This step toward democratization furnished governing power to the population of land-hungry agricultural settlers who had come from the eastern side of the Mississippi, their presence increasingly threatening the French minority who still largely controlled the fur trade. It also weakened the power of the territorial governor, whose claim to legitimacy still resided far away in the nation's capital.[46]

As Indian raids escalated during the war, so did resentment that American settlers harbored toward both French traders and the power of increasingly distracted decision makers in Washington. One group of Boon's Lick inhabitants, mostly migrants from Kentucky and Tennessee, justified in terms of self-defense their incursion on legally protected French commerce. Since the government of the United States refused to favor *their* interests over these "foreign" rivals, then, as one put it "we determined to protect ourselves." Others grumbled that federally appointed governors remained indifferent not only to the newly arrived Missourians' economic advantage but also their security. Governor Benjamin Howard, they said, spent more time attending to private affairs in his native Kentucky than he did to public ones in St.

Louis. An absent governor, especially in wartime, crippled the efficacy of the militia and delayed urgently needed administrative actions. Worse, the federal government viewed Missouri as a military backwater, which, compared to other theaters of the war, it was. At the start of hostilities in 1812, fewer than 250 regular troops guarded the territory, a number little augmented later, exposing the territory to oft-rumored British or Spanish conquest. Howard's successor in 1813, William Clark, addressed the troop shortage by entreating help from the Osages, to the further disgust of his territorial constituents, whose fresh memories of Indian "atrocities" made them distrustful of all tribes in the region.[47]

Clark's postwar Indian policy curried little more favor with his constituents than his wartime actions did. Perhaps recalling his gratitude to the Hidatsas, Mandans, and Nez Perce who saved his life during the "Corps of Discovery" days with Meriwether Lewis—or, just as likely, carrying forward Jeffersonian "philanthropy" under Madison's presidency—Clark dismissed whites' proposals that he exterminate their now-inconvenient Indian neighbors. Instead, he held a peacemaking council at Portage des Sioux in summer 1815 with representatives of a dozen tribes and thanked the Shawnees and Delawares for their help against the British. Then, following Jeffersonian land policy, he issued a stern anti-squatter proclamation that December, ordering white "intruders" on Shawnee and Delaware lands "to depart therefrom without delay." Bristling over the edict, white frontiersmen swarmed into those regions anyway, defying Clark to stop them and cursing his "insensitive" superiors in Washington, his French merchant allies, and the "monied" operators in St. Louis (including Clark himself) whom he favored.[48]

The white population of the Missouri Territory boomed after 1815. In 1818, apart from the opening of bounty lands, the federal government allowed public land to go on sale all over the territory. Proslavery migrants poured in from Virginia, Maryland, North Carolina, Kentucky, and Tennessee. Others followed the advance of the frontier, settling in Missouri because of the geographical proximity and cultural similarity to their previous homes southeast of the Mississippi River. Many new inhabitants filled the rich alluvial arc between the Mississippi and Missouri River valleys, a region promising abundant yields of tobacco and hemp despite smaller-sized plantations than the once-great Tidewater estates. The new planters and small farmers there shipped their crops to market via St. Louis, itself still less a city than a frontier settlement of wood-frame houses constructed by the earlier French in-habitants. Western settlers who opposed slavery, conversely, gravitated more to the legally designated free soil of the old Northwest. By 1820, some 56,000 whites, about 300 free blacks, and nearly 11,000 slaves lived in the Missouri territory—an increase from a total population of only about 3,000 ten years earlier and tripling the number of whites over nonwhites who remained. Meanwhile, ever larger numbers of white squatters, in defiance of federal land law, pushed farther and farther inland toward the Ozarks and brutally dispatched any Indians who got in their way, undercutting decades of inter-cultural goodwill. So resistant to governance, schooling, and culture were these lawless intruders that ethnologist Henry Rowe Schoolcraft, in his 1818 travels through the Ozarks, encountered one pioneer who acknowledged he had no idea who was president or even whether Missouri had achieved state-hood—nor did he care. Schoolcraft further reported how the often-witless parents of young boys in these wilds of the territory encouraged ultra-aggres-sive behavior, approving childhood quarrels in which they "frequently stab each other with knives." Some of the locals looked upon such defiance of good order as "a promising trait of character."[49]

Appalled by indifference to the rule of law, Clark stood his ground, no matter the cost to his own popularity. The Missouri Assembly, elected by white male citizens of the territory, prepared to thwart him as much as it could. Replying to his pro-Indian proclamation, the assembly resolved in Jan-uary 1816, and again in 1817, that the earlier Spanish government had never meant "the Scattered parts of Indian Tribes . . . to hold much Lands if any." Territorial lawmakers cited preceding grants to individuals living within the now-protected Indian domain (claims that a national land commission had mostly upheld), referring to the "considerable improvements" these white settlers had already made, and recommended removal of the Shawnees and Delawares to "some more remote part" of the territory, "better suited" to their "pursuits." The subtext was that neither Clark nor leaders in Wash-ington would dare mount an anti-squatter expedition in the West. Everyone knew that military force against one's own people held almost zero appeal in nation's capital. With Missouri's elevation to third-stage territorial status after 1816—the verge of statehood—the governorship had become elective, which meant the end for Clark.[50]

In short, the mass of white Missourians on the eve of the Missouri crisis in Washington held little regard for any faraway central government. Knowing that, few in Congress after 1815 would have viewed Missourians as much inclined to cooperate with any nationalist designs, short of those imposed upon such an obstreperous people. Westerners often used public occasions both to assert their identification with American Revolutionary ideas and to distance themselves from eastern authority. A July 4, 1817, celebration in St. Louis, for example, featured toasts that expressed local aversion to federal power. The revelers drank heartily to the "lead and fur trade of the country.—Certain sources of wealth and strength, if in the hands of individuals. But not otherwise." And also to the "Salt Springs and public lands in the territory.—May they be speedily offered for sale; better in the hands of individuals, than monopolized by the government." Celebratory occasions of one sort or another served as a "two-way mirror" whereby western leaders pandered to independent-minded local audiences while knowing full well that their statements would appear in newsprint and circulate back East as a message, and sometimes an implied warning, to federal lawmakers. It further enraged would-be settlers that wealthy St. Louis speculators, sometimes with prior knowledge of impending congressional decisions, often snapped up tracts released to the market for bargain prices, afterward kicking off squatters already there, then destroying (or taking over) their crops and buildings without compensation. Victims of such treatment blamed the government for their misfortune as much as they did the speculators. Those who saw matters in ideological terms sensed a corrupt, unrepublican alliance between the two. Rarely, however, did these "less-fortunate" squatters confess their own unholy intentions to resell for profit the government lands they had seized for nothing and "improved" scarcely at all.[51]

As for slavery, the growing presence of bondsmen over these years went unquestioned in the territory—a normality to the minds of settlers from south of the Ohio River, especially so because unfree labor never had been banned or unwelcome. The influx of slaveholders featured prominently in the commercial rise of St. Louis in the early nineteenth century. The city's population exploded between 1810 and 1820—particularly in the five years after the War of 1812—from roughly 1,400 to more than 4,500. Situated between the mouths of the Missouri and Ohio Rivers, no urban location in the West boasted greater promise for transportation, finance, and trade. Emigrants' guide author William Darby proclaimed in 1818 that the spot would become in time "the seat of empire" for the expanding nation. At the time of the Louisiana Purchase, the St. Louis district included 667 slaves; within

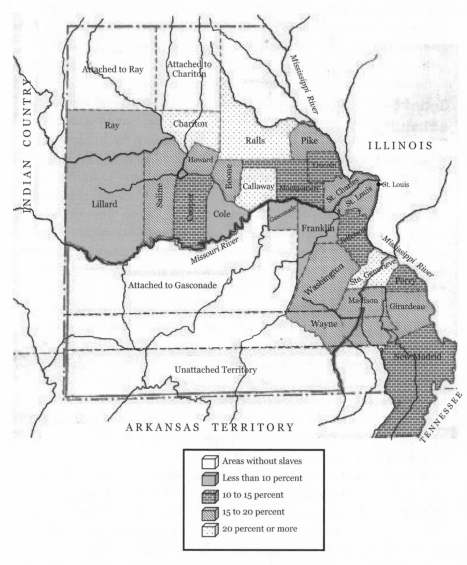

Distribution and Concentration of Slave Population in Missouri, 1820–21.
Drawn by Margot Gibson-Beattie.

Free and Slave Population in Missouri, 1821 (1824)

County	Free Whites	Slaves	Free Blacks	Indentured	Slave (%)	Free Black (%)
Boone	3,115	576	1	0	15.6	0.0
Callaway	1,354	443	0	0	24.7	0.0
Cape Girardeau*	(4,749)	(931)	(46)	(0)	(16.3)	(0.1)
Chariton	1,124	290	7	5	20.3	0.0
Cole	976	52	0	0	5.1	0.0
Cooper	3,031	440	12	0	12.6	0.0
Franklin	1,733	186	9	0	9.6	0.0
Gasconade	1,113	60	1	0	5.0	0.0
Howard	5,909	1,409	2	9	19.2	0.0
Jefferson	1,624	209	4	1	11.4	0.0
Lillard	1,210	130	0	0	9.7	0.0
Lincoln	1,459	211	2	2	12.6	0.0
Madison*	(1,352)	(291)	(5)	(0)	(17.7)	(0.0)
Montgomery	1,730	302	0	0	14.9	0.0
New Madrid	2,127	310	7	0	12.7	0.0
Perry	1,363	229	1	0	14.4	0.0
Pike	2,249	425	2	0	15.9	0.0
Ralls	1,324	353	1	2	21.0	0.0
Ray	1,644	141	2	2	7.9	0.0
St. Charles	3,309	733	11	5	18.1	0.0
St. Genevieve	2,398	717	62	4	22.5	1.9
St. Louis	6,422	1,603	141	24	19.6	1.7
Saline	995	178	2	1	15.1	0.0
Washington	3,179	560	2	0	15.0	0.0
Wayne	1,365	246	1	2	15.2	0.0
Total*	56,854	11,025	321	57	16.2	0.0

Source: Missouri Senate Journal, 1st General Assembly, St. Louis, MO, 1821, http://digitalcollections
.missouristate.edu (accessed June 21, 2014). Federal census returns for Missouri Territory in 1820 no
longer exist, having been either lost or destroyed.

*The Missouri census returns for 1821 did not include figures for Cape Girardeau and Madison
Counties. To give an approximate idea of population in those two counties at the time of Missouri
statehood, I have relied on Missouri's 1824 census. See *Missouri Senate Journal*, 3rd General Assembly,
St. Charles, MO, 1825, http://digitalcollections.missouristate.edu (accessed June 22, 2014).

little more than a decade, that number had swelled to perhaps 1,500. Talk of statehood now dominated public discussions in the territory, but repeated congressional delays only heightened the anger and distrust that many Missourians had long felt toward central government.[52]

One of the ironies of the Missouri crisis was that Missouri Territory, like the whole upper Louisiana region surrounding it, never threatened to become a large bastion of slaveholding or plantation-style agriculture in the first place. Its soil did not suit for cotton growing as a staple crop. The only area promising to come even close was the Boon's Lick region, along the Missouri River in north-central Missouri, its ground more inviting for tobacco production than the worn-out plantations of Virginia. Agricultural migrants had brought some 2,000 slaves there by 1820. Most of the slaves living in the territory belonged to growers of hemp, a crop already so uncertain that it needed federal tariff protection against the superior quality fiber that came from Russia. Early-nineteenth-century Missouri seems, therefore, to have presented an exception from the usual picture of white enslavers and African enslaved in the pre–Civil War South—a little less dehumanizing on both sides, perhaps, than slavery as practiced farther east and south.[53]

In fact, Missourians often fancied themselves as having developed a new-and-improved type of slaveholding society, free of plantation districts, that is, farms of twenty slaves or more. Yeoman families envisioned an order distinct from the grossly inegalitarian Lower South and Southwest—and more compatible with the democratized version of republicanism that now unfolded in the West. Historian Christopher Clark has described early Missourians as boldly "anti-developmental . . . as they attempted to insulate themselves from the financial and market pressures" that increasingly characterized economic life farther east. Even as banks contracted credit during the Panic of 1819, some confident Missourians saw a valuable opportunity to distance themselves from commercial brokers in the East. As one exclaimed: "It is high time for the western country to *abandon all commercial intercourse with the Atlantic cities—reject English and French gewgaws—make and wear their own clothing—wean themselves from foreign wines[,] spirits and other trumpery, and make every effort to create something like a balance of trade in their own favor by the only natural channel, the Mississippi.*"[54]

To most Missouri slaveholders, their world seemed hardly a "slave society" at all but only a "society with slaves," where, historian Diane Mutti Burke has said, "empathy and cooperation" characterized the relationship between owners and the owned at the household, extended-family, and neighborhood levels. As Missouri Indian agent George Silby reported in an 1813 letter, "we have but few slaves," and they were "all well fed & clothed & kindly treated." Vermont transplant Justus Post, despite migrating from a place hostile to slaveholding, congratulated himself on giving his five human chattels "victuals, clothes & and work in abundance." Another anonymous settler, averse to the more grandiose notions of cotton and sugar planters farther south, described the "blessings" he sought in life as simple and relatively modest: a few "faithful friends," a house chosen for "convenience rather than state," a "moderate but independent fortune," business enough to be "secure . . . from indolence," serving "no master" and possessing but a "few servants," and not being "led away by ambition, nor perplexed with disputes." Looking this way at Missouri's slavery seemed to add credibility to the "diffusion" theory, which held in part that as slaveholding freely expanded westward the practice would become more intimate, humane, flexible, and finally dispensible.[55]

What the slaves themselves thought remains, of course, a very different question, harder to answer. They left few accounts and carefully masked discontented feelings that might have elicited a master's wrath. Nonverbal signs of resistance appeared often enough, however: avoidance of work, theft, deception, hiding, running away, and surreptitious destruction of whites' property. Still, slave life in Missouri must have seemed far more agreeable than being sold south, the climate milder, tobacco and hemp cultivation more forgiving than cotton and sugar, the chances of being "hired out" more frequent, especially in St. Louis, where slaves doing odd jobs often kept part of their earnings. Nevertheless, few slaves received enough to purchase their own freedom; various local ordinances restricted their ability to socialize, stay out at night, or carry medicine (to prevent masters from being poisoned); and legal discriminations, such as the denial of the right to testify in court, discouraged an influx of free blacks. Missouri whites, like their southern counterparts, dreaded a growing free black population. Their oldest newspaper, the *Missouri Gazette and Public Advertiser*, in St. Louis, affirmed that the colonization movement, if ever "carried completely into effect," promised "a greater influence on the moral condition of the future people of this great Republic, than almost any measure which has been adopted." Unsurprisingly, the population of free blacks in Missouri declined precipitously between 1810 and

1820, from about 3 percent to less than a third of that.[56]

Apart from all this, however, loomed a "big picture" that many lawmakers in Washington saw more clearly perhaps than could westerners themselves. The political situation of the West in general had shifted dramatically since 1815—in ways that potentially weakened slaveholders there, heartened antislavery people in the North, and made a sectional showdown in Congress more likely than ever. Before that time, the westward expansion of slavery had been a conflict between East and West, with antislavery northerners squaring off against proslavery western planters, traders, trappers, and speculators like those who now dominated Missouri politics. Historically, those western slaveholders had gotten their way—not just because northerners in Congress feared South-North disharmony but also because the British and Spanish held the potential to aid a separation of western parts from the United States. After 1815, events had combined to eliminate European influence in the western states and territories, auguring well for westward growth but also, it seemed, for tightened federal authority. Proslavery westerners no longer held the easy leverage of courting a rival foreign power if eastern policymakers failed to please them. The occasion seemed ripe for aggressive antislavery politicians in Congress to try stretching the doctrine of implied powers farther than ever—this time to halt the westward spread of slavery.[57]

3 Impasse

IN EARLY November 1818, Isaac Riggs, editor of *The Cabinet* in Schenectady, New York, felt a little frustrated. His job was to report all the interesting news, but little *seemed* to be happening. No "extraordinary occurrences at home or abroad" awaited the nation's leaders, he all but lamented. Peace prevailed in the world, no wars loomed, revenue abounded, no taxes appeared necessary, the republic enjoyed prosperity "beyond example," "no grievances" demanded addressing, and "no emergency" called for attention. So he indulged in some predictions for the second session of the Fifteenth Congress, set to commence on the seventeenth of that month and terminate on March 4, 1819. One of the routine matters for lawmakers, he noted, was the probability of two western territories, Missouri and Alabama, being authorized "to form constitutions of state government, preparatory to their admission into the Union." These areas qualified with the requisite numbers in population, and "sound policy" recommended that they "be allowed to govern themselves." This, he added, would be wise, as "territorial governments are always excrescences on our system." On the whole, Riggs concluded, "we expect an animated and useful session, characterized rather by efficient action than by prolonged debate." If they read nothing else, upstate subscribers hardly would have sensed the approaching political gale that would infuse those words with thundering irony.[1]

In November 1818, the second session of the Fifteenth Congress gathered in Washington's old brick capitol, while workers under architects Benjamin Latrobe and Charles Bulfinch rebuilt the one British regulars had torched when they invaded Washington in the summer of 1814. The restored building, now in final stages of construction, promised to surpass its predecessor. A massive, gleaming structure standing high on a hilltop, the spacious new chambers for both houses, the connecting rotunda and the low wooden dome enclosed in copper—all promised a happy destiny for the still-undefined American nation. But for antislavery congressmen arriving that autumn, the processions of chained bondsmen passing outside their boardinghouse windows, resembling funeral marches, portended a very different future. While slavery ended gradually in the northeastern states and in the Northwest, the sale of slaves in the Upper South had grown more profitable than tobacco. Cotton already claimed distinction as a leading American export. Slave auctions became a more common sight than ever, even in Washington, the political heart of a country that appeared now more than ever a slaveholders' republic.[2]

During that second session, Jeffersonian Republicans would outnumber their Federalist adversaries 145 to 40 in the House and 28 to 12 in the Senate. But as the Federalist Party eroded after the Jeffersonian triumph of 1800, long-present strains within Republican ranks had grown increasingly distracting. The "Old Republicans," stubbornly loyal to the original Jeffersonian political economy of agricultural simplicity and free trade, deplored governmental "consolidation," followed strict construction of the Constitution, and relied heavily on states' rights doctrine to guard against the threatening tentacles of federal power. Moderate nationalists like Clay and Calhoun also rejected Federalist elitism, which they saw as antithetical to republican political and social values, but they accepted a strengthening of the federal government, advocated federally supported road and canal development, and, after 1815, embraced loose constructionist policies once associated with Alexander Hamilton's financial program: a national bank and federal promotion of manufacturing. These divergent groups and many political leaders around the country even disagreed on what "republicanism" now meant in a society so different from that of the 1780s.[3]

The first protective tariff in American history and the Second Bank of the United States both passed in 1816 with the help of many moderate southern votes and the signature of a Virginian chief executive, James Madison. Neither policy, those southerners *then* believed, controverted "states' rights" or endangered "state sovereignty." In theory, rapid commercial development in all parts of the republic would provide a mutually beneficial home market for the nation's farmers and other producers, while manufacturing and agricultural enterprises would keep the laboring population (both free and enslaved) fully employed and out of poverty.[4]

Outside the sphere of government, meanwhile, antislavery editors on both sides of the Atlantic flooded the mails with emancipationist literature. Antislavery reformers, too, wanted federal power employed for nationalist purposes—in their case, *moral* ends as opposed to economic ones. Recent disputes over the return of fugitive slaves had worsened relations between the sections. Angered by northern use of state anti-kidnapping legislation to shield runaways, as well as to protect free blacks, southern congressmen had called without success for a more potent fugitive slave statute in 1818. On the fugitive slave issue, ironically, it would often be northern legislators who asserted states' rights and southerners, even Old Republican types, who eagerly embraced federal power to protect slaveholders' interests. Referring sarcastically to the "republicans of the south" who conducted the "traffic in human flesh"—and to advertisements for the recovery of runaways that filled southern prints—a writer in the *Albany Gazette* doubted that many slave owners really wanted to "manumise" their blacks. The appearance in 1817 of John Kendrick's pamphlet *Horrors of Slavery* signaled an early radicalization of the antislavery movement. A Massachusetts abolitionist, Kendrick predated William Lloyd Garrison by more than a decade in demanding immediate emancipation. *Horrors of Slavery* assailed the gradualism of the colonizationists, asking how an institution so "impolitic, antirepublican, unchristian, and highly criminal" as slavery could possibly end except by one final, cataclysmic stroke. Among Kendrick's allies was George Bourne, an English-born Presbyterian minister in Virginia, whose extremist writings got him defrocked and chased out of the Old Dominion in 1818. In an 1816 pamphlet, Bourne had written that "every man who holds Slaves and who pretends to be a Christian or a Republican, is either an incurable Idiot who cannot distinguish good from evil, or an obdurate sinner who resolutely defies every social, moral, and divine requisition."[5]

The Tallmadge Amendment of February 13, 1819, gradually ending slavery in Missouri as a condition of statehood, not only reflected this kind of antislavery passion but also asserted a construction of federal powers that went far beyond the establishing of banks, tariffs, roads, and canals. It provoked a defensive barrage from the South unprecedented for its fierceness, drawing conspicuously on Old Republican rhetoric and revealing much more at stake for southerners than just Missouri. Georgia's Thomas W. Cobb, among others, launched the resistance. Did the New Yorker and the antislavery forces behind him know what they were about to do? "Did they foresee no evil consequences likely to result, if the measure were adopted?" Cobb demanded. "Could they suppose that the southern states would submit with patience to a measure, the effect of which would be to exclude them from all enjoyment of the vast region purchased by the United States beyond the Mississippi, and which belonged equally to them as to the northern states?" The Georgian's words vibrated with indignation. The Tallmadge Amendment would deprive Missouri "of one branch of sovereignty not surrendered by any other state in the Union, not even those beyond the Ohio." Could Tallmadge or anyone show "in what clause or section" of the Constitution this "right" was "expressly given, or from which it could be inferred?"[6]

As for slavery, some southerners might admit "its *moral impropriety*," yet there remained, Cobb roared, "a vast difference between moral impropriety and political sovereignty." In a culture of honor like his, the worst humiliation for a "gentleman" was the kind of "unmasking" or "pressing of the lie" about slavery upon the slaveholders that Tallmadge and his accomplices now inflicted. Cobb and many fellow southerners in the days and months to follow interpreted the Missouri controversy as an attack not just on slavery but on *them*—a long-brewing northern onslaught against their society and morals, their values of manhood and self-respect, their future hopes, and even their right to govern themselves.[7]

Tallmadge's motives tied equally to political pressures in his home state, the sectional stresses within the Republican Party, and the progress of the antislavery movement in general. And yet the big story of the Missouri crisis was the aggressive nationalism that antislavery northerners in Congress and many of their constituents back home now more often embraced. On its surface, the amendment seemed simpler and more innocuous than it really was. It proposed that "further introductory of slavery or involuntary servitude be prohibited," except for the punishment of crimes, and that "all children" born in Missouri "after the admission thereof into the Union shall be free, but may be held to service until the age of twenty-five years." The measure thus called for the kind of gradual emancipation adopted in nearly all of the northern states in the years following the American Revolution, a far cry from abrupt emancipation. If adopted, it would have required Missouri to operate only very slowly toward abolition. Children who were slaves at the time of admission would have remained enslaved for the entirety of their lives, and even *their* children would have been destined for half a lifetime in servitude. All of that, however, assumed congressional authority not only to influence the shaping of territorial government in the West *prior* to statehood but also to impose a broad social and economic agenda within new states *afterward* as well. To adopt that principle was to foretell the ultimate demise of the slaveholding South by curbing its westward expansion.[8]

For its time, Tallmadge's initiative carried more far-reaching and radically statist implications than it might seem looking back from today: "a wider scope of operation than, on the *face* of it, would be supposed," the *National Intelligencer* quickly noted—a condition for admission to the Union other than simply that the embryo state adopt a "republican" form of government. It was, as the *Intelligencer* rightly said, the "first instance of such a restriction being imposed on the new states," as opposed to new territories. The Northwest Ordinance had not *required* that states from that region be admitted slavery-free or remain so once admitted. Article IV, Section 3, of the Constitution—the territorial clause—had provided Congress with the power "to dispose of and make all needful Rules and Regulations respecting the Territory or other Property belonging to the United States," but that provision did not speak to the rights of new states upon entering the Union. The same section of the Constitution declared that "New States may be admitted by the Congress into this Union," but it authorized no restrictions on the *internal* social and economic practices of new states. Article IV, Section 4 required that "[t]he United States shall guarantee to every State in this Union a Republican Form of Government," but the Constitution neither defined "republican" nor implied an incompatibility of slavery and "republicanism." The Fifth Amendment in the Bill of Rights stipulated that "No person shall be . . . deprived of life, liberty, or property, without due process of law," and few had questioned that slave "property" fell under that protection. Finally, the Tenth Amendment provided that "powers not delegated to the United States by the Constitution, nor prohibited by it to the States, are reserved to the States respectively, or to the people," which southerners understood to assure that states might adopt, legalize, or preserve slavery as they saw fit.[9]

The several previous attempts to restrict slavery expansion into the upper part of Louisiana Territory, such as James Hillhouse's in 1804, had failed because less appeared at stake and, more important, because of their *timing*. In 1811, as the House considered elevating Missouri to second-stage territorial status, Pennsylvania Republican Jonathan Roberts had introduced a proposal to prohibit any further introduction of slaves, but others persuaded him that the approaching war with Britain superseded divisive concerns about slavery. Besides, westerners, already "infatuated with the spirit of opposition to the Government," needed no further incentive to revolt. The following year, Abner Lacock, another Pennsylvania Republican, had tried again, resulting in a mere seventeen House votes in favor. New Hampshire Republican Arthur Livermore, in April 1818, had proposed a constitutional amendment that would have barred admission of any more slave states, but with Alabama statehood pending, the House defeated that, too. But Missouri meant something different, partly because of when it applied and also its geographical location. To validate slavery there would protect the institution as far as two hundred miles north from the mouth of the Ohio River, the traditional dividing point between freedom and slavery.[10]

Beyond that, maintaining the balance in Congress between slave states and free states, a condition long considered vital to sectional peace, bore heavily on the Missouri dispute. When the Constitution went into effect in 1789, North and South had been close to even in population and wealth, with three-fifths of the slaves being counted for House representation and electoral votes. But over the following generation, economic development in the North had given that section a commanding advantage. By 1819, a free-state majority of 105 to 81 dominated the House. Southern influence in Congress had diminished at every census. In 1790, 49 southern House seats stood against 57 northern; twenty years later, only 79 to 107; and after 1820, a widened breach of 89 to 124. This meant the balance of power in the Senate, where the number of slave-state members remained equal to that of the free states, now loomed all the more critical. After Alabama's admission, that would make twenty-two slave-state senators against twenty-two from the free states. To restrict slavery from spreading further into Missouri could shift power in both houses against the South and promise *more* free states to come.[11]

Further, both Tallmadge on the Republican side and Rufus King on the Federalist wanted to revisit the three-fifths-clause dispute. That constitutional provision had been the *other* wellspring of southern influence in national politics, and slave-state forces would meet this new attack with all the venom they could muster. Earlier elitist assumptions that had justified extra power for slaveholders as a check against challenges to their authority from below no longer commanded the ideological sway they had in the 1780s. The notion that a stable republic depended so much on government protection of the propertied groups could not hold up in an age of increasingly democratic politics and emerging free-labor political economy. The offending clause mattered in close presidential elections and tight congressional roll calls. It had put Jefferson in the White House and launched the "Virginia Dynasty" that many northern Republicans now resented. Voices from the North, opposing the three-fifths rule and preferring that *no* slaves be counted for representative purposes, now asked whether the clause needed to apply *at all* in *new* states west of the Mississippi. Besides, stopping slavery at the great river would make repeal of the three-fifths clause inevitable after enough western free states entered the Union. With that aggressive northern supermajority, slavery, slave-state self-determination, planter-class authority, and white control over the black race *all* would be doomed. Aware of all that, Virginia's Philip P. Barbour retorted that if the three-fifths compromise in 1787 did not apply to the new states, then neither did the other critical compromises of that time, including that which entitled new states to a pair of senators apiece.[12]

For southerners, the fate of "diffusion" also hung in the balance. Slaveholders who worried about the volatility of slavery pinned their hopes for social order, and their profits from selling excess slaves, on the draining of the slave population westward. A *Washington Whig* correspondent thought it strange that the "sensibility . . . manifested by the gentlemen from the slaveholding states" did not seem to reconcile "with a repugnance to the principle of involuntary servitude, which most of them profess to entertain." But unless slave states could disperse westward this dangerously growing number of potential insurrectionists, answered Thomas Ritchie's *Richmond Enquirer*, "more slaves are kept here, and their condition is not ameliorated as fast as the natural course of events would direct. You do not lessen the evil of slavery; but you make it bear more heavily upon a smaller space." The *Charleston City Gazette* went still further, announcing that it would have "rejoiced" over the Tallmadge Amendment if its effect in Missouri could have been to "diminish the number of slaves in the United States or improve their condition," but in reality, it would only "concentrate that description of population." Philip P. Barbour, among other Virginians in Congress, would argue that spreading slavery over a greater surface would lessen the danger of slave insurrection and encourage the eastern slave master to be "more tender in his treatment to his dependants."[13]

Tallmadge had drawn together an unusually volatile mix of political forces at just the right moment. These elements had built to a climax not just in Washington but outside as well, reflecting rapid and massive changes in all sections—North, South, and West—over the previous decade or so. All converged on the nation's capital at once, involving not only the future of slavery and of the Union but also the question of federal power over new western states—and much more. While the international situation had shifted, the party equilibrium that once preempted sectional warfare had disappeared. Missourians, for their part, had a history of being stiff-necked and assertive, which could only intensify the controversy. Southern arrogance surged, as did the market for cotton and slaves. Northern sectional identity had crystalized as well, auguring new determination to end slavery expansion and promote a free-labor destiny for the republic. And yet, despite all of this, devotion to the Union remained strong in all sections. In all, Tallmadge's timing was perfect to rock the foundations of American politics.[14]

The Sectional North

Cobb had it right: It *was* a northern attack on the South, not just on slavery. However much early antislavery impulses in the North reflected authentic concern for the human rights of slaves and contempt for their masters, they also mirrored deep-seated cultural and economic anxieties of northern whites. Chief among those fears was that further expansion of slaveholding would mean the ultimate demise of *their* society, one that increasingly valued and identified with free-labor principles.[15]

In the hundred years or so before the Civil War, southern institutions and values changed far less rapidly than northern ones. As historian Bertram Wyatt-Brown aptly put it, "the quickly industrializing North, with its urban, polyglot populace, had increasingly little in common with the still agrarian, underpopulated, and deeply parochial South." Over the same period that northerners embraced state-by-state emancipation programs, a dynamic market revolution in the North gradually opened a new vision of political economy that made the expansion of free-labor capitalism just as crucial as the spreading of slavery now seemed to many southerners. Two rival systems now would vie for the economic future of the republic. In the "southern section of the union," a New York writer cautioned in 1817, "Slaves compose nearly the whole agricultural population—The class that [normally] constitutes the bone and muscle of every community." Were the southern model to prevail, then, what kind of people would Americans become? Work inspired not by "the natural motives" but by "violence and terror" could "never produce that persevering industry, and active ingenuity, which makes labor in some places so very productive," said another columnist in Delaware. If the new western states were to be divided into nonslaveholding and slaveholding, it would be assumed that migrants from the North and East would settle only in the free states, others only in the slave—two very different, incompatible Wests, forming separately. In that case, said the *Alexandria Gazette* soon after the Missouri debate first commenced, "we may therefore look to have in the former industry, orderliness, neatness, prosperity, comfort, prudence, and their adjuncts—in the latter, selfishness, laziness, slovenliness, wealth, generosity, hospitality and carelessness. *Utrum horum, mavis accepi*" (Take whichever you prefer).[16]

Reflecting on the controversy several months later, a Philadelphia editor illuminated the core reason why his readers cared so much about the Missouri question: "because they look to the western territories as the future home of themselves and their children." Apart from the abstract principles of moral rightness or government policy making, "their own individual happiness and interests" lay at stake. Would Missouri—and for that matter the entire trans-Mississippi frontier—become "poor, half-peopled, badly cultivated and insignificant . . . or rich, populous, flourishing, and enterprising"? Early in 1820, Boston's *North American Review* framed the conflict in similar terms: "The employment of slaves has an obvious tendency to banish that steady, cheerful, and active industry which is among the chief causes of national wealth and strength." For these writers and most interested northerners outside the crucible of Washington, the question of what kind of new society would take shape in the West—and how that society might ultimately affect *them* and their hopes for the future—was the main issue in the debate on slavery expansion.[17]

In the late eighteenth century, Philadelphia, Boston, and New York increasingly attracted free labor, mostly single young white men, with the

effect of diminishing the economic need for slaves in those cities. In Philadelphia, for example, the number of unfree workers had shrunk in 1783 to
6 percent of its growing labor force, down from about 40 percent in 1750.
Meanwhile, in New York City by 1820 some 20 percent of the population
had emigrated from European countries where the very idea of some people
holding others as slaves had fallen into moral disrepute. Historians have estimated that by 1820 roughly one-fifth of all workers in the country—twice as
many as in 1800—toiled for wages and not for masters of any sort. This shift
fitted comfortably enough with the northeastern rural tradition of household
work within the self-sufficient family. As free labor advanced in the North,
indentured servitude dwindled as well, essentially disappearing by 1820. The
formal apprentice system also declined, as the growth of urban populations
and labor supply freed both employers and workers from that kind of legal
compulsion. The early expansion of white manhood suffrage, eliminating
property requirements, contributed to the concept of equal political rights
to accompany the burgeoning worker pride in being a part of the "producer"
class. All of this coincided, too, with early stirrings of evangelical revivalism
in northern churches where the theological message reinforced congregants'
belief not only in divine expectations but also their own developing sense of
individual freedom and self-direction. The social respectability of wage work
and independent proprietorship in northern cities and towns, together with
the proliferation of small-scale farming around the North and Northwest,
helped to form in the free states a strong sense of sectional difference—and
with that, moral superiority—from labor practices in the slave states and the
prevailing economic values of the South.[18]

None of this social transformation denies that many northern businessmen, while touting the ethos of "free labor," unashamedly joined in the
mammoth profits from southern slavery-based production. Even as slaveholding ended by gradual emancipation, cotton helped to generate what
would become a vital textile industry in New England. Insurance companies in northeastern cities indemnified slaves as property investments to be
sheltered from loss. Wall Street firms in New York City started in business
as middlemen in the cotton trade. Again and again, the lords of the loom
conspired with the lords of the lash, as radical Massachusetts abolitionist
Charles Sumner would later concede. For that matter, the Tallmadge Amendment could be interpreted as just as much a challenge to other northerners
who espoused egalitarian principles more than they pursued them. Gradual

emancipation notwithstanding, most northern whites of the time would never accept blacks as their equals.[19]

Apart from Yankee complicity with slave owners and their own unmistakable racism, northerners could still look upon the growth of their regions, their towns and cities, and their range of economic pursuits with a pride of accomplishment that matched, if it did not exceed, that of the South. With the onset of the Panic of 1819, one might expect small employers and disappointed workers to forsake their faith in the emerging market economy and embrace more radical, class-conscious alternatives like the later workingmen's parties, but most did not. The earlier taste of prosperous times and fortunes in the making, along with whatever advantages of opportunity and character some had—better education, temperance, evangelical faith, or just a run of luck—fortified the belief of many northern laborers that their day would come and, at all events, their individual freedom to seek work for wages elevated them. A host of northern moralists, like Mordecai Noah in New York's *National Advocate*, interpreted the financial panic as punishment for straying from an earlier, agricultural, and localized economy. For that matter, one could find latter-day Calvinists who still saw *any* crisis, including the Missouri one, as signaling God's wrath. But economic nationalists, like Mathew Carey in Philadelphia, Hezekiah Niles in Baltimore, and Clay in Congress, countered these rustic lamentations with a more forward-looking agenda. Subsistence-level agriculture, however "virtuous," did nothing to expand markets. Besides, too many Americans tilled the land already, whether on scattered small farms or sprawling plantations. A comprehensive free-labor economy required much more. "A nation of pure agriculturalists cannot be numerous," Niles had instructed in 1817, "unless there are lords and peasants, masters and slaves." Better to pursue a government-encouraged program of home manufactures, aided by road and canal development, to protect American producers from foreign competition—the growth schema that began as President Madison's postwar economic "platform" of 1815 and would continue as Clay's "American System" in years to come.[20]

Still, if sectional pride mushroomed as much in the North as in the South, so did economic pressure to compromise on Missouri in spite of growing antislavery pressure not to. Devotion to the Union resonated heavily in the North, as well as in much of the South and West, as did belief in the limiting of federal government power, hence the cross-sectional strength of the Jacksonian Democratic Party during the 1830s and 1840s. Even among northern antislavery nationalists, Carey, for one, acknowledged that Congress possessed the constitutional right to impose restrictions on both territories and new states, but to exhaust so much time debating the Missouri issue only distracted from more urgent matters in a time of economic and sectional crisis. "The great questions regarding the manufactures, the bankrupt system, and the public lands," he would complain, remained unsettled when Congress adjourned in 1819. The economic welfare of the Union as a whole ought to supersede this kind of sectional wrangling. Regarding protective tariffs, for example, Carey asked, "What measures in support of the commerce and manufactures of the eastern and middle states could be expected from the southern members, when they saw no disposition on the part of the former to make reciprocal concessions, and supposed their own peculiar interests neglected?" The worst scenarios foretold either dissolution of the Union over the slavery question or, nearly as threatening, an independent Missouri positioned to command navigation of the Missouri River.[21]

"I Can Only Say, Let It Come!"

Some congressmen saw nothing much to debate. Missouri was not Illinois. Slavery had never been outlawed there. No territory legitimately open to slavery had ever been denied statehood on its own terms. Even if Congress *could* prescribe details of government for a new state, other than it be "republican" in form, that power would be "nugatory," said Henry Clay. Once admitted to the Union, any state had the unquestioned right to amend its constitution and govern itself as its people saw fit. Certainly he wanted to soothe southern congressmen who now felt betrayed by their northern brethren, but he also knew that the Constitution protected slaveholders. At stake for him were the votes in Congress needed to pass further protective tariffs and internal improvements bills that economic-nationalist Republicans wanted. Many of them would rather accept slavery, and even fit it within the American System, than make an issue of it now.[22]

On the second day of the debate, Monday, February 15, 1819, the rhetoric intensified, northerners mostly sidestepping the question of state sovereignty in favor of a loftier moral vision for expansion. The way this Missouri question would be resolved, cried Tallmadge's fellow New Yorker John W. Taylor, would "decide the destiny of millions" who would in years to come fill frontier America all the way to the "Western ocean." If southern "Gentlemen" had "tried slavery and found it a curse," then let them exclude it from the territory in question—"plant not its seeds in this uncorrupt soil." The thirty-three-year-old Taylor practiced law in Ballston Spa, a tiny village in eastern upstate New York, near Saratoga Springs and known for its health-restoring mineral waters. He had served in the House since 1813, never regarded as a very prominent member—until *now*. A Jeffersonian of nationalist convictions, he had sided with the War Hawks during the war, supported the Second Bank of the United States and the protective tariff, and in principle favored federal funding of roads and canals. Clay had regarded him highly—until *now*. Taylor argued that under the territorial clause and the power to admit new states, Congress held "unlimited" authority, including the right to prohibit the further introduction of slavery. If "enlightened" southerners were sincere about ending slavery, here was their chance. And yet, how many northern men, even those of conscience, would have accepted an economic loss comparable to that of a prime field hand—estimated between $800 and $1,100 in 1819? Attacking more in the language of abolitionists like Kendrick and Bourne, Timothy Fuller of Massachusetts followed by reminding House members that slavery stood inconsistent with the Declaration of Independence, making slaveholders men of suspect political character, less than true republicans.[23]

Others went even further. Never mind questions of constitutional interpretation, declared New Hampshire's Arthur Livermore: Slaveholders and anyone else who did not oppose slavery stood equally culpable. Beyond mere politics, here stood a defining moment for American civilization, the opportunity "if not to diminish, at least to prevent, the growth of a sin which sits heavy on the souls of every one of us," a precious chance to "retrieve the national character, and, in some degree, our own." The Constitution did not specifically *impose* slavery, but it did establish liberty, he contended. "Let us no longer tell idle tales about the gradual abolition of slavery; away with colonization societies, if their design is only to rid us of free blacks and turbulent slaves." In response, Edward Colston of Virginia warned that Livermore's confrontational words could not be contained within the walls of Congress. When it reached the ears of slaves, as inevitably it would, this kind of talk could "excite a servile war," endangering the lives of southern whites. Northerners who did that, Colston exclaimed, deserved "no better fate" than that of Arbuthnot and Armbrister, the two British subjects that Jackson had captured, court-martialed, and shot in Florida during the Seminole campaign of 1818.[24]

Cooler heads tried to intervene on the southern side. For Philip P. Barbour, it was a question more of legal logic than of passions on either side. The essential point, he thought, was that Congress had no constitutional power to dictate such terms of admission to Missouri. To do so would be to encroach on the sovereignty of Missouri and, by extension, on all future states to be brought into the Union. Historians have viewed this position as a sectionalist smoke screen, an "indirect defense" of slavery. But that is to underestimate the depth—indeed, the history—of southern fear that northern leadership would erase their right to self-government, just as British tyrants once had tried. Barbour consistently had taken the antinationalist, strict-constructionist side on the major economic questions of the post–War of 1812 years, opposing the national bank, voting against the tariff, and denying funding for improvements. State sovereignty, he believed, provided the bulwark against overreaching federal authority.[25]

In addition, Barbour now coupled a faith in slaveholders' paternalism with this aversion to the nation-state. True, slaves in the South constituted a form of property, yet many slaveholders treated them "as the most valuable, as the most favored property" and with a sympathy that binds "one man to another, though that other may be our inferior," he claimed. Virginia slave owners who had carried their human chattels to Missouri had done so not only because their labor was "peculiarly necessary" but also because honor and obligation could not permit these dependents to be left behind. Coming from one not known for personal reservations about slaveholding, Barbour's argument persuaded no one on the other side. Even so, while few southern voices had yet embraced the "moral rightness" of slavery, they left no doubts about the right to decide its operation and destiny for themselves.[26]

On February 16, 1819, the Committee of the Whole voted 79 to 67 to include the Tallmadge Amendment in the Missouri bill, but upon its report to the House the following day, Missouri's territorial delegate John Scott ripped into the majority, his words echoing Barbour and Cobb. To impose this "unconstitutional inhibition" on Missouri, Scott cried, invoked not-so-distant memories of the American Revolution, hastening the time "when the General Government might, in turn, undertake to dictate to them on questions of internal policy." Scorching exchanges followed. Tallmadge, fed up and exhausted, glared at Cobb: "If a dissolution of the Union must take place, let it be so! If civil war, which gentlemen so much threaten, must come, I can only say, let it come!" But if the South would confine slavery to the original slaveholding states, "where you found it at the formation of your Government," he continued, they would "stand acquitted of all imputation"—not much of an olive branch if it meant their loss of the West. More than that, extending the three-fifths clause to slave states beyond the Mississippi, Tallmadge asserted, "would be unjust in its operations, unequal in its results, and a violation of original intentions."[27]

Their morality questioned, their "republicanism" doubted, their Americanism impugned, and their influence threatened, some southern congressmen had heard quite enough. Cobb of Georgia had already demanded that Tallmadge withdraw his amendment, lest it kindle "a fire that all the waters of the ocean cannot put out, which seas of blood can only extinguish." Southern fire-eating defiance registered with force. Its tactic, now historically familiar, repeated the same threat issued since the 1780s: The price of any federal restricting of slavery would be disunion—in violent style quite possibly. Such talk reflected more than just tactical considerations, however. Southern honor lay at stake as well. As historian Kenneth Greenberg has explained, "[T]he difference between having and not having honor was the difference between having and not having power," and if a northern critic encroached on that cultural territory, a white southerner worth his salt had to resist the attack with all the force of language and, if necessary, action that he could summon.[28]

The initial House vote on the Tallmadge Amendment, on February 16, 1819, reflected bipartisan support in the North both for restricting slavery and expanding free labor. The first part of the amendment—to forbid the future entrance of slaves into Missouri—passed the House 87 to 76, northern Republicans and Federalists voting in favor 86 to 10; the South, 66 to 1 against. Given the slim majority, one Washington correspondent sighed, "[C]an we blame Europeans for their sneers," seeing how barely "the equal rights and liberties of mankind as guaranteed by the constitution" had been "saved in our House of Representatives?" The second part—to liberate slaves born after Missouri's admission at age twenty-five—carried more narrowly in the House, 82 to 78, the North voting 80 to 14 aye, the South, 62 to 2 nay. Eleven days later in the Senate, where slave states held the power to block Tallmadge, the amendment failed 22 to 16 on the first part, 31 to 7 on the second. The voting, again, went almost completely along sectional lines. Only two House members from slave states, both born in the North, sided with the amendment; ten free-state members opposed the first clause and fourteen the second, while no one from a nonborder slave state supported either clause. The ban against further introduction of slaves into Missouri would have passed in the Senate were it not for the opposing votes of five free-state members, including both Illinois senators, Edwards and Thomas.[29]

The Fifteenth Congress ended on March 4, 1819, as did Tallmadge's brief career in Washington, without a decision on the Missouri question. Meanwhile, a parallel debate had unfolded that February over the newly defined territory of Arkansas, where the proportion of slaves stood at about 11 percent in contrast with Missouri's roughly 16 percent. Here, New York's Taylor had played Tallmadge's role, introducing a similar amendment in the House to restrict slavery in the region immediately south of Missouri Territory and north of the state of Louisiana. This, too, shocked the South, as it represented a more sweeping antislavery challenge to its *middle* region than any since Jefferson's in 1784. On Arkansas, however, antislavery members had proved more pliable—just barely—than on Missouri, with Taylor's proviso failing by a vote of 89 to 87, northern members voting 86 to 15 in favor, southerners 74 to 1 against. Arkansas Territory sat at a latitude south of Kentucky, noted Ezekiel Whitman of Maine, who favored the Tallmadge Amendment but also the "conciliatory" strategy with Arkansas. "We must go on as we have begun," he concluded, "admitting some States with, and some without any restriction." In the Senate, the measure lost 19 to 14, with slave-state votes unanimously opposed and four from the Northwest (again including Thomas and Edwards) joining them. The bill to organize Arkansas into a separate territory in the southern half of the Louisiana Purchase finally passed, its slaveholders' "rights" intact, but after such a close call southern congressmen had reason to worry how long they could hold back the northern attack when a new Congress convened the following December.[30]

For now, Missouri statehood stood "lost between the Senate and the House of Representatives on the question of slavery," complained Thomas Hart Benton's *St. Louis Enquirer.* For another year the territorial government would continue in Missouri. Meanwhile, the bill to admit Alabama, as expected, had become law without any restricting of slavery there. How Missourians would react remained uncertain, but the *Enquirer* guessed that "some timid people, thinking Congress omnipotent and that next year their slaves will be surely lost, will sell off their property at a sacrifice, and remove away." Further emigration of slaveholding families from the southern and western states might be checked, while that from "the New England states will increase, under the hope of gaining supremacy in this country." But the columnist, probably Benton himself, considered the fears of the former and the hopes of the latter both to be "delusive." Missourians would have more allies next time around—southern men "waked up to the danger" of growing federal government power. And even if "the worst came to the worst," and Congress in 1820 were to pass a law "to suit the views of the New England politicians," would Missouri submit? The *Enquirer* answered emphatically: "No! never! and those who suppose her capable of such pusillanimous submission" knew nothing of the people or the region. If Congress had passed the bill restricting slavery, it would witness "a specimen of Missouri feeling in the indignant contempt with which they would have trampled the odious restriction under their feet, and proceeded to the formation of a Republican constitution in the fullness of the peoples' power."[31]

By contrast, Tallmadge and Taylor must have relished the kudos they received back home. Said one New York sheet, "This shews that the sentiments of men of consideration in our country, are becoming more and more correct on this interesting subject." It looked now as if "the evils of slavery are to be confined to the territory which they now occupy, and are not to be extended over any other portion of our country." The news inspired free-labor advocates all over the North. Antislavery Americans had cause for hope "that the enterprising and hardy race of men who are settling the new regions of territory will not feel themselves degraded, but elevated, by the idea, that the soil which they own is to be cultivated by *freemen*, not *by slaves*," said the *New York Daily Advertiser*. The New York Manumission Society, in a special meeting headed by New York City mayor Cadwallader D. Colden on February 23, 1819, resolved the further introduction of slavery into "our states or territories" to be "irreconcilable with the genius of our government and institutions, and hostile to the political, moral and social interests of our common country." It, too, congratulated Tallmadge and Taylor for "their manly and persevering efforts" to prevent the expansion of slavery and to elevate the character of New York state.[32]

Even though the amendment asked for less in Missouri than emancipationists had achieved in New York, Tallmadge had shattered southern nerves, leaving them rawer than ever. On one level, the furor produced by the amendment disputed the social, economic, and political future of the Mississippi Valley. But on another, it looked like nothing less than a moment of truth for the Union as a whole. While slave-state leaders feared the erosion of their power in Washington, few northerners had ever been happy with the three-fifths clause or a westward-expanding application of it. The Missouri fight tested what remained of the Jeffersonian political alliance between North and South—especially New York and Virginia. Many northerners stuck with Tallmadge, but how long could Jeffersonian Republican leadership put up with a fight that promised to split their party—and the nation—along sectional lines, North versus South?

Fallout

Over the next several months, as economic depression spread across the country, mounting anxieties about the future of the Union added further distraction for an already worried populace. The controversy proved hardly confined to Washington politics. Many ordinary Americans cared deeply about the fate of their country, registering their sentiments via the newspapers and pamphlets they bought, public meetings and celebrations they attended, organizations they supported, representatives they sent to state legislatures, and ultimately their choice of men worthy to sit in Congress. Such popular concern swept through the South and West, as well as the North. The *New-Hampshire Sentinel* cited reports in early June 1819 that the "fate" of the Missouri bill had produced "great excitement in the territory proposed for admission, and in the slave-holding States generally." Even if media "propagandists" had whipped up public opinion on the sectional crisis, the fact remained that they could not operate alone; their market of information-consumers still decided what to read and how to respond.[33]

Many southerners, already fearful of slave unrest, wondered whether radical northern rhetoric would now incite their bondsmen to rebellion. To them, as to their congressmen and senators, northern efforts to restrict slavery smacked of growing federal power, combined with virulent anti-southern feeling. At the very same time, the Second Bank of the United States also had come to symbolize the danger of national consolidation. On the other side, northerners more and more suspected southern designs to spread their vile institution far and wide, beginning with slaveholders' intentions to lay their clutches on the entirety of the trans-Mississippi West. Meetings throughout the free states called on congressional representatives not only to support the Tallmadge Amendment but also to stand at all costs against a rising slaveholders' threat to the republic.[34]

Just three days after the congressional session ended, the Supreme Court generated another round of anti-federal reaction with its *McCulloch v. Maryland* ruling, which held the Bank of the United States to be constitutionally valid and exempt from state taxation. Much of the blame for the Panic of 1819, especially in the South and West, had fallen upon the bank and its president, William Jones, whose financial mismanagement contributed to the chaos. But the real villain, southern writers said, was the "implied powers" doctrine. Virginia, even more than the Lower South, would epitomize anti-federal extremism in 1819–1820, and Old Republicans there wasted no time in saying "we told you so." The decision in the Supreme Court did nothing to exonerate bank officials from their share of the responsibility, but Chief Justice John Marshall's neo-Hamiltonian reasoning proved infuriating to many, including the "Richmond Junto," a group of ardently anti-nationalist Old Republicans that included Spencer Roane, Thomas Ritchie, and others who resented growing federal power. A pair of essays in Ritchie's *Richmond Enquirer*, beginning on March 30, 1819, and signed "Amphictyon" (now attributed to Judge William Brockenbrough of Richmond), launched their counteroffensive. "It is necessary that the laws which regulate the daily transactions of men should have a regard to their interests, their feelings, even their prejudices," Amphictyon seethed. "This can better be done when the territory is of moderate dimensions, than when it is immense; it is more peculiarly proper too in the situation of our society, where we have been always accustomed to our own laws, and our own legislatures, and where the laws of one state will not suit the people of another." Those words could apply just as easily to Missouri.[35]

The second essay railed against the alleged implications of Marshall's aggressively nationalist doctrine: What would stop Congress from funding roads and canals wherever it pleased, creating "boards of internal improvement," incorporating companies under federal authority, establishing universities, and even founding churches—all under "implied powers"? Roane followed with another series under the pseudonym "Hampden," decrying "consolidation" and fully deploying the anti-statist tradition against the spread of centralized tyranny. He warned against the arming of Congress with a *"general power of attorney"* to legislate on any matters it wished.[36]

Soon after, the Virginia House of Delegates issued a set of resolutions in support of Missouri's cause, expressing a sense of alarm as intense as that of Missourians but, so far, without the implied threat of disunion. The author,

Briscoe Gerard Baldwin, represented Augusta County, practiced law in Staunton, and enjoyed a reputation in Virginia as a political scholar and orator. He, too, emphasized the inviolability of the states, without which slaveholders lay equally vulnerable everywhere. Congressionally imposed restrictions would degrade "the sovereign character" of the Missouri people in forming their own constitution or form of government. Success of the Tallmadge Amendment would mean not only foisting an anti-southern will on Missouri but also "the exclusion of the inestimable right to alter the same hereafter as those people may deem necessary for their prosperity and happiness." Beyond just the Missouri question, here was a "most serious and portentous danger to the sovereign rights reserved to the states; alarming as it respects the future liberties of the people; and tending immediately to weaken the strong cement of mutual concession and confidence, in which the foundation of our happy union has been laid." Another writer in the May 21, 1819, *Richmond Enquirer* provided a spicier sample of the anti-federal passions swirling in the Old Dominion at the time: "If we should unfortunately fail in support of our principle, the certain effect will be to make all the territory west of the Mississippi, and north of latitude 36, a Yankee country, governed by the sniveling, sanctimonious doctrines in politics and religion which, as a Virginian, I early learned to abhor."[37]

Out west, most Missourians agreed on one thing: the injustice of their territory being singled out when other western states had entered the Union with slavery by their own choosing and without controversy. One enraged inhabitant, identifying himself in May 1819 as "A ST. LOUIS MECHANIC," condemned the "eastern aristocrats" now in control of the "domineering, unprincipled party" in the House of Representatives who had made Missouri's admission part of their program to achieve "a consolidated government" in Washington. "The day is approaching," the writer warned, "when the people of Missouri will show to their enemies that they not only know their rights, but also, if occasion requires, they have still enough of 1776 left, to fight for them." Neither he nor his neighbors would "submit to the mandates of eastern Jesuits," he vowed, mingling anti-Catholic fears with anti-federal ones.[38]

It was not that all Missourians supported slavery; far from it. Take for example the experience of Humphrey Smith, an antislavery native of New Jersey who had settled with his family as squatters on public land near Boon's Lick. Outspokenly opposed to slavery, he vowed to do all he could in the cause of freedom. One night, a proslavery mob beset his house, dragged

Smith out of bed, beat him with clubs, administered twenty or thirty lashes for good measure, knocked his wife down, and "otherwise abused" her "in a shocking manner." Before leaving, the lawless invaders announced their intention "to kill or drive out of the country" any man who opened his mouth against slavery. Not coincidentally, Smith later found himself outbid for his land by a slaveholder when auction time came around, losing his improvements to boot. Newspaper reports of such behavior could have done little to soften the resolve of pro-Tallmadge restrictionists in Congress. In another case, the editors of the two newspapers in St. Louis, the antislavery Irish immigrant Joseph Charless of the *Missouri Gazette* and Isaac N. Henry, Thomas Hart Benton's proslavery partner at the *St. Louis Enquirer*, also differed vehemently. The rivalry between the two journalists even degenerated into an ugly fistfight on the street early in 1820. When Rev. Joseph Piggot tried to restrain the combatants, Wharton Rector, a friend of Henry's, pulled a pistol and threatened to "blow him through" if he interfered. All the same, the gritty Charless, though nearly fifty and twice Henry's age, got the better of his opponent, sending him away with an "unjointed" shoulder.[39]

Less colorful, but more revealing, a set of resolutions published in the *Missouri Gazette* after a citizens' meeting at the St. Louis home of Elisha Patterson included a condemnation of slavery as contrary to "freedom" and to "the laws of nature," one of the country's "greatest evils." If not checked, it would "eventually end in an entailed hereditary misery on our future posterity, and bring upon us their just censure, as well as the judgment of a just, but *angry God.*" Yet the same group viewed "with jealousy any attempt made in congress to usurp from us, any right with which we may be legally vested by any treaty of cession, or guaranteed to us by the constitution of the United States." Slaveholding in Missouri ought to end, they believed, but Missourians should end it themselves, in their own way, instead of the federal government forcing that result upon them. Beyond that, one public meeting after another condemned the presumption that Congress had any right to restrict their slavery. The 1803 treaty with France, various public speakers and newspaper columnists insisted, bound the United States to guarantee citizens of states carved from the Louisiana Territory the same rights and privileges as those of the older states, meaning the fate of slavery in their state was theirs alone to determine. Others, like Benton, said the restrictionist position reflected a longstanding eastern contempt for the West, envy of its resources, a desire to inhibit its growth or gain control of its commerce. Taking that sentiment a step further, one bold resident of Franklin, Missouri, promised in a dinner toast in May 1819 that he and his fellow citizens would "defend their rights"—including the right to own slaves—"even at the expense of blood."[40]

Transplanted Missouri resident Nathaniel Beverley Tucker voiced provincial indignation more powerfully than most. Born in 1784 near Petersburg, Virginia, and a son of prominent legal scholar St. George Tucker, the younger Tucker had grown up in an unusual plantation family. The anti-nationalist influence of his older half brother, John Randolph of Roanoke, had impressed him deeply. Tucker and his family had been part of the post–War of 1812 flood of migration to the Missouri Territory, arriving there in 1816. Thanks to acting governor Frederick Bates, another one-time planter-class Virginian, he quickly received appointment as a circuit court judge. Around Tucker's farm near St. Charles, Missouri, about 20 miles northwest of St. Louis, gathered a small enclave of upper-class, slaveholding former Virginians and South Carolinians, living contiguously, some of them blood relatives. These neighbors reinforced Tucker's political views as well as his social aspirations. They deplored excessive government, planned, like him, to stay in Missouri, and held every intention to keep the slaves they had brought to cultivate their fields. Tucker styled this a "true Virginia settlement," a country gentleman's paradise, replicating in the West the old Upper South he had once known. For such people, the Tallmadge Amendment boded far more than a gradual phasing out of slavery; it threatened the very reasons they had gone west, assailing their cherished vision of a new, improved, socially homogenous, and more secure republican world than the one they had left, and with the right men in charge.[41]

In five essays published in St. Louis's *Missouri Gazette* during the spring of 1819, Tucker contended that Congress had no authority even to consider requiring Missourians to emancipate their slaves. According to states' rights theory drawn from his father's edition of Blackstone, Tucker saw the Union as a compact among sovereign states, and the Tenth Amendment protected the states from being violated. As for the territories, neither the original sovereignty, vested in Missouri's people before statehood, nor the property rights of those inhabitants, which included slaveholding, could rightly be disturbed by federal power. In Tucker's eyes, Tallmadge's proposal amounted nearly to a criminal punishment where there had been no crime—in essence, it was both a bill of attainder and an ex post facto law violating the federal Constitution. Further, the territorial clause in the Constitution applied only to territories as federal property, not matters of local governance or the right of citizens to keep enslaved workers. The same held true for determining the future of slaves' progeny and the right to ban free blacks from Missouri. Reports of the Supreme Court's *McCulloch* decision had reached Missouri at about the same time that Tucker and others crafted their reactions to the debate on the Tallmadge Amendment. That news, together with the growing clamor in the Northeast for protective tariffs, continuing federal control of public lands, and mounting interest in federal support for internal improvements, connected ominously to the new threat of federal encroachment on state-building in the West.[42]

Grand juries all over Tucker's northern circuit in Missouri also registered contempt for congressional meddling with their "right" to construct a frontier society as they, and no outsiders, saw fit. In the early republic, such grand juries, operating usually at the county level, not only determined grounds for criminal prosecutions but also considered a wide range of public matters. They consisted of twenty-three citizens assembled to address anything from road repair and delinquent behavior of elected officials to formal protests against governmental policies. Grand jury pronouncements, in turn, circulated among newspaper editors all around the country. At a meeting in St. Louis on Saturday May 15, 1819, a grand jury that included Alexander M'Nair and David Barton unanimously declared Congress to possess no right "to control the provision of a state constitution, except to preserve its republican character." The House majority supporting the Tallmadge Amendment had acted "contrary to the rights of the state, and to the welfare of the slaves themselves." Missouri statehood, they said, was a matter of law and not the *will* of Congress. Then came a more radical assertion: The people of the territory had the right to "meet in convention by their own authority," forming a constitution and a state government, "whenever, hereafter they shall deem it expedient to do so." If Congress in its next session were to deny them again, Missourians could interpret that as "an attempt to expel" them from "the federation of the States," rendering them justified in exercising what amounted to a right of revolution rooted in popular sovereignty—in other words, secession from the territorial fold of the United States and formation of a separate slaveholding republic west of the Mississippi.[43]

And why not? Congress was not *required* to admit Missouri in 1820— or perhaps ever. Nothing had been predetermined about the physical dimensions of the republic. Dissatisfied leaders and their constituents had dreamed of alternative political geographies almost since the beginning. Even Jefferson had mused that parts of the Louisiana Purchase *might* break away. No one knew how far the "federative principle" reasonably extended. Nor had events on the ground established that Madison was right, and Montesquieu wrong, that a national republic could work in such a large country—one now much more vast than in 1789. Only the future communication and transportation revolutions—telegraph and railroad technology—would settle that lingering question in the affirmative.[44]

Others at the time sensed the possibility of a newly independent Missouri, standing outside the United States and drawing neighboring parts into its political orbit. Mathew Carey deplored the "harsh and discordant sound of disunion," the hostile airing of "separate views, interest, and feelings." The "blessings" of the federal system had not been so clearly evident in the western states as in the East, its power even less so. It disconcerted Carey and other promoters of a modern fiscal-state that the farther west one went, the fewer ties of dependence on the old states one found. "State functionaries" and, as in Missouri, territorial legislatures performed the main business of government. They knew Washington "in hardly any other capacity than that of a great landholder and collector of purchase moneys," and its "visitations" had not been more welcome "than those of private persons with similar claims." If "thrown out of the attraction of the present sphere," why would they *not* "revolve in another system," finding their "liberty, security, and prosperity" that way, to "be enjoyed without the aid of the United States"? Other new states, too, might prefer to "get on without . . . the expense of a general government," Carey warned. Worse, the loss of Missouri could end expansion of the United States to the northwest: "supported or even not opposed by the states immediately around her, and commanding by her situation the navigation of the noble river from which she derives her name."[45]

The possible loss of the West also occupied the "repeated conversation" between Secretary of War John C. Calhoun and fellow South Carolinian William Lowndes. The two men roomed together in Washington during the Missouri controversy. Both agreed that Missouri had to be regarded as a sovereign state, the only question being "whether she should be a State in or out of the Union." As Calhoun later recalled, "[a]ll saw that if Missouri was not admitted, she would remain an independent State on the west bank of the Mississippi, and would become the nucleus of a new confederation of States extending over the whole of Louisiana." No one really wanted that, but it remained for the northern members "to devise some means of escaping from the awkward dilemma in which they found themselves."[46]

Less fearful of disunion, the Baltimore protectionist writer Daniel Raymond drew on political economy to bolster the restrictionist side. In his 1819 pamphlet "The Missouri Question," Raymond argued that undercutting the diffusionist argument once and for all would win the West for free labor. Far from diminishing the evil in the old states, Raymond declared, the allowing of slavery west of the Mississippi would "have directly the contrary effect, . . . preventing the southern states from ever ridding themselves of that curse." Analyzing population data, he arrived at five conclusions: one, the number of free blacks increased by procreation nearly 50 percent *less* over twenty years than the white population in nonslaveholding states; two, by reproduction the slave population of blacks increased *faster* than the number of free blacks; three, the white population in slave states increased 30 to 40 percent *less* over twenty years than in free labor states; four, a slave population increased by procreation *faster* than the white population in a slave state; and therefore, five, "*in proportion as you restrain the increase of a slave population, you promote the increase of the white population.*" All that boiled down to a simple realization: The more slavery expanded in the fullness of time, the sooner the number of blacks in America would outstrip that of whites, even if many former slaves might be colonized in Africa.[47]

It required no argument, Raymond went on, "to prove that slaves are less industrious, and less faithful in their labours, than a free white population who labour for their own benefit, and reap that which they sow." Add to that the mounting potential for "mischief, misery, insurrection, bloodshed and desolation to our country and our [white] race." If southern states insisted on keeping, increasing, and expanding slavery, then, he prophesied, the "day of desolation and wrath is sure to overtake us." Apart from economic forces, the examples of Kentucky, Tennessee, Alabama, and Mississippi had established that slavery expansion did *not* lessen the slave population in the primary slave-supply states of the Carolinas, Virginia, and Maryland. Instead, the effect had been only to shower individual slave raisers and slave traders with windfall profits. An obvious conclusion therefore followed: Allow slavery to root any further, and Americans would never be rid of the institution.[48]

Farther North, however, radical editors treated their readers to more blistering fare, rooted in moralistic premises. In Stockbridge, Massachusetts,

R. H. Ashley's *Berkshire Star* blasted Congressman Henry Shaw for his vote against restriction and implored voters against supporting him: "your religion forbids it!—your virtue forbids it!—and your everlasting peace and happiness both here and hereafter forbid it!" The indecisive first round of the Missouri debate also reenergized antislavery passions in Tallmadge's home state of New York. Theodore Dwight's anti-southern *Daily Advertiser* called slave states "*the regions of despotism* in our country." If the restrictionist cause were to fail, then "the SIN OF SLAVERY" would be "fastened" on the region beyond the Mississippi and "THE DEATH WARRANT OF THE POLITICAL STANDING AND INFLUENCE OF THE FREE STATES WILL BE IRREVOCABLY SEALED." One of the largest public gatherings on Missouri took place in the assembly room of the City Hotel in Manhattan on November 16, 1819—a meeting of some two thousand participants. Its chair was Matthew Clarkson, a Revolutionary War hero and old-school Federalist, who in the New York assembly had introduced one of the state's earlier gradual abolition bills and now led the Bank of New York. Peter Augustus Jay, eldest son of John Jay and a former president of the New York Manumission Society, addressed the overflowing crowd and concluded with another set of resolutions, adopted without opposition. These asserted that slavery had become "a great political as well as moral evil, derogatory to the character of the nation, dangerous to the safety of its inhabitants, and opposed to the benign spirit and principles of the Christian religion." All present pledged themselves "to prevent, by all constitutional means," the further extension of the evil. Those means included a "clear and indisputable power . . . to prohibit the admission of slavery into any state or territory hereafter to be formed and admitted into the Union." They formed a twenty-seven-man committee of correspondence, mandated to persuade "individuals and public bodies in this and other states" and request cooperation and support in checking "the progress of slavery."[49]

In a pamphlet on the Missouri issue, twenty-eight-year-old New York City lawyer Joseph Blunt maintained that to extend slavery was to further a system "repugnant to the fundamental principles of a republic," serving "local prejudices" whose influence already endangered the welfare of all. The experience of republics from antiquity forward had taught that power left uncontrolled led to corruption and ruin. So it was, he thought, with slaveholders: their inhumanity, "caused by avarice," given free reign; their "malignant" and "licentious" passions unrestrained, their tyranny manifested in urging bondsmen "to labour beyond their strength by stripes and torture." Apart from considerations of justice and humanity, Blunt, too, cited five practical reasons for condemning slavery: (1) "It impoverishes the country." (2) "It has an immoral tendency." (3) "It endangers the peace of the republic." (4) "It paralyzes our arm in time of war." (5) "It is contrary to republican principles, and stains our national honor." Any free men, "feeling more interest in their occupations," he contended, would labor to greater advantage than slaves.[50]

Blunt cited pre-cotton-boom statistics from 1810 that showed the aggregate wealth of Massachusetts to exceed that of Virginia, South Carolina, and Georgia combined: $25,636,644 to $22,545,509. As for the "demoralizing" effect of slavery, he offered an argument similar to Jefferson's in *Notes on Virginia*: When "the lowest order of citizens is very ignorant and depraved, the corruption gradually seizes the adjoining members, until the nobler parts are invaded, and the disease pervades the whole body." Revolutionary events in Saint-Domingue and other Caribbean revolts had for some time sounded "warning voices, crying aloud" to southern planters: "You are on the brink of ruin." Beyond this, the question lingered whether in time of war a nation, "one-sixth of whose subjects are discontented and rebellious," could stand fit to enter a contest with a foreign enemy. After all, foreign foes before had exploited that vulnerability. And not least, slavery left a "foul stain" on the image of the republic, causing "enlightened Europeans"—those favorably disposed toward republicanism—to be "continually shocked at the glaring inconsistency of our conduct and principles."[51]

Of the antislavery memorials sent to Washington at the start of the Sixteenth Congress, two of the most persuasive came from ad hoc groups of citizens in Connecticut and Rhode Island. In Hartford, John T. Peters, the leading Republican on the Connecticut Supreme Court of Errors and founding president of the Hartford Auxiliary Colonization Society, chaired a public meeting of citizens on December 3, 1819. They started by declaring slavery to be "utterly repugnant to the principles of a republican Government." It became, they resolved, "a duty the American people owe to their republican character . . . to prevent the further extension of slavery," which they considered also "contrary to the spirit of our free and excellent constitution, and injurious to the highest interests of the nation." Peters composed the attached petition, along with Thomas S. Williams, a Federalist lawyer from Mansfield who had served in the Fifteenth Congress and would later become Chief Justice of Connecticut and president of the American Tract Society of New York; Rev. Thomas H. Gallaudet, who in Hartford had co-founded the first

American school for the deaf; and Sylvester Wells, a physician and member of the state senate.[52]

The Hartford document militated powerfully against the admission of newly acquired territories on an "equal footing," embracing one of the most extreme arguments on the restrictionist side. Congress had every right to impose restriction on new states carved from territory acquired after 1789, they contended, because the compromises made in the federal constitution applied to the original states *only*. Thus, any trans-Mississippi territories that might enter the Union "lie out of the limits" of those bodies that made those original compromises. That made "fallacious" the argument for "the absolute and entire sovereignty" of such new states. Therefore, the three-fifths and fugitive slave provisions in the Constitution need not apply in the far West. These had been part of a "bargain" that "ought not be stretched in its applica-tion to any *new* parties, without the consent of all those who *originally* made it." For their own safety and that of the Union, why not keep the "contagion" of slavery "within the narrowest possible limits"? Diffusion, however well-in-tentioned, would only spread "this terrible moral disease into regions which are yet unsullied by its contamination." Better, too, for "a bold and hardy yeo-manry" to comprise the population of the West—"tillers of their own soil, and its most able defenders."[53]

In the Newport statehouse, Thomas G. Pitman, who then served as gen-eral treasurer of Rhode Island, presided over another heavily attended meet-ing of local citizens just before Christmas in 1819. Reacting to a circular let-ter from a like-minded group in New York, the Newport petition opposed the introduction of slavery into *any* state or territory. It further noted that making Missouri a slave state, "to say nothing of its utter inconsistency with the genius of our republican institutions," would greatly boost illegal slave imports—a problem that Rhode Islanders understood all too well. After all, geography had located the outlet of the Mississippi and its tributary waters, emptying into the Gulf of Mexico, "in a region, beyond almost any other in the Union, open to an illicit trade." This, combined with the domestic in-crease of slaves already in Missouri, would lead to an increase "a thousand-fold greater than if the slaves were confined . . . to the states now holding them." So much, then, for the diffusionists' argument. As for political econ-omy, slavery had been introduced into America "in an unenlightened and fanatical age," the memorial continued, "and knowing . . . its effects on the state of agriculture, the manufacturing and mechanic arts, and generally on

the industrious and profitable habits of a people, and their domestic peace—
to think of introducing such a state of things, and of choice, too, into a new
country, is . . . inconceivable."[54]

As slavery expanded westward, southern leaders tried harder to defend
their no-longer-so-regretted institution. Meanwhile, their attackers, alarmed
by a widening cultural gulf between North and South, reviled slavery as an
institution that now weighed more heavily on *their* consciences than on those
of slaveholders themselves. All this resulted in widespread anxiety that the
country might split into not two, but three (or more) separate, distinct, and
rival political entities—in the West, the South, and the North. Historian Matthew Mason has noted that antislavery ideas in the abstract rarely motivated
northern people beyond their just lamenting the injustices that slaveholders
perpetrated upon southern slave laborers. But when the opponents of slavery
could make a more tangible case that the labor system of the South, and the
values that underlay it, directly threatened northern economic interests, civil
liberties, and hopes for the future, then mere belief quickly converted into
concern, advocacy, and movement. The same held true on the slaveholding
side, especially when southern planters sensed more at work against them
than just fundamental differences of political economy. By 1820, so many
Americans had invested so much in the dream of westward expansion—on
personal, regional, sectional, and national levels—that serious talk of *whose*
West it would be mattered deeply. The question of what kind of society would
prevail there, and what sort of economy, labor system, and political impact
it would bring, had generated concern enough to mobilize public opinion
everywhere in dramatic ways.[55]

4 Compromises

CONGRESSMAN JOHN FLOYD expected to answer at home for his behavior in the House of Representatives. "You have learned, by this time, the fate of the Missouri Bill, which perhaps excited more alarm, than has ever been felt in this country upon any subject," he told his Lexington, Virginia, constituents on March 11, 1820. Floyd infused his words with palpable caution. And for good reason: He had just been one of the few Virginians to vote *for* the Missouri Compromise.[1]

As in much of the great Shenandoah Valley, large numbers of Scotch-Irish and German migrants from Pennsylvania had started settling the Lexington area in the mid-1700s. Many abhorred slavery and regarded the institution as a sure route to economic stagnation. As a "Valley Poet" would lament in 1821: "The deed of wrong I now deplore, I know I cannot mend; [b]ut hope that slaves will bleed no more [w]here mercy finds a friend." Given such sentiments, slaveholders in Lexington and scattered around Rockbridge County, like those throughout the valley, kept a lower profile than their Tidewater counterparts.[2]

Because he had grown up in Kentucky before settling in western Virginia, Floyd sympathized with the voices of the frontier and would later add his own to the clamor for further territorial expansion. A physician by profession, he had lived in Philadelphia as a young man and studied medicine at the University of Pennsylvania. His experience as an army surgeon during the War of 1812 had made him nationalistic in spirit, but he tempered this devotion with a belief that "sovereign" states had given over completely to the national government only the powers of making war and peace and of regulating interstate commerce. That understanding of federal power placed him comfortably among fellow Jeffersonian Republicans in Virginia. Although he had kept his own counsel in the debate on Missouri, Floyd probably stood no more opposed to slavery in 1820 than the rest of the state's House delegation. With no wish to rile his conflicted constituents, he saw the issue as a matter of state choice. But like many southerners, what shocked Floyd about the Missouri debate was the vastly expanded, constitutionally unspecified, notion of government power lurking in the restrictionists' arguments—and with that, a complete disregard for Missouri's own preference. In years to come, he would follow the changing political climate in Virginia toward strict constructionist and states' rights advocates like John Randolph, Philip P. Barbour, Littleton Tazewell, Thomas W. Gilmer, and other "Old Republicans." Some politicians of this type would eventually become Jacksonians; others would gravitate to John C. Calhoun's newfound, increasingly aggressive, southern sectionalism.[3]

It saddened Floyd to witness so much hostility toward what everyone now called "the *compromise*." He assured the slaveholding contingent among his Virginia neighbors that the law's provisions would be confined to territories, containing no direct threat to the slave states. "That our friends to the North are *entirely ignorant* of the nature of slavery to the South, we know," he avowed, and "that many of their opinions are founded in prejudice, we cannot doubt." Still, something owed to the "honest intentions" of good legislators on both sides who had engineered what still seemed a precarious agreement, "such men as Kinsey, Stevens, Storrs, Bloomfield and others in the House of Representatives—and Hunter, Lanman, Parrott, Edwards and Thomas, in the Senate." Their "boldness and independence, worthy of imitation in all future times," had breasted the tempest of "popular indignation" for the sake of preserving the country, Floyd judged. A short but terrible contest, it had "looked to *disunion, civil war,* and all its concomitants on the one side, or the even prosperity of the Republic on the other." That prosperity, that future for the republic, he thought, had been "secured alone by the success of this measure."[4]

If there was cause for hope now, Floyd might have thought otherwise had he been able to foresee his own destiny—and the reason he would later become ardently proslavery. In 1831, when the deadliest slave insurrection in Virginia's history erupted in Southampton County—Nat Turner's rebellion—the governor of the state would be none other than John Floyd. Fifty-seven white victims, including women and children, were to receive a dose of vengeance by the hands of armed bondsmen. The insurrectionists drew inspiration this time not from revolutionary Saint-Domingue but from the liberating thrust of evangelical Christianity, which slave owners would quickly blame on meddling northern clergymen and abolitionists. In the meantime, however, Floyd's 1820 stance on Missouri apparently satisfied voters in his district; they would reelect him four consecutive times in the decade to come.[5]

"Equality is equality"

The continuing crisis, further heated by intemperate out-of-doors commentary in the months before, entered a new phase when Washington lawmakers assembled again in December 1819. As the Sixteenth Congress opened, Republicans outnumbered Federalists 30 to 10 in the Senate, and their House majority had swelled to 157 against 26. But on the Missouri question, the North-South sectional split within the Republican Party counted more, while the handful of cross-sectional votes—especially free-state representatives who would vote on the southern side—would matter *most*. That December, Maine applied for admission as a free state, enabling anti-restrictionists to argue that bringing Missouri and Maine into the Union together, both on terms of *their* choosing, was only fair. So said Henry Clay, newly reelected House Speaker, a position that in those days carried the powerful leverage of granting (or denying) coveted committee assignments. "Equality is equality," Clay announced when the Missouri Enabling Bill again came before the Committee of the Whole on December 30, "and if it is right to make the restriction of slavery the condition of the admission of Missouri, it is equally just to make the admission of Missouri the condition of that of Maine." Another fierce debate ensued, but the enabling bill again passed the House, still containing the controversial restrictionist part.[6]

Clay did not at first expect the Missouri question to lead into such dark and treacherous waters. He had presented the Missouri Territory request for admission in December 1818, hardly thinking the matter would take so long to resolve. He wanted the territory admitted quickly; some of his friends and family lived there. But more important, Clay envisioned the new state as part of a grateful western constituency that would help propel him to the presidency. Now, the Tallmadge Amendment had opened a sudden crevice under Clay's political fortunes, threatening the sectional harmony essential to his "American System" of economic improvement: protective tariffs, roads and canals, and tight federal control over public lands.[7]

Clay journeyed back to Washington in December 1819 deeply worried about the economic depression now sweeping the country, and especially the falling agricultural prices, bank failures, and farm foreclosures he had seen all over the West. That included personal financial losses. Making matters worse, a calamitous drought that summer had left precious hemp, tobacco, and cotton crops shriveling in the fields. All the more reason, he thought, for the House and Senate to settle the Missouri imbroglio and move on to pressing economic subjects, along with Latin American independence, and the sticking points that had delayed Senate ratification of the Adams-Onís Treaty.[8]

Many historians have regarded Clay with suspicion, underestimated his economic vision, and dismissed him as a mere political opportunist, especially on slavery. According to a recent biography, he sank to his "moral nadir" during the Missouri crisis. Another prominent study labels him as "a kind of quarterback for the slaveholders," as well as "the man who rallied the awakened South to resist the Tallmadge Amendment." Such characterizations add little understanding of Clay or of his role in the debate. His words and actions must be taken in context, judged not by how opponents saw him or against prevailing values of today. True, while he supported colonization, he objected to Tallmadge and sided with the anti-restrictionist, proslavery opposition. At times, he spoke of slaves as contrasting with northern factory workers in terms that sounded much like arguments that southerners would advance years later: slavery a "positive good" worth keeping, more than just a necessary evil. While otherwise eager to stretch the powers of Congress on economic policy, he denied that Congress had constitutional power to dictate the status of slavery within new states.[9]

And yet, there was much more to him than hypocrisy fueled by political ambition. It frustrates historians that Washington scribes did not record Clay's initial speeches on the Missouri question, nor did he write out his remarks or prepare detailed notes beforehand. We know those speeches affected listeners powerfully. On February 13, 1819, and again on February 15, Clay had risen against the Tallmadge Amendment. Neither speech found its way into the record, but the main points may be inferred from his opponents' responses. First, he endorsed the "diffusion" theory, finding it compatible with colonization. As reported later in the *National Intelligencer*, John W. Taylor said that Clay had "pathetically urged us to withdraw our [Tallmadge] amendment and suffer this unfortunate population [the slaves] to be dispersed over the country. He says they will be better fed, clothed and sheltered, and their whole condition will be greatly improved." Second, Clay protested the attachment of conditions on Missouri's admission. Timothy Fuller of Massachusetts said Clay had argued "that Congress has no right to prescribe any condition whatever to the newly organized States, but must admit them by a simple act, leaving their sovereignty unrestricted." Third, Clay contended that Article 4, Section 2 of the Constitution—"The citizens of each state shall be entitled to all the privileges and immunities of citizens of the several States"—further protected the right of Missouri citizens to decide for themselves on the matter of slavery, as slave owners elsewhere, like anyone else, stood entitled to take their property into new states and territories that permitted slaveholding. Fuller objected that "to make one portion of the population the property of another, hardly deserves to be called a privilege, since what is gained by the masters must be lost by the slaves."[10]

The Missouri question raised an obvious moral issue, but few politicians of national prominence had the luxury to see it *only* that way. Put simply, Clay's economic nationalism did not extend to aggressive federal action on slavery. While a lifelong slaveholder, Clay *did* believe the institution degraded white masters as well as the black men and women it victimized. Like Jefferson, he also thought diffusion would increase the proportion of whites in slaveholding areas so that eventually the price of free labor would fall to the point that slave labor could not compete. Fears of emancipation in the slave states would lessen, strengthening the liberal-minded support for gradual abolition like that of the North. Slaveholding, rendered transient rather than permanent, thus would be phased out. Economic interest, and not moral opposition from the North or destabilizing pressure from Congress, would end it.[11]

After the Fifteenth Congress adjourned in March 1819, Clay had seemed less preoccupied with Missouri than with the unfolding economic crisis, especially the rumors that the Lexington (Kentucky) branch of the Bank of the

United States had been slated for closing. The branches of the federal bank in the West and the South had already been instructed to suspend their issuing of notes, meaning that remittances eastward had to be made in specie, bills of exchange issued by European banks, or the notes of reputable banks located in the Northeast—all in short supply for westerners. Equally distressing for the West was the continual specie drain eastward from federal land purchases.[12]

The same crisis, of course, afflicted Missouri's economy, but differently. There, as in the farthest western states like Indiana and Illinois, resentment of federal institutions and policies flamed all the more, which meant rapidly fading support for nationalists like Clay and a resurging of anti-government radicalism like that of Illinois senator Ninian Edwards and Missouri's Thomas Hart Benton. Clay scrambled to mitigate political losses. Following the dinner circuit to New Orleans that spring, he spoke of the "intimate connexion between the prosperity of the Deep Southwest and that of the section of the country to which I belong." Meanwhile, President Monroe had departed Washington on March 30 on his own tour of the West and the South, reaching Nashville in early June. Accompanied by Andrew Jackson, Monroe went to greet crowds in Kentucky while Clay, to his frustration, "encountered unusual delay" in his return from the Mississippi Delta. Eyeing the presidency in 1824 as much as his budding rival Jackson, Clay tried to recoup support in the West and South for protective tariff policy. "The best remedy for hard times," he announced at a dinner in Hopkinsville, Kentucky, in early July, is "[i]ncreased production—diminished expenditures."[13]

Thus, for Clay, the ongoing Missouri crisis represented a distraction from business that mattered more to his political economy. And yet, as the Sixteenth Congress unfolded, Missouri also would offer an opportunity for him to raise political capital in the South and West: in the role of heroic mediator. Knowing the bitter statehood fight would resume that December, the Speaker had already implored House colleagues, as they readied to head home in March 1819, to put aside the "momentary irritation" and the "unkind expressions" that had recently fallen in "the heat of debate." Let these, he said, "be consigned to oblivion" in the belief that all sides had favored "the prosperity of our common country."[14]

Of Clay's speeches on the Missouri question that *did* survive, that of December 30, 1819, is probably the most suggestive of his motivations. It concerned Maine's application for statehood. On December 8, Massachusetts representative John Holmes had introduced a petition from the state's "district of Maine" asking for admission, and the Committee of the Whole addressed the Maine application three weeks later. In what followed, Clay assumed the role he coveted most, short of the presidency: leading spokesman of the West. Although not philosophically opposed to Maine's entry, he insisted the larger question had to be settled first, and that was whether "certain doctrines" of a disturbing nature, "which, if persevered in, no man could tell where they would end," were to be sustained. He later replied sharply to Arthur Livermore's contention that the Missouri and Maine questions were unrelated. Are we, Clay demanded, to accept the view that "because . . . Missouri was acquired by purchase, she is our vassal," subject to "conditions not applicable" to states on the eastern side of the Mississippi? If so, he declared, that doctrine was "an alarming one, . . . that there are any rights attaching in the one case which do not in the other; or that any line of distinction is to be drawn between the Eastern and the Western States."[15]

For both political and philosophical reasons, Clay leaned toward federal partnership with the states, though stopping short of "states'-rightist." He knew that many westerners, as well as southerners, bristled at being treated as "second-class" in any sense and resented any federal intrusion on their "sovereignty." He also believed that republicanism in America required that all members of the Union stand on an equal footing, no state intrinsically inferior to another. In that sense, Clay like other southerners regarded self-government, not slavery, as the fundamental issue in the Missouri debate. But he also revealed privately how much the spreading talk of disunion really bothered him. He feared that a malicious sectional realignment of political parties—North against South—would almost certainly occur unless compromise could be reached. He reported to Frankfort (Kentucky) *Argus* editor Amos Kendall on January 8, 1820, that many in Congress believed the whole debate intended to array "one portion of the U. States against another; and there is some reason to apprehend that this sinister design may be effected." Two weeks later, he vented to Adam Beatty that he heard members of Congress uttering the words "civil war" and "disunion" almost without emotion. Even outside Washington, "the subject of *disunion* is discussed in the circles with freedom and familiarity," Clay grumbled to Leslie Combs on February 15, having just heard that people in Richmond "are all in a flame; indignant at the idea of any compromise." Such "allusions to separation" only "some years ago" would have been regarded as "criminal," he exclaimed to Horace Holley just a couple days later.[16]

By this time, the battle had transferred to the Senate. "I fear from what I see that the southern States, by persisting in abetting the claim of Missouri, will more estrange the majority of this & the eastern part of the Confederacy, than any previous circumstances have done at any time," the southern-sympathizing Philadelphia editor Robert Walsh Jr. commented to James Madison on January 2, 1820. A day later, the Missouri bill emerged from the Senate Judiciary Committee *minus* the restrictionist provision. Pennsylvania senator Jonathan Roberts twice tried to restore the antislavery thrust of the measure, first in a futile effort to have the bill recommitted, and then, on February 1, losing 16 to 27 in a floor vote. For the next two weeks, fears of inevitable disunion escalated wildly. William Pinkney of Maryland and others speaking for states' rights won accolades from fellow southerners, including many in the Virginia state legislature. For southern moderates like Virginia's James Barbour, however, the pressure to compromise mounted. It came not only from the fear of disunion, which he shared, but also the belief he expressed privately to James Madison that if the question were kept open, then Maine would be admitted to statehood without Missouri, "the whole territory to the west of the Mississippi will be taken from us," and "[Rufus] King or [DeWitt] Clinton will most probably be the next President." Meanwhile, on the restrictionist side, Rufus King on February 11 made the case for northern sectionalism with such force and, it appeared, so little willingness to compromise, that slaveholders in the audience reportedly "gnawed their lips and clenched their fists" as they listened.[17]

King, of course, had been present in Philadelphia when the U.S. Constitution was written. Inveighing against the three-fifths clause and deprecating the acquisition of the Louisiana Territory in the first place, he added that if Missouri restriction did not prevail, then the northern people ought not submit. One scribe who heard the speech from the Senate gallery wrote that King's exposition had been "more alarming to the friends of our Union (whether federalists, or republicans,) than any thing which has hitherto been written or spoken upon the subject." Unsurprisingly, most of the disunionist talk had come from the southern side; northern Republicans held no desire to share the ignominy of the 1814–1815 Hartford Convention, where disgruntled New England Federalists had pondered the idea of the

northeastern states seceding. A New Hampshire newspaper later claimed
that "not a *single* word like it" had "fallen from the lips of a member north
of Maryland." And yet, a few days after King's speech, Pennsylvania senator Walter Lowrie disconcerted moderates by announcing that if forced to
choose between alternatives of dissolving the Union or extending slavery
over the whole of the western country, he would take the former.[18]

At last, on February 16, after the Senate agreed by a vote of 23 to 21 to join
the Maine and Missouri bills, Jesse B. Thomas, one of the new proslavery
senators from Illinois, proposed what turned out to be the critical compromise amendment to prohibit slavery in the Louisiana Purchase territory
north of latitude 36°30' (except for Missouri). Ironically, that was the same
demarcation line between slave and free territory that John W. Taylor had
urged, without success, after the defeat of his amendment to bar slavery expansion into Arkansas Territory several months earlier. Also at that time, the
anti-compromise *New York Daily Advertiser* had warned that such a dividing
line "would be fraught with dangerous consequences," just as likely to "sow
the seeds of discord in the government" as the restrictionists' position might
be. A slaveholder himself, Thomas, like his cohort Edwards, favored' establishing slavery in the new state of Illinois, where the voters at large remained
sharply divided on the question. Spotting a political opportunity, Thomas apparently figured he could win support from a majority of Illinoisans on *both*
sides of the slavery issue by bringing Missouri and Maine into the Union
on their own terms, thus preserving the principle of state self-determination
and the balance between slave and free states. On the next day, February 17,
the Thomas Amendment passed the Senate by 34 to 10, while the Maine-
Missouri bill, with the 36°30' provision attached, succeeded by 24 to 20. One
crucial shift was that both the Thomas Amendment and the admission of
Maine and Missouri together proved acceptable to the slave state senators,
who voted in favor of these provisions 14 to 8 and 20 to 2, respectively—
clearly a sectional pattern.[19]

Now, could Clay get the House to accept the Thomas Amendment in place
of Tallmadge's? The restrictionist majority there remained solid, but only by
a thin margin; a three-vote change would turn the tide. The Pennsylvania
nationalist John Sergeant had picked up where Taylor left off as leading voice
for the restrictionists. "[W]e, who are in favor of the restriction," said a correspondent for the *New York Evening Post*, "expect much from Mr. Sergeant."
Allied with Pennsylvania governor John McKean's faction of the state's

Jeffersonian party, Sergeant claimed several influential Federalist friends in Philadelphia as well. He could appeal to antislavery northerners of both political parties. "It is to no purpose, to say, that the question of slavery is a question of State concern," Sergeant proclaimed during a speech that lasted for six hours. "It affects the Union, in its interests, its resources and character, permanently; perhaps forever." Meanwhile, a more consequential drama unfolded, not on the House floor but in the political backrooms of the city. These deals, not speeches at the Capitol, would determine the ultimate fate of the Missouri question. Leading politicians, most importantly President Monroe, who commanded patronage favors, threw their persuasive powers and political influence behind the Thomas compromise—and thus found the votes they needed.[20]

The Clay-Thomas compromise that would finally pass consisted of three simple elements: Missouri admitted without restriction on slavery, Maine as a free state no longer part of Massachusetts, and a line at 36°30' prohibiting further introduction of slavery in the northern part of the Louisiana Purchase. Knowing that most northern congressmen still opposed the compromise and that it would still fail in the House as a package, Clay rearranged the provisions into two separate parts and drove both through with the help of the minority of representatives who supported the whole. Southern members backed the 36°30' restriction narrowly, 39 to 37. The border states (Delaware, Maryland, and Kentucky) voted 16 to 2 in favor. Virginia opposed it 18 to 4. The other slave states recorded 19 yeas against 17 nays. Now the bill went on to the president's desk, where Monroe waited eagerly to usher it into law.[21]

Who got the better of the deal? The South. Outside of Virginia, most southerners thought so at the time. Several historians have noted how few southern leaders ever believed that they had actually "compromised" in any serious way. The threat of disunion had worked its magic once again. Granted, only 39 percent of the congressmen from the South Atlantic states who had supported the Thomas proviso returned to serve in the Seventeenth Congress, while 70 percent of those who opposed it did. That fact probably attests more to the post-Missouri strengthening of Old Republicanism in the South than to any widespread public sense that the compromise had gone against them. If one looks at the map, of course, antislavery forces received the largest territorial share of the Louisiana Purchase. But most southerners accepted the free-labor semi-encirclement of Missouri, at least for now.

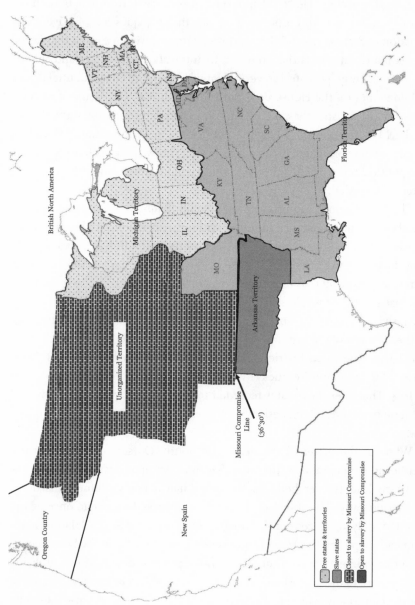

Missouri Compromise of 1820. Drawn by Margot Gibson-Beattie.

After all, the free soil part above 36°30' lay far above the traditional Ohio River dividing line between slave and free states. Few regarded that region as promising for plantation-style agriculture or likely to be settled soon in any case. The compromise line would establish a more formal division between "North" and "South," free states and slave, than had existed before, making more likely the eventual acquisition of Texas and the areas beyond, along with a war with Mexico to get them. "If we are cooped up on the north," Ritchie wrote in Richmond, "we must have elbow room to the west."[22]

Nevertheless, the slave states got what they wanted most: a victory of state self-determination and, with that, a temporary repulsing of antislavery nation-building designs for the trans-Mississippi West. As for slavery, that victory included a northern concession that no federally mandated emancipation would occur in new states; the power to ban slavery could apply (for now) only in territorial development as it had first with the Northwest Territory. The fate of the institution in the slave states remained a uniquely southern concern, off limits to outsiders—the ongoing sine qua non for southern acquiescence to a union with the North. The compromise also established in policy the hitherto informal practice of admitting new states in twos for sectional parity, the entry of Maine with Missouri keeping voting power balanced in the Senate, so critical to slave-state agency.[23]

Beyond the Missouri confrontation, the southern fear of aggressive nationalism, more deeply rooted now than ever, would manifest more often—and, at times, decisively—on economic issues, too. This trend also would reflect the spreading of Old Republican values and beliefs, primarily (but not exclusively) in the slave states. Along with the varied effects of the Panic of 1819, lingering memory of the Missouri crisis would help make southern votes for protective tariffs, federally funded roads and canals, continued national control of public lands, and, ultimately, a renewal of the Second Bank—in short, key ingredients of Clay's American System—far scarcer than before.[24]

"Doughfaces"

From the restrictionist perspective, the Missouri settlement of 1820 seemed less a "compromise" than a capitulation of the northern antislavery opposition. Viewed that way, particular scrutiny falls on the fourteen northern congressmen who voted for the compromise, along with four others conspicuously absent. The irascible John Randolph contemptuously dubbed them "doughfaces" (northerners who voted with the South), and the label stuck. Only five of the eighteen doughfaces in the House returned to the next Congress. Of the thirteen sent home, some lost for reasons not directly connected to Missouri. Still, many northern newspapers "blacklisted" the dough-faced congressmen and senators. Some of those lawmakers saw the light only as it emanated from their own burning effigies. Charles Kinsey of New Jersey, Connecticut's James Stevens, and Samuel Eddy of Rhode Island—the three restrictionists who changed their votes—invited special scorn back home. In early April 1820, a group of Carlisle, Pennsylvania, citizens paraded through the streets and cremated a figure of David Fullerton, a Republican merchant and banker from Greencastle, for his vote on the Missouri question. To a pole they affixed a transparency bearing the words "Fullerton & Slavery." Soon thereafter, Fullerton resigned his seat and opted against seeking renomination.[25]

Several northern members who voted against restriction later addressed their constituents in the public prints, often with elaborate epistles justifying their conduct. "It would appear," a northern editor smirked, "that some of the '*dough faced*' gentry are now alarmed for their re-election." The *Rhode Island American* quipped that three of the New Jersey House delegation had sided with the restrictionist majority until they got to "the fork in the roads." Perceiving that one of those paths led to dissolution of the Union, "they turned short about, and joined the stiff-necked *minority* of the south." The immediate backlash in the North against the compromisers, said the *New Hampshire Sentinel*, arose not from "party difference" or any other cause than their votes for the extension of slavery—an "honorable" public reaction, manifesting "a virtuous indignation against the course their Representatives saw fit to adopt," and revealing "the open, manly and persevering efforts of the friends of freedom."[26]

For some senators up for reelection in their respective state legislatures, the same story applied. Starting with the ones that John Floyd cited in the March 1820 letter to his Virginia constituents, William Hunter, a Federalist senator from Rhode Island, had practiced law in Newport before going to the Senate in 1811. He had chaired the Committee on Commerce and Manufactures during the Fourteenth Congress but left Washington in March 1821, denied Rhode Island's nod for reelection. He had voted "wrong" on Missouri. James Lanman, fifty-two, a Republican from Connecticut, served only one term in the Senate, from 1819 to 1825. Classically educated at Yale, he practiced law in Norwich and had been state's attorney for New London County, a state legislator, and a delegate to the 1818 Connecticut constitutional convention before the legislature picked him for the Senate. But the Missouri question instilled long memories, and Lanman's vote cost him his seat. John Fabyan Parrott, a fifty-two-year-old Republican from Portsmouth, New Hampshire, who identified with the nationalist Adams-Clay faction of the party, also entered the Senate in 1819 and remained for just one term. Such was the penalty for his compromise vote. That leaves Edwards and Thomas of Illinois who, of course, had voted with the South all along.[27]

As for Floyd's friends in the House, the story becomes more complicated. Kinsey, a forty-seven-year-old paper manufacturer from New Prospect, New Jersey, changed his mind on the Tallmadge Amendment, which he, with a majority of the House, had supported throughout the Fifteenth Congress and until the end of the Sixteenth in early March 1820. By this time, many New Jersey citizens stood adamantly opposed to any further extension of slavery. Antislavery forces there had organized under the leadership of the seventy-nine-year-old Elias Boudinot, a lawyer, former congressman, and one-time president of the Continental Congress. Later in life, Boudinot turned his energies to funding Presbyterian missions and advocating the human rights of Indians and blacks. In 1816, he had helped to found the American Bible Society and served as its president. In Burlington, on August 30, 1819, Boudinot and a group of fellow antislavery men met to demand a statewide meeting to be held in the capital, Trenton, two months later. The October gathering attracted a massive crowd, including the state's governor and members of the legislature. They approved a set of resolutions and a statement that they "would view, with unspeakable pain and mortification, any measure adopted by the federal legislature, tending to extend and perpetuate slavery among us; and holding out encouragement and temptation to the dealers in human flesh to continue their infamous trade, in defiance of the laws of the land, and the more sacred will of Heaven." Soon after, the New Jersey legislature issued resolutions to the same effect. Boudinot along with Joseph Hopkinson, one-time Pennsylvania Federalist and former House member who had moved to Bordentown, New Jersey, William Newbold, a Quaker merchant and manufacturer, Episcopal rector Simon Wilmur, state assemblyman James Parker, and Samuel Emlen, a Quaker abolitionist and philanthropist from Burlington, all agreed to "correspond with other persons and bodies" engaged in supporting similar principles.[28]

In February 1820, in a special election to replace John Condit, who had resigned, Kinsey had won by a landslide over seven other contestants, his 3,213 votes topping his closest opponent, James Parker, by 2,692 ballots. Republicans in Paterson, New Jersey, counted on him to support "the manufacturing and agricultural interests" of the state, which a continuing stalemate over Missouri could only prevent him from doing. Kinsey read too much into the one-sided margin of his election if he thought himself at liberty to disregard the expressed will of his constituents on the slavery question. One columnist offered a word of advice for future New Jersey congressman: "Perhaps the great popularity of Mr. Kinsey as manifested . . . has proved his ruin, by leading him to count upon a support which will not, which cannot be continued, when the known sentiments and wishes of the people are disregarded."[29]

If one takes Kinsey at his word, it was devotion to the Union that inspired his shift. Congressmen now had to ask whether their experiment in free government should be broken asunder over a dispute on the division of territory. In the end, he said he could not bring himself to risk that "disastrous" prospect. How much had southerners really demanded? Not an *equal* division of the public domain west of the Mississippi, a "common property, purchased with the common funds of the nation." They had agreed "to fix an irrevocable boundary, beyond which slavery shall never pass," surrendering to "the claims of humanity and the non-slaveholding states . . . nine-tenths of the country in question." Could northerners rightly insist that they concede the remainder, especially when "religion and reason" might still prevail against slavery in parts of the South where the cultivation of cereals instead of plantation staples might ultimately make "the labors of the slave unprofitable"? Further, if compromise had failed, what kind of political realignment would likely result? An "unhallowed . . . political ascendency," Kinsey answered, embittered northern and southern factions against each other, their leaders driven by "lurking ambition, the bane of all government." Refuse the compromise, and "this arena of the national council becomes the theatre of discord."[30]

Perhaps, but voters at home did not swallow it. Kinsey would never return to Congress after his term expired on March 3, 1821. Recriminations for his Missouri vote came quickly from antislavery citizens in New Jersey. "The electors in the eastern part of the State will not give them their suffrage," an anonymous "REPUBLICAN VOTER" told "the Freeman of New-Jersey" in regard to three House candidates for reelection, Kinsey along with Joseph

Bloomfield and Bernard Smith. "The part the gentlemen took in the Missouri question, and their final vote in favor of SLAVERY, has unquestionably ruined their popularity in this region of the country: politically, they are dead as a doornail." That public meeting at Trenton, as well as the state legislature, it turned out, had been "conclusive" in expressing the "feelings of the public."[31]

The same fate awaited Bloomfield. Also a Republican, he had served as a major in the Revolutionary War and practiced law in Burlington before being elected as governor in 1801, a position he held for eleven years. He was sent to the Fifteenth Congress and again to the Sixteenth, but voters who deplored his compromise vote in 1820 denied him reelection after that. The only consideration his critics offered was that "he hoisted no false colours"—had voted with the "advocates of slavery" all along, never misleading Jerseyman as to how his Missouri vote would fall. Even so, his pro-compromise position on "the unfortunate Missouri bill," a Newark editor declared, would render his selection as a candidate "inexpedient" and his election "impossible."[32]

The fifty-two-year-old James Stevens, a Republican from Fairfield County, Connecticut, had served in the House off and on since 1804. His career in Washington would end with the Missouri crisis as well. Like Kinsey, Stevens tried to explain his vote in a speech that he undoubtedly expected to be reprinted back home. The compromise did not satisfy him, he said, as he would rather have seen no further introduction of slaves into Missouri and worried that the 36°30' line would later be extended to the Pacific and thereby "perpetuate the evil we seek to remedy" and create "a perpetual rallying place for party." But as he saw the matter, even higher considerations lay at stake. "A precipice lies before us, at which perdition is inevitable," and who would "not tremble for the consequences?" If compromise might inspire a new alignment of parties, failure to compromise would certainly do so. Walking away now from a bargain, however imperfect, would create "ruthless hatred," eradicable "jealousy," and "a total forgetfulness of the ardor of patriotism." Stevens recalled President Washington's 1796 admonition to his countrymen that they avoid *both* party and sectional conflict—all the more valid when parties threatened to form along sectional lines. Future restriction without disturbing the right of slaveholders to keep slaves they already had and the offspring of those might have allayed party feelings, Stevens thought. But most of his northern and eastern brethren had not been willing to settle for that—and many not for *any* compromise. The same applied for many northeastern constituents, including Stevens's.[33]

And finally, Henry Randolph Storrs, thirty-three, a Federalist lawyer born in Middletown, Connecticut, and an 1804 graduate of Yale, had moved to New York and represented Jefferson County. Voters in his district elected him to the Fifteenth and Sixteenth Congresses, but his Missouri vote cost him renomination in 1820. He would return to the House a few years later as an Adams man, later opposed to Jacksonian democracy. Within days after the 36°30' agreement, antislavery writers in New York attributed his anti-restrictionist support to the influence of the pro-southern "Bucktail" faction. Storrs, one upstate editor wrote, could not resist the "blandishments of the southern gentry," and "being habitually indolent and fond of entertainments and sumptuous living, he was easily won over to the slaveholding interest by the assiduous attentions of southern men of higher stations, and by frequent invitations to participate in their banquets." Another New Yorker, Henry Meigs, voted against restriction, while two, Caleb Tompkins and Walter Case, turned up missing for the vote. Those three also lost reelection to the next Congress.[34]

Maine

The new "Pine Tree State," aptly nicknamed, had been part of Massachusetts even though physically separate from its parent commonwealth. Festering disagreements over land speculation and settlement rights, along with resentment over the failure of Massachusetts to defend Maine against British invaders in the War of 1812, had inspired a secession movement there. In 1819, Massachusetts agreed to permit the separation if voters in Maine approved, which they soon did. Although eager to enter the Union in 1820, many Maine residents balked at being tied to the admission of another slave state. Nearly three weeks before the Tallmadge Amendment, a January 1819 meeting of inhabitants in the small Kennebec County town of Vassalboro, in southern Maine, had anticipated that possibility—and objected strongly. Following town leaders Moses Sleeper and Jacob Southwick, the group declared a preference for "remaining forever in our present situation" rather than "being admitted on ignominious terms, or giving the semblance of a sanction to the violation of the rights of humanity." One year later, a Brunswick resident, Henry Putnam, even set this anti-compromise sentiment to verse:

If the South will not yield, to the West be it known,
That Maine will declare a *King* of her own;
And *three hundred thousand* of freemen demand
The justice bestow'd on each State in the land.
Free whites of the East are not blacks of the West.
And Republican souls on this principle rest,
That if no respect to their rights can be shown,
They know how to vindicate what are their own. . . .
South and West, now be honest, to MAINE give her due,
If you call her a child, she's an Hercules too.
A Sister in Union admit her, as free;
To be coupled with slaves, she will never agree.[35]

Maine newspaper exchanges in the months preceding the compromise had reflected a complex range of opinion, however. Some considered delaying Maine's statehood over a matter so geographically remote to be a needless sacrifice. Others equated Missouri's struggle for autonomy with the struggle of Maine's people to escape their subjection to "Federalist overlords" in Boston. While regarding slavery "*with abhorrence, as inconsistent with the first principles of republican government,*" Portland's *Eastern Argus* in January 1820 nevertheless cautioned "to let not our holy indignation lead us to intermeddle too hastily with our neighbor's affairs." Others saw Maine as more deserving of admission than Missouri in the first place. "What!" exclaimed the *Hallowell Gazette*, "after erecting southern and western States, almost by the dozens, and constituting every Territory beyond the Alleghanies, which contained thirty or forty thousand inhabitants, an independent member of the Union, shall Maine, containing three hundred thousand inhabitants, with wealth, and strength, and talents in proportion, the *first* and *only* applicant from the North, be spurned and refused?" For that matter, "who is Missouri?" demanded the *American Advocate*. "A nursling of Spanish bigotry, and French despotism," it had contributed nothing to the American Revolution or the adoption of the federal Constitution. Further, the *Eastport Sentinel* warned, "Should our application fail in consequence of its being connected with the Missouri question, it will produce in Maine a state of feeling in relation to the general government which we should exceedingly deprecate."[36]

Even after the compromise in March 1820, controversy continued to swirl in Portland, where the two principal sheets, the *Argus* and the *Gazette*, took opposing sides. The former defended the pro-compromise votes of the two Massachusetts representatives from Maine, John Holmes and Mark Langdon Hill, while the latter assailed them. As Republicans, Holmes and Hill faced lingering Federalist challengers at home. Those local rivals, among others, had no intention of letting voters forget the two pro-compromise votes from Maine that made a key difference in the 90-to-87 margin to strike the anti-slavery proviso from the Missouri bill. Despite the partisan wrangling, which accompanied genuine philosophical differences, both men afterward would be elected to Congress, Hill to Maine's House delegation, Holmes to the Senate. One columnist for the *Argus*, styling himself as "KENNEBEC," reminded readers of the value of sectional harmony to Maine's producers of beef, fish, butter, cheese, potatoes, and manufactured goods—and in return sugar, cotton, and freights for their shipping. "The prosperity of the South will give life and activity to every species of industry in the north," the writer argued, "and if they [southerners] are crippled and depressed, the evil will just as certainly fall by a rebound on us." Holmes and Hill had voted the "general interest of the nation" and should rest assured "the people of Maine will give them full credit for their exertions." The *Gazette*, by contrast, consigned both men to its "black list," reserving harshest condemnation for Holmes, who had collected certificates from senators avowing that if Missouri had not been admitted without restriction, then Maine would have been left out, too. "Now these certificates must have been obtained either before or after the question was decided," the *Gazette* noted. "If afterwards, what are they good for? If before does it not amount to evidence of *mutual pledges* between the parties, viz. Mr. Holmes on one side and these southern Senators on the other." Lamenting the lingering quarrel in the press, the pro-compromise editor of the *American Advocate*, in the trading town of Hallowell, asked "[w]hy this reluctance to let go of the Missouri question, and why thus abuse those who have put it to rest?" The prescribed answer: "Does it not look as though it were true, as has been suspected, that they [the *Gazette* and its backers] intended it as a stalking-horse for the attainment of power?"[37]

Holmes, an ardent voice for Maine's separation since 1816, had opposed the Tallmadge Amendment from the beginning, one of only six free-state representatives who did. Allied with William King (brother of Rufus), Albion Keith Parris, John Chandler, and *Argus* editors William Pitt Preble and Ashur Ware, Holmes had chaired the committee that wrote Maine's proposed constitution in 1819 and envisioned statehood as strengthening Republican Party control at home and promising political advancement for himself. Holmes had struck a close enough friendship with Clay, political and otherwise, that the Speaker had appointed him as one of the five House members on the eight-man conference committee that hammered out the details of the March 1820 compromise. Pressured to defend his Missouri vote, Holmes insisted in his public "Letter to the People of Maine" that scheming anti-Jeffersonian, anti-southern politicians had manufactured the whole controversy, but he followed William King's private advice to refrain from mentioning by name Federalists like Rufus King or the Clintonian faction in New York, lest he "offend" powerful men or lose the favor of some. Although openly anti-restrictionist from the start, he said his office had "never received a letter in protest" from his constituents until after antislavery propaganda from a November 1819 meeting of New York abolitionists had circulated around Maine. His private sentiments, conveyed to William King in late March 1820, revealed a bit more: "[T]he restrictionists of our [Maine] delegation will either get up a newspaper or throw themselves into the arms of the federalists. Their object will be two fold—one to create a party against the *State administration* and the other to be looking towards a *northern combination* against the Presidential election after next [1824]."[38]

A more extensive rationalization came from Hill, a forty-seven-year-old Jeffersonian merchant and shipbuilder from the coastal town of Phippsburg, at the mouth of the Kennebec River. While vilified in the local press for flip-flopping, Hill's natural inclination, he said, had been to favor restriction for Missouri, but he finally judged it best to act otherwise. He cited several reasons, but none suggested antislavery belief strong enough to trump the obvious commercial ties that he and his neighbors pursued with the South. That complimentary economic relationship had grown apace since about 1800. William King, a prominent Bath, Maine, merchant and fervent supporter of the compromise, who in 1820 would become the first governor of the state, had been the first Maine shipper to plunge into the lucrative New Orleans–Liverpool cotton trade that would thrive right up until the Civil War. This prosperity for traders, manufacturers, and businessmen in southern Maine would go far to dampen the moral outrage against slavery.[39]

Hill echoed Holmes's defense that persistence in the Missouri restriction would have sunk Maine's chances for statehood, thus blasting its hopes and wasting the time and money spent "in making preparations for self-government." Further, in averting the likely use of force against an unwilling

Missouri, he said, "you quiet the slave-holding States" and "inhibit slavery from a territory [north of 36°30'] larger than all the original thirteen United States, in exact conformity to the ordinance of 1787." Three months earlier, in private, Hill had told William King that favoring compromise really had little to do with either defending or opposing slavery. "I am for going as far as anybody to restrict slavery, if it can be done without setting the United States on fire," he wrote, "for I think the welfare of eight million of whites . . . of more importance than a question about the black population and that the preservation of the Union and the admission of Maine, of more importance, than the doubtful right by the constitution to meddle with state sovereignty." Much farther south, former president Madison, having received from Hill a copy of the epistle to Maine constituents, thought the statement "well calculated to assuage the party zeal" that the Missouri question had generated. Eventually, "these stormy subjects will . . . blow over," Madison counseled, "and the people on the return of calm, be more disposed to consider wherein their interests agree, than wherein their opinions differ."[40]

Monroe

Had the Missouri bill come to him with the Tallmadge Amendment included, President Monroe would have vetoed it. As a nationalist, he primarily wanted a bill that he could sign to keep the country in one piece. As a politician, he needed a compromise perhaps even more than Clay because continuing support in his home state of Virginia depended on it. When Monroe became president in 1817, his main political objective had been reconciliation and, when necessary, compromise. He wanted to bring peace between increasingly disparate factions of his own Republican Party and also rival parts of the nation, especially the South and New England. He wanted a Massachusetts man, John Quincy Adams, to be secretary of state partly for that reason. His administration, Monroe imagined, would mark the end of both destructive party conflict and sectional strife in American politics, as if to fulfill the hopes that President Washington expressed in the 1796 Farewell Address.[41]

After completing a goodwill tour of the Northeast, Monroe concluded that people there, who appeared in droves to welcome him, now wished as much as he did to push aside unpleasant memories of New England opposition to the War of 1812. "I have seen enough to satisfy me, that the great mass of our fellow-citizens, in the Eastern States are as firmly attached to the union and to republican gov^t. as I have always believ'd or could desire them to be," he gushed to Thomas Jefferson in late July 1817. The same assurance featured, too, in Monroe's First Annual Message that December. "Local jealousies are rapidly yielding to more generous, enlarged and enlightened views of national policy," he proclaimed, wishfully. After the admission of Illinois in 1818, he wrote without irony in his Second Annual Message that "[b]y increasing the number of the States[,] the confidence of the State governments in their own security is increased and their jealousy of the National Government proportionally diminished."[42]

Here Monroe seemed to foreshadow his view of Missouri's rights. Like Clay, he wanted the states themselves to determine whether they would have slavery. As the controversy reached its height in February 1820, the president's hopes faded. He told his Virginia friends that northeasterners had perpetrated the conflict—conniving, power-hungry Federalists who, whether or not "attached to the union," still despised Republican Party rule. "The object of those, who brought it forward," he told Jefferson, "was undoubtedly to acquire power, & the expedient well adapted to the end, as it enlisted in their service, the best feelings, of all that portion of our Union, in which slavery does not exist, & who are unacquainted with the condition of their Southern brethren." Further, the northeastern restrictionists, he suspected, aimed to stymie the growth of the West generally, blocking the addition of slave states indebted to Republican policymakers for their very existence. And if, in frustration, the western territories were to split away from the United States, the alleged schemers figured, then so much the better for the Northeast. Thinking of John Jay and Rufus King, Monroe recalled the unsuccessful Jay-Gardoqui negotiations with Spain in 1786, in which Federalist diplomats offered to accept a closing of the mouth of the Mississippi to American commerce for twenty-five years. "The dismemberment of the Union by the Allegheny Mountains, was then believed to be their object," he asserted, and while "a new arrangement of powers, is more particularly sought on this occasion, yet it is believ'd, that the anticipation of even that result, would not deter its Authors from the pursuit of it."[43]

In truth, of course, it had never been the Federalists at all but northern Republicans who had launched the Missouri crisis and provided strongest support for the Tallmadge Amendment. Even so, the possibility of a new, anti-southern political party combining the two groups still loomed. What

Monroe feared most was a sectional split within his own party. Along with a host of well-orchestrated political maneuvers, he was using the Federalist "threat" to unify his Republican camp as much as possible. With regard to Missouri and the expansion of federal power, he faced the most serious problems in his own backyard: Virginia and other slave states. Both the Missouri crisis and the Supreme Court's decision in *McCulloch* had enraged Virginia's Old Republicans. As state legislators in the Old Dominion went about selecting candidates for presidential electors in early February 1820, prior to adoption of the Thomas Amendment, rumors circulated that if Monroe consented to a bill restricting slavery in the territories, then they would look for a new president. But if he were to go against restriction, New Hampshire's William Plumer Jr. observed, "he loses all the north, where his best friends now are."[44]

While Monroe exerted his influence behind the scenes, he confided again to Jefferson his distrust of sectional dividing lines—a wariness that Jefferson shared. Considerations of discretion and restraint in western policy making sometimes recommended that lawmakers refrain from using powers they held. "I never doubted the right of Congress, to make such a regulation in [the] territories, tho' I did not expect that it would ever have been exercised," Monroe confessed. A strict division at 36°30' would only make further westward expansion more difficult to consider and, when undertaken, a source of further sectional acrimony, involving "difficulties, of an internal nature, which menace the Union itself." The whole Missouri fight had "excited feelings & raised difficulties, of an internal nature, which did not exist before," Monroe told Andrew Jackson in May 1820, implying also that such unpleasantness had not *needed* to exist. Better now, for one thing, to soft-pedal the acquiring of Texas—"to pause before we push matters to a dangerous extremity." And to Albert Gallatin a few days later: "Internal considerations, of which the discussion of the late Missouri question will have given you a just view, are favorable to moderate pretentions on our part."[45]

Meanwhile, at the War Department, Secretary John C. Calhoun indulged in cautious optimism. He told private correspondents that the worst of the crisis apparently had passed. The acrimony of the debate had weakened the attachment of the southern and western people to the Union, but, as he too instructed Jackson in June 1820, "the agitators of that question have, in my opinion, not only completely failed; but have destroyed to a great extent their capacity for future mischief." The following August, he soothed his Maryland friend Virgil Maxcy, suggesting that the only real danger now threatening the Union would be an erroneous *perception* in the slaveholding states that the North actually meant to undermine their property in slaves. "Should so dangerous a mode of believing once take root, no one can calculate the consequences; and it will be found, that a reagitation of the Missouri question will tend strongly to excite such a belief." And in October, Charles Tait in Alabama opened another letter from Calhoun assuring him that no "premeditated struggle for superiority" between North and South had seriously existed. Granted, there were a few in the free states "who for private objects" wished to create such a showdown, but "their number is very small" and "wholly in New York, and the mid[d]le States." For now, he advised, "[w]e to the South ought not to assent easily to the belief that there is a conspiracy either against our property, or just weight in the Union."[46]

In public, Secretary of State Adams also endorsed the compromise. It was the best settlement that could be effected under the Constitution as it was, he thought, and preferable, at least for now, to putting the Union at hazard. Privately, however, he registered serious doubts and, indeed, outrage. For one thing, Clay's legislative tactics disgusted him, especially the way a law perpetuating slavery in Missouri, and perhaps in all of North America, had been "smuggled" through both houses of Congress, "victorious by the means of accomplices and deserters from the ranks of freedom," with the "dishonesty" of coupling the bill with the admission of Maine. But Adams knew that the real fault lay in the Constitution itself, which "sanctioned a dishonorable compromise with slavery." For that, no remedy existed except a revisiting of the "morally and politically vicious" bargain between freedom and slavery that had resulted in governance by "slave representation." Perhaps it would have been a "wiser" and "bolder" course, he mused to himself, "to have persisted in the restriction upon Missouri, till it should have terminated in a convention of the States to revise and amend the Constitution." The outcome of that, he thought, would have been a new Union of thirteen or fourteen free states, "unpolluted with slavery," in the hope of rallying the other states eventually to the standard of universal emancipation. "If the Union must be dissolved," he prophesied, "slavery is precisely the question upon which it ought to break. For the present, however, this contest is laid asleep."[47]

Even after the Missouri crisis had shaken this "era of good feelings," the misnomer that historians have employed for the period, Monroe sat relieved. What the compromise had really prevented was not the revival of the

Federalist Party but a break-up of his own Republicans along destructive sectional lines. "Surely our government may get on and prosper without the existence of [opposing] parties," he would tell James Madison in 1822. "I have always considered their existence as the curse of the country." Americans in truth had no entrenched, European-style aristocratic orders in need of political organizations to protect property and position against threatening middle- and lower-class elements of society. Here, the challenge was to succeed in "the experiment whether there is sufficient virtue in the people to support our free republican system of government." Still, Adams foresaw the future better than Monroe did. Even if the Missouri Compromise had rendered that "experiment" a little more tenable than before, how long could it last?[48]

Monticello

Meanwhile, on an isolated mountaintop some five days' ride south from Washington, seventy-seven-year-old Thomas Jefferson lifted his quill to answer a letter from John Holmes. The Maine senatorial aspirant had enclosed a copy of his "Letter to the People of Maine," apparently hoping for an expression of approval from the former president, something quotable. Jefferson's optimism for the nation's future now seemed to be evaporating. He knew, however, that any political commentary in this letter would find its way into the press, so he fashioned the prose for public effect. Because Holmes was a northerner who broke sectional ranks, the famous Virginian could operate through *him*, too—by warning off the North from further action on slavery. The "momentous question" of slavery expansion into the far West, "like a firebell in the night, awakened and filled me with terror," Jefferson wrote. "I considered it at once as the knell of the Union." He knew, of course, that antislavery northerners had been trying to restrict that expansion for three decades, as he had himself in 1784. To others, the former president expressed less alarm, although to John Adams in December 1819 he had mused that in the days of the Revolution, from the Battle of Bunker Hill to the Treaty of Paris, "we never had so ominous a question [as the Missouri crisis]," and he thanked God he would not live to witness its ultimate outcome.[49]

What might that outcome be? As for slavery itself, Jefferson had never worried as much about its impact on blacks as he did the effect it had on whites, on both their personal behavior and their politics, and its destructive potential for the Union. He had long registered doubts on the fitness of black

Americans for citizenship. In *Notes on the State of Virginia*, he concluded that the African race was incapable of sensitive feelings; their very blackness made them politically untrustworthy and incapable of higher reasoning or an appreciation of the sublime. Recalling the practice of white slavery in republican societies of ancient times, he denigrated American slaves and free blacks for coming nowhere close to the intellectual achievements of some Roman slaves.[50]

As of 1820, while the letter to Holmes exaggerated his actual fears, Jefferson's concern about the political threat of slavery and his valuing of the Union remained authentic enough. His 1784 method for ending the institution was not so far from Tallmadge's in 1819 (or Lincoln's in 1860): stop its westward expansion. Now he, like one southerner after another in the Missouri debate, believed it more important for "diffusion" to remove blacks from the Old South. Congress had left open that window of opportunity. Further, he hoped the United States would someday annex Texas and Cuba—without the sectional acrimony that had accompanied Missouri.[51]

Beyond all that, he worried that northeastern Federalists might still revive their party by uniting the North against the South on the moral issue of slavery. But the drawing of a geographical line at 36°30', he thought, only had intensified the basic dilemma of cultural survival set against human rights, with no way to reconcile the two. Better to draw no lines at all and try to reduce the barriers between the sections instead of building new ones. He said the division marked not just a separation on the map but an assertion of opposing principles, moral and political, that would "never be obliterated; and every new irritation will mark it deeper and deeper." Having taken their stand, it would be hard for southerners ever to back down. With luck, and the help of men like Holmes, the North might further give way. "But as it is, we have the wolf by the ear," he despaired, "and we can neither hold him, nor safely let him go. Justice is in one scale, and self-preservation in the other." Holding that "wolf" at bay now meant as much the restraining of northern aggression as it did the controlling of the slave population.[52]

Round Three

Just when it looked as if the Missouri storm had passed, a further crisis threatened. Passing the compromise in early 1820, Congress had, in a sense, agreed to admit the Missouri Territory to statehood on condition that it draft an acceptable constitution, and no one would have expected this final step to generate additional controversy. A defiant Missouri convention, however, produced a document that would make it illegal for the state to free slaves without their owners' consent. That provision not only permitted slavery but made the institution impossible to end by state action. Further, the proposed constitution required the Missouri legislature to make whatever laws that might be necessary "to prevent free Negroes and mulattos from coming to and settling in this State, under any pretext whatever." This barring of free blacks from the state would violate Article IV, Section 2 of the federal Constitution, which stated that "citizens of each state shall be entitled to all Privileges and Immunities of citizens of the several states."[53]

Behind Missouri's actions, in part, blazed western indignation against the federal government. Anti-statist political belief, dripping with resentment of faraway (especially northeastern) decision makers, appealed widely in the newest states, now probably more in Missouri than any. Financially stricken westerners blamed Bank of the United States mismanagement in distant Philadelphia for the financial panic. Western radicals demanded all sorts of nostrums—reduced prices, free grants to the poor, endless relief to credit purchasers, preemption for squatters, cession of lands to the states—to break the tight-fisted grip of Congress on federal lands. There seemed at first little point for Missouri lawgivers to include such inflamatory constitutional statements other than to defy the restrictionist element in Congress. After all, its legislature could later have adopted the same policies without codifying them now in fundamental law. Following the long, angry debate of 1819–1820, the Missouri constitution carried "the appearance," said a columnist in Maine, "of an experiment on the patient and compliant temper of the national legislature." Viewed in the broader context of mounting anti-national anger in the West, however, Missouri's latest expression of contempt for federal power becomes more understandable.[54]

Self-appointed media spokesmen for Missourians, although still divided themselves on slavery, freely expressed disdain for those in Washington who had tried to impose restrictions on their own governance without their consent. A March 4, 1820, commentator in the *St. Louis Enquirer*, who invoked both ancient Roman and English Commonwealth tradition by signing himself as "cato," thought the "designs of the *north*" had become easy enough to discern. "New York is making *rapid strides* towards that power which is to give law to the Union," the writer avowed, "and the control over the great country west of the Mississippi, is no small part of her plan." If antislavery men in Washington could "*demand* a constitutional abolition of slavery in the state," could they not equally insist that "all free negroes and mulattos may migrate to the proposed state," vote in elections, serve as witnesses and jurors, hold "offices of trust," become senators and representatives, or "intermarry with the whites of Missouri"? Would the next step be to limit the amount of land a man could own, require Missourians to vote for "the *great men* of New York for president," demand support for a "general emancipation of all the slaves of the Union," decree that "no bank except a branch of the bank of the United States shall be established in Missouri," or insist that its senators and representatives in Congress "be chosen exclusively from the *honorable class* of emigrants from New England, New York and Pennsylvania"? Ohio, Indiana, Illinois, Tennessee, Alabama, Mississippi, and Louisiana all had once also been part of United States territory, yet Congress had claimed no further right to restrict them after statehood. Would it now pronounce Missouri's proposed state constitution inadmissible because of its specific exclusion of free blacks?[55]

This new controversy also mirrored rumblings of dissatisfaction elsewhere around the country. Even before Congress approved the Thomas Amendment, various southern newspapers expected further trouble. One, Samuel B. T. Caldwell's *Genius of Liberty* in Leesburg, Virginia, on February 8, 1820, anticipated an ongoing threat of government consolidation from the growing northern majority, whose *professed* opposition to black servitude only masked the true motivation: thirst for absolute power. "We are thoroughly satisfied that the extent of the impending calamity is not generally perceived," Caldwell said. "We are likewise satisfied that thousands of the good citizens of these free and united STATES have been deceived by public disclaimers against slavery." As further evidence that the Missouri controversy had yet to subside, a large public meeting assembled about a month later in Boston to protest the compromise and called for further meetings to do the same. In dismay, the *Boston Patriot* echoed the feelings of pro-compromise northerners. Already the slave states had shown "the greatest liberality" in conceding territory by way of ending this "serious and alarming conflict." How could there be any repealing of the compromise anyway, as it now stood "in the nature of a contract, which cannot be violated"? Did northeastern radicals wish to go on risking civil war? A writer for the *Baltimore American* gave a dire answer to that question in late November 1820, observing the "awful foreboding" of another gathering storm, beginning with antislavery northerners determined to refuse Missouri admission after all and citing the anti-black provisions in its constitution as a pretext: "The Missouri business is now lugged into every question—it is the grand machine by which the real enemies of the country, the advocates of a dissolution of the Union, intend to raise themselves into power."[56]

Although Congress could object to its banning of free blacks and mulattoes, Missouri in fact had asserted little that other states, including most northern ones, did not already practice. Several states at the time, including Massachusetts, New York, Tennessee, and North Carolina, did recognize free blacks as citizens, and no specific provision in the U.S. Constitution had made skin color a bar to citizenship. On the other hand, antislavery conviction, however ardent, had never precluded intense prejudices against blacks in either West or East. Whites in Kentucky, Indiana, and Illinois also had gone to considerable lengths to discourage free blacks. All three of those states denied African Americans the right to vote, intermarry with whites, testify in court against whites, or attend public schools. They made it a crime for whites to conceal fugitive slaves or to bring in slaves with the idea of freeing them. Kentucky in 1808 had passed a law prohibiting free blacks and mulattoes from entering the state, but unlike the one Missouri now proposed, its constitution had not mandated such a policy. Right after being admitted to the Union, Illinois had instituted the most brutal anti-black code in the North, with everything but specifically closing the state's boundaries to them. Before settling in Illinois, any black or mulatto (understood as more than one-fourth black) had to provide a court-sealed certificate of freedom along with background information on himself and his family. At the county level, overseers of the poor in Illinois held power to require of any former slave a bond of $1,000 as proof that he or she would not become a public charge—and to remove by force any who did not comply.[57]

For that matter, few white Americans anywhere thought the Declaration of Independence, with its promise of equality, had been meant to offer anything for blacks, including emancipated ones. In the United States, "there is no place for the free blacks," Nathaniel Macon of North Carolina had observed during the Missouri debate—"no place where they are not degraded." Otherwise, "the society for colonizing them would not have been formed." Behind those words lay a conviction heavily reinforced since the War of 1812, especially in the southern states. Wartime experience against British invaders had intensified slaveholders' fears of slave insurrection and slave flight from their masters, neither of which had federal authorities shown much interest in preventing at the time. If rulers in Washington would not, or could not, defend slaveholders' property rights in a time of crisis, would they do any more in peacetime? Even before the war, southern states and localities had started tightening regulations on both slaves and free blacks. After 1806, any manumitted former slave in Virginia had to leave the state within one year, a provision that Old Dominion authorities enforced all the more scrupulously after the war. Delaware in 1811 had closed its borders to free blacks, South Carolina steadily moved toward banning them from entry, and Georgia prohibited further manumissions altogether.[58]

No doubt any clause in a state constitution, if against that of the United States, "would be a nullity," as James Madison judged privately. Congress could not "vary the political equality of the States, or their Constitutional relations to each other or to the whole." Lawmakers in Washington *could* have chosen to take Missouri's action not as a deliberate affront to northern restrictionists but just a short step beyond that of Illinois, easily amendable. The result, however, was another verbal firestorm in both houses—a *second* Missouri crisis that threatened to unravel the narrowly achieved sectional agreement of the previous session. Antislavery congressmen, many representing states that welcomed blacks little more than Illinois or Missouri, would insist on elimination of the offending clause before Missouri finally could be admitted. In November 1820, a select committee of the Senate put forward a resolution admitting Missouri to the Union. John Eaton of Tennessee, later one of President Andrew Jackson's "Parlor Cabinet," as opposed to the informal "kitchen cabinet," offered an additional proviso that nothing in the resolution be construed as giving congressional approval to "any provision in the Constitution of Missouri, *if any such there be*," that might contravene the privileges and immunities clause. The purpose of this statement was apparently to raise the obvious question of Missouri's autonomy. At that point, South Carolina's William Smith again took a radical view of state self-determination in defense of Missouri. He noted that free blacks had already been relegated to inferior status practically everywhere; it would be no great stretch to see them as such under the federal Constitution and thus permit Missouri's exclusion as differing little enough from any others.[59]

Meanwhile, the mood of the House had changed when the antislavery New Yorker John W. Taylor, on November 15, 1820, briefly replaced Clay as

Speaker. The Kentuckian's personal finances had delayed his return trip to Washington. Taylor's contentious election on the twenty-second ballot foretold, as President Monroe told Madison, "a disposition" among the antislavery restrictionists "to revive the Missouri question, in the temper displayd in the last Session." The House referred Missouri's constitution to a select committee, headed by the ailing William Lowndes of South Carolina. Lowndes, like Clay and Calhoun, had been a War Hawk and later a supporter of the National Bank and protective tariff bills in 1816. Reconciling economic nationalism and defense of states' rights had proved no problem for him before. As far as he was concerned, Missouri was already a sovereign state, and therefore no further conditions could be attached to its admission to the Union. If something in its constitution conflicted with the supreme law of the land, it was the business not of Congress but of the courts—"judicial cognizance," as Lowndes phrased it. His voice now muted by terminal illness, he proposed on November 23, 1820, that Missouri be "admitted into the Union on an equal footing with the other states, in all respects whatever." But on December 13, the resolution perished by a House vote of 79 to 93.[60]

When Clay finally arrived in January, he found himself again immersed in the kind of acrimony he desperately wanted to see dispelled in favor of other business. And again, he undertook the role of mediator in spite of the smoldering resentment of those, John Randolph in particular, who disliked being shut out by his parliamentary tactics. At last, on February 26, 1821, the House passed a resolution that Missouri's admission be finalized on "equal terms" with the original states, but only upon the "fundamental condition" that the prohibition against free blacks in its constitution "shall never be construed to authorize the passage of any law . . . by which any citizens . . . of the States of this Union shall be excluded from the enjoyment of any of the privileges and immunities to which such citizen is entitled under the Constitution of the United States." Further, Missouri legislators would be required, by "a solemn public act," to assent to this condition for its admission to be "considered as complete." In short, the Missouri legislature had to declare, without amending the controversial clause in its constitution, that the exclusion of free blacks meant not what it clearly said. It did so on July 26. On August 10, President Monroe declared the agreement on Missouri statehood to be final.[61]

Story concluded? Not quite. In 1825, Missouri casually repudiated the agreement by passing a law excluding negroes and mulattos from entry at its borders unless they could present naturalization papers verifying their citizenship, knowing full well that no such papers could exist. The U.S. Constitution had given the power to institute a uniform naturalization policy to the federal government, and at that time Congress had limited the privilege to "free, White persons." In 1847, still practicing the politics of defiance, the state legislature formally nullified the "fundamental condition" Congress had forced it to accept in 1821. Their act went unchallenged. That scarcely noticed event finally ended the so-called Second Missouri Compromise.[62]

5 Aftermath

MANY CONSIDERED Higbee's Tavern the best drinking hole in Lexington. Good bourbon flowed plentifully. On special occasions, prominent Kentuckians showed up to dine, conduct business, smoke their tobacco, and imbibe heartily. The town trustees favored the place for their monthly meetings, and the local militia gathered out in front for training exercises. In addition to the popular inn, John Higbee, one of Lexington's foremost entrepreneurs, owned a grist mill, a powder mill, a distillery, and a hotel in South Elkhorn. Like many Kentuckians, he also had speculative land investments in the western part of Missouri. For that reason, it gladdened him to see the state now securely in the Union, thanks largely to the town's most celebrated citizen, Henry Clay.[1]

Clay had departed Washington in mid-March 1821, eager to shore up personal business still in chaos from the financial panic. After his return to Lexington, friends and supporters threw a huge public dinner for him at Higbee's on May 19. Two or three hundred guests arrived to greet the man they credited most for settling, at long last, the two-year crisis. The gathering included the new Missouri senator, Thomas Hart Benton, now a grateful admirer but soon to become Clay's political archrival. Benton blamed northerners for instigating the Missouri agitation and mostly credited southern flexibility—and Clay's House leadership—for ending it. The agreement, as he saw it, had come for the sake of sectional peace and to prevent a realignment of parties along North-South lines. Benton's view would darken in time, however. "This was called a 'compromise,'" he wrote many years later in his memoir, but in truth it had been "all clear gain to the antislavery side[,] . . . an immense concession" by the nonslaveholding States. "It was a Southern measure, and divided free and slave soil far more favorably to the North than the ordinance of 1787." The ordinance had divided things about equally; the compromise of 1820, he eventually judged, "gave about all to the North."[2]

Everybody, of course, toasted the guest of honor: "Union his motto; conciliation his maxim; firmness and independence his principle of action." When Clay finally rose to speak, he reflected on the session of Congress just completed. Its recognition of newly independent governments in South America pleased him, but he lamented the failure of further federal protection for domestic manufacturing. In the immediate wake of the Missouri fight, with fears of northern-inspired federal consolidation still raw, slave-state opposition had scuttled the Baldwin tariff bill of 1820, 49 of 52 slave-state representatives casting nays in the House, 15 of 16 southern votes favoring postponement in the Senate. Turning to the reason for the occasion, however, Clay acknowledged the "awful importance" of having achieved an "amicable settlement" of the Missouri question. Most critical had been "those strong feelings of attachment to the Union" that had prevailed—the "deep conviction," shared in all parts, without which "our country would be exposed to the greatest calamities, rent into miserable petty states, . . . convulsed by perpetual feuds and wars." He made sure to praise northern swing voters in the House, "who nobly risked their personal popularity for the good of the whole nation." As for "those few unprincipled men" who had pursued their own "flagitious ambition" by exploiting the "honest prejudices of the people" and the "unhappy divisions" among them, "there ought to be no indulgence." And yet, perhaps some of them had been impelled by an "honest zeal," misdirected. With the crisis now passed, Clay thought "mutual forbearance and mutual toleration should restore . . . concord and harmony in our country."[3]

In coming years, Clay would emphasize colonization more than diffusion as the only sensible—and, for southern whites, the only *safe*—way to end slavery in America while averting a disastrous and interminable war between the races. Immediate emancipation, he insisted, would make matters far worse than the evils of slavery. Northern radicals who advocated that, like New Yorker Lewis Tappan with whom Clay corresponded, would be better off refraining from "foreign interference" in a problem that was the South's to solve. When Tappan retorted that slaveholding was a sin, Clay sarcastically wondered why "there were no sins at the north to engage the exertions of Christian philanthropists." As he aged, and as the antislavery crusade gained further momentum in the North, the Kentuckian would condemn the "real ultra Abolitionists," who pursued their object "at all hazards, and without regard to any consequences, however calamitous they may be." To those radical agitators, he said, "the rights of property are nothing," the deficiency of federal powers "is nothing," the "contestable powers" of the states "nothing," and a "dissolution of the Union, . . . nothing." And the worst of nightmares, if immediate emancipation ever prevailed with no way to remove the population of former slaves, he could see only one outcome: Either "the white man must govern the black, or the black govern the white," resulting in "a civil war that would end in the extermination or subjugation of the one race or the other."[4]

Political writers not just in the South but scattered increasingly around the West feared a revival of the "consolidationist" program of the old Federalists, now coming from northern Republicans. What if abolitionism, as voiced in the Missouri crisis, combined now with the economic nationalist agenda of New York, Pennsylvania, and New Jersey? Many such commentators regarded the Missouri fight as just the opening foray of a long, bitter struggle between rival beliefs on governance. "Further attempts are to be made to wrest from the new states, about to enter into the American confederacy, the power to regulate their own concerns," warned Thomas Ritchie in November 1820. Another stalwart of the so-called Richmond Junto, the slaveholding Virginia agrarian John Taylor, said the same—and much more—in a pair of widely circulated treatises—*Construction Construed and Constitutions Vindicated* (1820) and *Tyranny Unmasked* (1822). In these works, Taylor discovered the "true" safety of the Union not in Federalist-identified nation-building strategies but in sources like natural law, Antifederalist arguments in the ratifying conventions of 1788–1789, and Madison's "Virginia Resolutions" of 1799. "The idea of a balance of power between two combinations of states, and not the existence of slavery, gave rise to this unfortunate, and . . . absurd controversy," Taylor wrote of the Missouri crisis. Further, the majority could no longer be trusted to "make fair bargains," but instead only "sacrifice the interest of some states and individuals to advance that of others." For him, the 1820 crisis highlighted once again the "true" character of federal government as a necessary evil, meant to protect property rights but all too susceptible to perversion, corruption, and power grabbing. From that anti-national formulation followed a radical states' rights doctrine that stressed vigilance and obstruction as serving the best interests of the general welfare.[5]

In Missouri, meanwhile, the furor gradually subsided. Economic distresses at last superseded the sectional one. The post–War of 1812 boom, driven by an exploding population and soaring land prices, had come to a halt. Land purchasers who had taken advantage of generous federal credit provisions, in place since 1800, now found themselves mired over $2 million in debt to the central government—a further irritation to those who never trusted Washington in the first place. Private borrowers faced foreclosures right and left, unable to unload property for even a twentieth of the amount it might have fetched four years earlier.[6]

Nonetheless, while passing through Missouri a decade later, Presbyterian clergyman and travel writer Robert Baird would marvel at the extensive forest products; the precious mineral deposits, especially lead; the corn, grain, tobacco, hemp, and cotton he saw growing there. He also thought "a decided moral change" had occurred, one that would bring slavery "to an end in this State, and also in Kentucky and Tennessee." So much for prophesy. Slavery in Missouri, now secured by law, remained well lodged. So too was the memory of the nasty attacks on both sides that had preceded the Missouri Compromise. At best, few could ignore the internal inconsistency of the 1820 agreement and its questionable chances of lasting.[7]

On one side, the Missouri debate had dramatized the view that the spreading of slavery in America must be ended. In this respect, the opposition to slavery had anticipated Free Soil principles and the ideological foundation of Abraham Lincoln's Republican Party. On the other side appeared some of the earliest and most ominous claims that slaveholding contributed something positive, worth preserving. Those on the restrictionist side contended that the nation could atone for allowing the sin of slavery and, through an empowered nation-state, prevent its further expansion. Anti-restrictionists insisted that state self-determination undergirded republicanism and that Missouri deserved unconditional statehood no less than all previously admitted states had. The dispute had taken place all around the country—North, South, and West—as well as in Congress. Journalists, politicians, clergymen, lawyers, orators, and ordinary citizens—from town meetings and church suppers to taverns and banquet halls—had debated the implications of the sectional question. That question involved conflicting views on the nature and legitimate manifestations of governance in a republican society as much as it did the future of slaveholding in America. Compromisers in Washington congratulated themselves on preserving the American experiment in republicanism, keeping faith with the founding fathers, and restoring a semblance of sectional harmony. But that told no more than half the story. If ending the controversy by compromise had banished for a time the unnerving specter of disunion, Missourians and their slave-state allies had asserted self-respect and a traditional contempt for distant, seemingly insensitive government authority.

Sum of All Fears

In the last days of spring 1822, white Charlestonians may have just narrowly escaped one of the bloodiest terror attacks in American history. Many blamed it on the published antislavery speeches delivered in Congress during the Missouri crisis, widely circulated in the press and read eagerly throughout the nation. One of those readers, they said, was a free black man living in Charleston: Denmark Vesey.

Although possibly born in Africa, Vesey's family roots and early childhood were known only to himself and perhaps his closest intimates. His original name, Télémaque, was the same as the title character in a popular French novel of that time. If he received the name in Africa, that would have made him one of historian Ira Berlin's "Atlantic creoles," with ties to both Africa and Europe. Sometime around 1780, it appears, young Télémaque found himself packed in a slave cargo of 390 captives headed for Saint-Domingue. His striking physical appearance, the story goes, impressed the captain, Joseph Vesey, so much that he later arranged to keep the young slave for himself. In years to follow, Denmark became literate, acquired skills as a ship's carpenter, and may have witnessed some of the revolutionary tumult in the Caribbean. This life aboard ship continued until 1799, when by incredible luck he held the winning ticket in the Charleston East Bay lottery—with a prize of $1,500. Almost immediately, he purchased his freedom for $600, set up his own carpentry business, and acquired a house at 20 Bull Street in Charleston. A local newspaper reported that he had accumulated $8,000 worth of property in the city by 1822.[8]

For all of this, Vesey could not escape the maddening limbo between the white and slave worlds. Apart from the contempt of whites who resented his economic status and the humiliating regulations governing the activities of free blacks, Vesey's regular liaisons with several slave "wives" kept him tied to the enslaved community. His income as a carpenter never exceeded just two-thirds that of his white counterparts. When he joined the Hampstead branch of the African-Methodist church in 1821, he encountered the suspicions of Charleston whites who sensed the potential danger of all-black assemblies. But on the whole, the city's internal security had been lax. Despite rumors of a thwarted slave conspiracy in upcountry Camden in 1815, Charleston patrolmen often neglected their duties. Arsenals sat practically unguarded.[9]

The belief had persisted among slaves living in Charleston and throughout the plantation South that a great king would someday free them from their bondage. Slave preachers and spiritual music often reinforced the message that their deliverance was coming—and not just in an afterlife. "If thou wilt walk in my statutes and execute my judgments, then I will perform my word with thee," the Old Testament pledges. During the American Revolution, and again during the War of 1812, a fulfillment of the promise did arrive for many, thanks to invading redcoat forces carrying out the mandates of *their* monarch. Afterward, some African Americans expected the British to continue as their "greatest earthy friends and benefactors," as the black abolitionist David Walker predicted. But for others who remained in chains, no one really knew who the next liberator would be, when or from where he would come, what allies he might enlist, or how that miracle of freedom would unfold—only that such assurance remained and, if justice prevailed in the world, a great day of jubilee would finally dawn.[10]

Vesey might have had a better opportunity than most blacks to make that dream a reality. By 1820, South Carolina was the only state where the black population exceeded the white population, by a margin of some 265,000 to 237,000. Although it commanded attention, that imbalance did not necessarily alarm whites at the time as much as one might suppose. They could find reassurance in the odds against *successful* slave insurgency, especially if abolitionist agitators from outside, including those in Congress, could be kept quiet. The constant presence of white observers on every plantation and in every town, the unfamiliarity of most slaves with their geographical situation, the limited places of refuge for slave rebels, the supposed improbability of their collecting stores of firearms and other weapons, the absence of a common language among slaves of recent importation, and, of course, the fear of death for themselves and of white reprisals against their loved ones—all of these factors mitigated the danger of a massive slave uprising. Free blacks like Vesey did, however, present a more complicated issue of policing. The augmented privacy of their lives, their relative freedom of movement, their greater knowledge of the world outside the slave quarters, and the greater likelihood of their having reading and communication skills made whites nervous about them. And yet, despite those suspicions, plantation owners and white townspeople often left doors unlocked and windows unlatched at night. To have done otherwise would have conceded an inherent distrust of the genteel slaveholding society that they believed so worth preserving.[11]

If Charlestonians had grown complacent about the danger of slave insurrection, they must have been somewhat less so after the 1790s slave revolution in Saint-Domingue on the Caribbean island of Hispaniola. In the years prior to the Louisiana Purchase, Emperor Napoleon's New World focus had been not so much on the continental mainland but on that particular colony, then the world's foremost supplier of sugar and coffee. The idea had been to use mainland Louisiana as a source of lumber and agricultural produce to house and feed French planters and slave workers living on the island. But the coming of the French Revolution had inspired, in 1791, a slave revolt that turned into a full-fledged revolution. With French military forces occupied in Europe, the rebels had picked a good time to strike. By 1798, the black majority, by then in control of the colony, had put an end to slavery. After signing the short-lived Peace of Amiens with the British in 1802, the French emperor sent an armed force to crush the rebellion. They captured its leader, Toussaint L'Ouverture, but failed to overcome his guerilla fighters and their most decisive ally, yellow fever. Without Saint-Domingue, France's vital sea lane through the Caribbean to New Orleans no longer lay under Napoleon's control, and his main reason for keeping Louisiana had melted away. So the aspiring master of Europe decided to cut his losses, grab what profit he could for the territory by selling it to the United States, and redouble on neutralizing his implacable foe, Great Britain.[12]

White Americans had reacted with mixed emotions toward the Saint-Domingue revolt. Before Jefferson's party came to power, President John Adams had welcomed the spread of the republican revolutionary spirit there so long as the island's rulers proved willing to encourage trade with the United

States and refrained from attempts to export servile insurrection to the North American mainland. Southern Federalists went along with the northern contingent of Adams's party, believing a stable government in Saint-Domingue, governed by anyone but revolutionary France, preferable to a possible spread of French Jacobinism and radical class conflict. Vice President Thomas Jefferson and his southern followers, more Francophile than the Federalists, worried more about the proliferation of slave uprisings and less about the implications of the French radicalism.[13]

While 1790s abolitionism had remained confined to states and localities, the news from Saint-Domingue circulated wildly among blacks in the United States, especially those who lived in urban centers. In 1799, free blacks in Philadelphia, at that time temporarily the nation's capital, agitated for Congress to embrace the cause of human rights but found little sympathy there. Blacks raised their voices for freedom in New York as well, particularly in New York City. Receiving no encouragement in Virginia, except from private advocates like St. George Tucker, gradual emancipation efforts failed also in Delaware and Maryland. But Tucker, a judge and law professor at the College of William and Mary, warned fellow southerners in 1796 that the "calamities" occurring "like a contagion" in the West Indies ought to be taken as a "solemn warning" of what might soon happen much closer to home. Those words would seem chillingly prophetic when, in 1800, an enslaved blacksmith named Gabriel and a number of co-conspirators, expecting to replicate the events in Saint-Domingue, failed in a plot to launch a slave revolt in Richmond, capture Virginia governor James Monroe, and demand for his return the freeing of all slaves in the state. Although nothing came of it, "Gabriel's Plot" darkened the collective memory of Virginia's slaveholders for years to come.[14]

Slave conspiracies and insurrections had occurred before in South Carolina, too, but nothing compared with the 1791 rebellion in Saint-Domingue. In general, things had been pretty quiet since the Stono Rebellion in 1739, when a literate slave and twenty conspirators had recruited about sixty others before going on a killing rampage that took about twenty-five white lives before the militia crushed the insurgents near the Edisto River. Over the decades of relative calm, South Carolinians for the most part regarded their slaves as compliant and trustworthy. Masters' worries had dissipated. The slaves supposedly had made peace with their condition, accepting it as best for them. Only a year after the Missouri crisis ended, however, Denmark

Vesey's plot would lift the aspirations of his followers, a number still un-known to this day, while chilling the blood of South Carolina whites as never before.[15]

By the early 1820s, Charleston's residents had come to regard their city as the epitome of southern beauty, refinement, and grace. Its prosperity had skyrocketed with the growth of the plantation-based, cotton-producing econ-omy of the post-Revolutionary South. Its 1820 population of 25,781 made it the sixth largest city in the United States. Trouble lay buried in that statistic, however. Charleston's blacks—12,652 enslaved and 1,475 free—dangerously outnumbered its 11,654 whites. The slaves—domestics and artisans, dock workers and other common laborers—did most of the work in the city, and many had grown angrier and more restless than they appeared.[16]

According to the *Official Report* released afterward, a major insurrection plan probably started to form in Vesey's mind sometime around 1817 or 1818. His carpenter's trade gave him close contacts with other black craftsmen in the city and its environs. Some of his key accomplices would be skilled work-ers, including Monday Gell, a harnessmaker, and Peter Poyas, a ship's carpen-ter. Even Governor Thomas Bennett's most trusted house servants, Ned and Rolla Bennett, went to meetings at Vesey's home, gathered money, reportedly hid weapons, and deluded the governor's family. Slaves often learned how to take the measure of "ole massa" and to exploit the foibles of their owners. In Vesey's parlor, visitors received instructions and encouragement, read Bible verses, prayed, and (by later white accounts) discussed the Missouri debate, which signaled to them a mounting attack by radical northerners on slav-ery in the United States. Widely circulated in newspapers and pamphlets, the powerful speeches by Missouri restrictionists, like Rufus King's in the Senate, easily reached and reportedly inspired Vesey and his co-conspirators. Vesey also traveled, sometimes as far as eighty miles outside Charleston, into the heavily black plantation districts, spreading news and secretly recruiting additional supporters.[17]

As later testimony fashioned it, they planned to strike under a dark moon at 12:00 a.m. on July 14, 1822—also, coincidentally, Bastille Day in France. First, vital munitions, roads, and docks had to be secured. Then, Vesey's band would move throughout the city, slaughtering as many whites as possible, children and adults alike with no hesitation, no mercy. Hundreds would per-ish, many while they slept. This bloody chore completed, the insurrectionists would torch the city and then proliferate into the countryside, widening the rebellion as much as possible. Finally, Vesey and some of his companions, fortified with valuables and provisions, would board ships and flee to Saint-Domingue to be greeted there as triumphant fellow revolutionaries.[18]

About a month before launch date, however, the plot started to unravel. It had been too long in developing. For all the care Vesey took in selecting accomplices, it proved not careful enough. Peter Devany Prioleau, a slave who belonged to Colonel J. C. Prioleau, exposed the existence of a conspiracy but could give no further details. Charleston authorities, skeptical after questioning a few suspects, finally dismissed the information as idle talk and suspended their inquiries, but they remained wary enough to plant spies.[19]

Although better-advised now to scuttle the plan, Vesey decided instead to move the deadly moment forward to June 16, while taking the precaution of destroying his records and other evidence. Within days, another slave accomplice, William Paul, lost his nerve and cracked. Further investigations followed. Then, on June 15, the revised date for the insurrection having been leaked, panic swept the city. Officials called out the militia, but few whites slept soundly that night. Vesey now abandoned his plans, probably sent out word to dispose of stockpiled weapons, and took flight. A search party discovered him a week later, hiding in the slave quarters of one of his wives.[20]

Following all that, a special tribunal of white authorities in Charleston evaluated charges against 131 blacks, condemning thirty-five, including Vesey, to be executed by hanging. White constables carried out the sentences in the early morning hours of July 2. The tribunal ordered another thirty-seven of the accused to be banished outside U.S. boundaries. The full extent and numbers involved in the Vesey plot, unknown at the time to whites and most blacks, remain a mystery today. Given the restrictive structure of slave society, some Charlestonians questioned how extensive the conspiracy *could* have been, and so have historians. But the shocking thought of brushing so close to a bloodbath still lingered. Charlestonians would not again look upon their human chattels with misplaced confidence, nor again tempt the fate that nearly befell them in summer 1822. "The present system of patrolling is too weak," cautioned the *Charleston Courier*, a glaring understatement. The legislature promptly strengthened security measures, restricted the freedom of slaves to assemble, constrained their movements, and withheld access to Bibles. "If the citizens will faithfully perform the duty enjoined on them by the Patrol Laws," Governor Bennett announced, "I fear not but that we shall continue in the enjoyment of as much tranquility and safety, as any State in the Union."[21]

Post-scare reaction in the South laid the blame on northerners, particularly those on the antislavery side of the Missouri debate. After the trial, Bennett downplayed the whole episode, but his excessive reassurances revealed plenty of lingering anxiety. Perhaps embarrassed by the involvement of his own slaves, he pointed eagerly to outside agitators. "Materials were abundantly furnished in the seditious pamphlets brought into this state by equally culpable incendiaries," Bennett contended in a widely circulated statement. Along with these, "the speeches of the oppositionists in Congress to the admission of Missouri" had "a serious and imposing effect" on the "machinations" of certain conspirators who "could read and write with facility." Many southern newspapers leaped to the same conclusion. Several sheets reprinted an account referring to the confession of Jack Purcell, one of the more prominent conspirators, as evidence "that the evil foretold, from the discussion of the *Missouri Question*, has been, in some degree, realized." Even three years later, in August 1825, the *Daily Georgian* told its readers that the effects of northern interference, "official or unofficial," lay now exposed. "For years our Constitutional right of Representation was assailed by all the arts of sophistry and the ingenuity of talent; our character has been assaulted, and the state of society among us, misrepresented in the vilest manner." But the Missouri question, "under the specious cast of humanity and religion," had been "the most direct attack . . . made upon the prospective influence of the south." After the executions had been completed, Congressman Joel Poinsett in August 1822 privately blamed the actions of the "miserable deluded conspirators" not on Vesey as much as the "discussion of the Missouri question at Washington," which such "unfortunate half-instructed people" could only have interpreted "as one of emancipation." A month later, Isaac Harby's *Charleston City Gazette* cited the "Missouri poison" that antislavery politicians had now laced into southern society. Another Charlestonian, John Moultrie, in a letter to his brother-in-law Isaac Ball, added, "[i]n these times of emancipation freedom and liberality, the Southern States will be in constant apprehensions [of] insurrection."[22]

The northern press, of course, interpreted the events in South Carolina very differently. "It is hardly necessary to suggest that the discussions on the Missouri question were not begun until more than a twelvemonth *after* the negro plot was concerted," observed one antislavery editor in Illinois. Trial testimony reported that Vesey also had read to his followers from the Bible—how the children of Israel had been delivered out of Egypt from bondage. Why not, then, contend that Christianity answered as much for the discontent of Charleston's slaves as the Missouri question? Further, some pointed out, antislavery spokesmen in the Missouri debate had refrained from encouraging slave insurrections, even warning the South against the common practice of letting emancipated blacks mix with slaves. James Tallmadge himself had said, "I had learned from southern gentlemen the difficulties and dangers of having free blacks intermingling with slaves." He had, further, urged against prohibiting slavery in Alabama because, surrounded as it was by slaveholding states, "the intercourse between slaves and free blacks could not be prevented, and a servile war might be the result." Afterward, some northerners resented slave owners' efforts to hold others accountable for their own mistakes. One writer in the *National Gazette* condemned "the injustice, indecorum, and we may say rashness, which have been displayed in using on this occasion, the topic of the Missouri controversy." Southerners needed to understand: It was not the work a few radical antislavery agitators in Congress, "but whole legislatures, and great bodies of citizens of all professions and classes, who took a direct and earnest part . . . in the Missouri question." But still, "the great majority" in the free states "deprecated and condemned all attempts on the part of the negro slave, to obtain his freedom by violence."[23]

In all, however, the message from the South registered clearly: Slave labor remained workable, reasonable, and necessary. The system sufficiently safeguarded whites, despite the occasional aberration. Slave owners seldom mistreated their blacks and gave them little justification for rebellion, southerners insisted. Vesey-type conspirators appeared rarely but would, in any case, be thwarted by careful patrolling. Slave unrest, if it did occur, owed to the subversive work of radical northerners who advocated excessive federal power to target not only slaveholding but the entire southern way of life. And, not least, no further debate on the issue of slavery would be tolerated at the national level of government.[24]

In the wake of the Vesey scare, South Carolina passed the Negro-Seamen Act of 1822, a law requiring free black seamen of whatever nationality working aboard foreign or domestic ships to be held in custody while at port within the state's boundaries. The captain of each vessel could redeem these sailors only by paying a $1,000 fine for each or serve a two-month imprisonment himself, while any jack-tars remaining unclaimed went thereafter to the auction block. While reflecting the intensified distrust of free blacks generally, the law also illustrated the same power struggle between nationalism and state sovereignty that had manifested in the Missouri controversy. Rejecting the supremacy of federal law, South Carolina now asserted its own legal autonomy. Echoes of Missouri's 1821 attempt to ban free blacks from entering the state could not be missed. After state courts upheld the statute, U.S. Supreme Court justice William Johnson, riding circuit in South Carolina, heard an appeal in the case *Elkison v. Deliesseline* (1823) and declared the Negro-Seamen Act an unconstitutional violation of the congressional power to regulate interstate commerce. South Carolina quickly defied Johnson's decision by expelling from the state Samuel Hoar, a Massachusetts attorney who wanted to challenge the law in the U.S. Supreme Court, thus forestalling a ruling in Washington and foreshadowing the Nullification Crisis of 1832, in which South Carolina would again contravene federal law by declaring the tariffs of 1828 and 1832 "null and void" within state boundaries. Disinclined to confront South Carolina and prompt yet another sectional crisis on the heels of Missouri, President Monroe refrained from enforcing Johnson's decision, seeming to encourage further exclusionary legislation in the South against free blacks.[25]

The following year, however, the Marshall court, still reviled in the South for its 1819 *McCulloch* ruling, indirectly addressed Johnson's district court decision within the framework of the 1824 *Gibbons v. Ogden* case. This controversy pitted the state of New York, which had issued a steam-shipping monopoly to the firm of Livingston and Fulton, against a 1793 federal law that regulated the coasting trade of the nation. The court held that federal law superseded state law, under the supremacy clause in Article VI of the Constitution, and affirmed the plenary power of Congress to regulate navigation as well as trade between the states, including all coastal waters and navigable rivers inland—another bold assertion of federal power, bound to stir further anger in the South. But in what appeared a deliberate gesture to soothe antinational firebrands in South Carolina and elsewhere, the court also left the door open to states' regulation of their internal commerce where such action did not conflict with prior federal legislation.[26]

Planters and Plain Republicans

Aside from the financial panic's political impact, nothing contributed more heavily than the Missouri crisis to the realigning of factions and parties in the years following 1820. By the time of the Tallmadge Amendment, the first American party system—the rivalry between Jeffersonian Republicans and their Federalist adversaries—had collapsed. Except for enclaves here and there, the Federalists had declined as an organized political force. President Monroe, like Washington before him, had hoped for a golden era free of political conflict, without the partisan struggles that had rent the body politic and undercut the unity of Americans along competing ideological, if not sectional, lines. And yet, behind the deceptive smokescreen of post–War of 1812 reconciliation lurked bitter animosities. Even within Jeffersonian ranks simmered resentments between purist Old Republicans on one end of the spectrum and governmentally assertive nationalists on the other. Similar antipathies divided and animated state politics as well.[27]

The role of the Panic of 1819 here seems clear enough. Resulting from overly rapid market shifts and social dislocations that Americans scarcely comprehended at the time, the economic crisis had transformed political consciousness and inflamed old antagonisms in all parts of the country. Overextension of bank credit and reckless land speculation in frontier areas featured heavily among the immediate causes. Anger mounted especially in the South and West, as more and more citizens faced banks foreclosing on their mortgages. Farmers who lost their land and workingmen their livelihoods often blamed these misfortunes on favoritism in government policies and an impersonal market that all too often seemed to reward the rich and victimize the poor. Many regarded the mismanaged Philadelphia-based Bank of the United States as the main perpetrator, resenting the implied powers doctrine underlying that institution, along with the nationalist Supreme Court that had now vindicated its existence. It was the same resentment of growing federal power that had found expression in the Missouri debate and, in years to follow, would help shape quarrels on other key issues of the 1820s and 30s, especially the tariff, internal improvements, and land policy—as well as banking and finance.[28]

But also the question remained whether party conflict would reflect lingering sectional divisions over Missouri. Or would disparate interests reconstitute again along ideological and economic lines at least vaguely similar to those that had separated Federalists and Jeffersonian Republicans? Since the 1780s, sectional antagonisms, especially between North and South, had been most pronounced, and threatening to the Union, at times when vibrant two-party conflict did not exist. The slavery issue and related southern fears held far less potential to cut the republic in two when other compelling issues divided the parties, dictated partisan loyalties, and structured political behavior *within* North, South, and West. Compromises, achieved within a framework of party conflict, had been and in the pre–Civil War period would continue to be the traditional means of keeping sectional extremism at bay. Putting it another way, as historian Peter Knupfer has said, "The problem for political leaders was not to keep slavery from becoming a national issue but to keep it from becoming a party issue." Congressional votes had tended to follow sectional allegiances until quarrels between Federalists and Republicans in the 1790s changed that pattern into one of interparty competition. Following the gradual decline of the Federalist Party after 1800, sectional polarization returned, manifesting itself most disturbingly in the Missouri question.[29]

Northern restrictionists' efforts to govern the admission of Missouri had strengthened Old Republicans in the South, who thought they detected a comprehensive nationalist conspiracy to usurp states' rights while at the same time threatening the destruction of slavery. Evidence of this post-Missouri shift in favor of southern rights, strict construction, and resistance to growing federal power showed in the presidential election of 1824, where five contenders, all nominally Republicans but representing contrasting political impulses and philosophies within the party, sought the White House. Early on, John C. Calhoun, wavering from his previous nationalism, dropped from the running and eventually settled for the vice presidency. Secretary of State John Quincy Adams and House Speaker Henry Clay, both of the nationalist wing, still sought the prize. So did Monroe's treasury secretary, William H. Crawford, and the upstart hero of New Orleans, Andrew Jackson. Adams appealed most to New Englanders, including former Federalists and antislavery men who had rallied behind first the anti-southern spirit of the Hartford Convention in late 1814 and then the Tallmadge Amendment. In general, they shared the vision of an active, more-empowered central government. Clay, despite losing support from antislavery northerners because of his "proslavery" engineering of Missouri statehood, drew support from the middle Atlantic and northwestern states where voters especially wanted protective tariffs and internal improvements. Crawford, a favorite of the Old Republicans and the nominee of the Republican congressional caucus, suffered from the post-Missouri backlash against Washington insiders as well as his incongruous support for the Second Bank of the United States.[30]

That left Jackson, whose military reputation remained his claim to fame. Yet "Old Hickory" quickly came to represent far more than just the profession of arms. Never mind his true identity as a wealthy, slave-owning Tennessee cotton planter and land speculator, Jackson made a perfect antiestablishment—and anti-eastern—standard-bearer for southerners and westerners eager to vent their resentments against the familiar politicians. Those targets included the types of northerners who had tried to violate the principle of state sovereignty for Missouri. Jackson's unquestioning acceptance of slavery and his fame as an Indian killer especially solidified his appeal in the slave states. Shrewdly, he and his operatives also focused their campaign on public fears that "corruption" at the national level of government now endangered the future of republicanism, undercutting the traditional liberties that Americans had fought the American Revolution—and, for that matter, the War of 1812—to secure.[31]

The "corruption" theme, of course, could apply in all kinds of contexts, depending on individual voters' perceptions, but it always referred to the core belief that power naturally encroached on liberty, requiring eternal vigilance to sidetrack the onslaught of government tyranny, lest republican citizens themselves become slaves to overly empowered men of no principle. Americans looking for corruption could find it almost wherever they looked, from cabinet investigations, the mismanagement of the National Bank prior to 1819, and the idea of government subsidies for internal improvements to the ongoing federal control of public lands in the West, continuing protective-tariff agitation, or the recent attempt in Congress to restrict slavery from (and within) newly admitted states. Jackson himself, like the voices opposed to the Tallmadge Amendment, insisted that the process of degeneration had already begun and would continue apace unless stemmed by someone promising to save the republic, as he now did. He would become *the* rallying figure—and ultimately the symbol—for every kind of anti-government anxiety of his age. His Jacksonian followers, moreover, positioned themselves to exploit effectively the state-by-state expansion of the franchise that would eventually include all adult white males—an overpowering force for both the democratization and the popularization of political conflict in America.[32]

Appealing especially to voters in the new western states, the Carolinas, and those in the middle-Atlantic region who resented the "privileged elite," Jackson claimed a plurality of both the popular and the electoral votes in 1824. But failing the required majority in the Electoral College, he could only stand by and watch as the House of Representatives, supposedly under Clay's influence, conferred the presidency on Adams instead. Clay's subsequent appointment as Adams's secretary of state further embittered Jacksonians and fueled their accusation that a "Corrupt Bargain" had kept conniving nationalists in power and boded a further threat to states' rights and republican liberties. It also pointed toward some kind of realignment of politicians and voters that would result in a second American party system.[33]

In the mid-1820s, many political observers recognized the danger that this new party realignment might form along sectional lines, the Missouri crisis leading to an ongoing political war over slavery in all its ramifications. No one saw this more clearly than certain northern politicians like Isaac Hill in New Hampshire and Martin Van Buren of New York. Van Buren especially (and his New York "Bucktail" faction) would play the most decisive role in forming the Jacksonian Democratic Party as a deliberate North-South coalition, beginning with a revived New York-Virginia alliance in the 1820s. "Political combinations between the inhabitants of the different states are unavoidable," he wrote *Richmond Enquirer* editor Thomas Ritchie in January 1827, "& the most natural &, beneficial to the country is that between the planters of the South and the plain Republicans of the North." Instead of the question being "between a Northern and Southern man," the letter continued, "it would be whether or not the ties, which have heretofore bound together a great political party should be severed." Party functionaries and the voters themselves "would have to decide between an indulgence in sectional & personal feelings with an entire separation from their old political friends on the one hand or acquiescence in the fairly expressed will of the party, on the other."[34]

The restoration of two-party competition by the early 1830s—the Whigs coalescing in 1833–1834 as an anti-Jacksonian political party, sectionally balanced and equal to the Democrats in voting strength—resulted in a limited containing of the slavery issue, just as the earlier rivalry between Federalists and Jeffersonian Republicans had. The so-called Jacksonian era marked a suppression of antislavery agitation in the *formal* sphere of politics. As far as the westward expansion of slavery was concerned, the Missouri Compromise had settled the matter for the foreseeable future—at least until further terri-torial acquisitions led to renewed controversy. At other political levels, how-ever, the less-formal "bottom-up" mobilization of abolitionist activity—the radical journalists like William Lloyd Garrison, formation of the American Antislavery Society, petition campaigns, activism in churches and other reli-gious organizations, rising numbers of militant African Americans—signaled a surge of antislavery activity apart from the equally vibrant, ongoing clash between Democrats and Whigs on economic issues rather than sectional ones.[35]

Outside that formal sphere, antislavery activists lamented the way politi-cians in Congress had ended the Missouri question by compromise rather than confrontation. The appearance in 1821 of Quaker editor Benjamin Lun-dy's antislavery newspaper, *The Genius of Universal Emancipation*, highlighted the renewed discussion on the future of slavery. In 1829, David Walker, a free black from North Carolina who had relocated to Boston, published a tract entitled *An Appeal to the Coloured Citizens of the World*, which urged slaves to revolt. Garrison's *The Liberator*, first published in 1831, advocated immediate emancipation and scorned the idea of financial compensation to slavehold-ers who agreed to release their slaves. In response, southern planters, espe-cially in areas of South Carolina and Virginia where the black population outnumbered whites, reacted with growing sensitivity to any talk of slavery being abolished. Apart from inviting reprisals against former masters, eman-cipation would entail the "surrender of $300,000,000" in property and "rev-olutionize the whole character and habits of the people of the South," cried a pseudonymous writer for the *Richmond Enquirer* in 1825.[36]

Over the years after 1820, abolitionists again and again condemned any kind of political deal-making on a question of fundamental morality like slav-ery as bargaining with the devil. For Jeremiah Gloucester, a former slave and pastor of the Second African Presbyterian Church in Philadelphia, the Mis-souri Compromise had settled any remaining question of whether slavehold-ers and their northern accomplices *ever* wanted slavery to be abolished. If they did, he asked in 1823, then "why would they have opened a new avenue in Missouri, for the admission of slaves" and "why did they not admit her in to the union on the grounds that they should not admit slaves into their territory?" Another black abolitionist, James Forten, pondered the Missouri settlement, the growing wealth and political agency of the cotton states, and the recent passage in Congress of the Gag Rule to ban abolitionist petitions

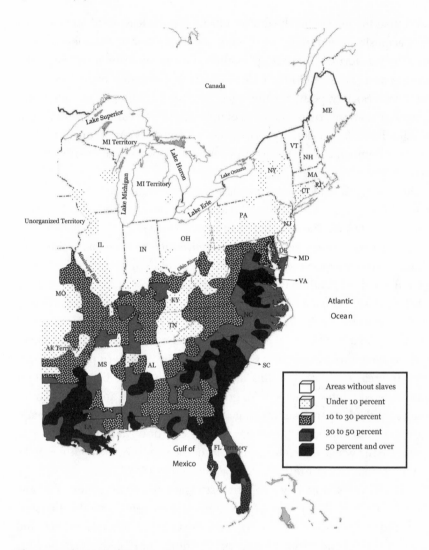

Slavery in the United States, 1830.
Drawn by Margot Gibson-Beattie.

from being received there. He told the Ladies' Anti-Slavery Society of Philadelphia in 1836 that he felt "as one should feel who sees destruction, like a
corroding cancer, eating into the very heart of his country."[37]

Further, in a letter to Henry Clay in 1839, Gerrit Smith, the wealthy New
York landowner, philanthropist, reformer, and abolitionist, who in 1859

would provide funding for John Brown's ill-fated raid on Harpers Ferry, vilified the Kentuckian as favoring an increase in the number of slave states. The evidence: Clay's "unholy compromise" of 1820, "in which tranquility was purchased at the expense of humanity and righteousness." Writing for the *National Anti-Slavery Standard* in March 1850, James Russell Lowell would denounce the political history of the nation not as a story of compromises but of "conspiracies by which Good has been uniformly betrayed." And, of course, Garrison, who never had any respect for the 36°30' deal in the first place, protested the admission of Arkansas as a slave state: "This is another Missouri question. No pains, no expense should be spared to flood the House with remonstrances," he implored the "Friends of the Antislavery Movement" in April 1836. An advocate of "immediate emancipation without expatriation," he assailed the continuing support for colonization, as well. Referring to him as "the author of the Missouri Compromise," Garrison would scold Clay privately in March 1849, "you have done more than any other to lengthen the cords and strengthen the stakes of oppression." In addition, "[t]he work before us is not the limitation but the extinction of slavery," Garrison would tell the Reverend Nathan R. Johnston in October 1860. "Ours is not a geographical conscience, 'bounded by 36 degrees, 30 minutes, North latitude.'"[38]

Expansion, War, and Wilmot

To whatever extent such antislavery appeals garnered attention in the wider public sphere, the reconfiguration of the Democratic Party, along with the 1830s emergence of the Whigs, now deflected political passions from the slavery issue. In every national election, each of these major parties strove to maintain an internal coalition of northern and southern wings. Without that, neither could remain viable against a unified rival.

Economic issues divided the two sides, while North-South sectional conflicts remained mostly submerged. To help ensure sectional unity, the Democrats in 1832 adopted a two-thirds rule for presidential and vice-presidential nominations, meaning a candidate had to command strong support in both free and slave states. The Whig Party acted similarly. Interests of party solidarity influenced policy too. When the newly independent, proslavery Texas Republic in 1836 sought to join the United States, for example, President Andrew Jackson held back for fear of fracturing his party over the slavery issue in an election year. On the Whig side, however, ardently proslavery president John Tyler, who had gained the office only by William Henry Harrison's death, and who already had alienated his own party by opposing its nationalist economic program, invited a new confrontation in 1844 by seeking Texas annexation at all costs. Just like that, a generation of fragile intersectional calm nearly ended in a single injudicious stroke. Another round of disputes, as bitter as the Missouri crisis, suddenly threatened. But in the end, the Texas issue proved more partisan than sectional, 90 percent of Whigs opposing annexation, 81 percent of Democrats supporting. The Lone Star Republic, its southern and western boundaries still ambiguous, thus would enter the Union in March 1845 by the unusual means of a joint resolution of Congress.[39]

Meanwhile, Democrat James K. Polk of Tennessee, so similar to Jackson politically that supporters dubbed him "Young Hickory," won a narrow presidential victory over the Whig nominee (and anti-expansionist) Henry Clay and the Liberty Party's James G. Birney. During the campaign, Polk had promised to compensate Democratic free-soilers for the impending annexation of Texas, which he, too, favored, by securing the Oregon Country by some means from Great Britain, either by war or negotiations. The addition of Texas, Oregon, and also California—completing a coast-to-coast republic as promoters of "Manifest Destiny" envisioned—now became the overarching political goal of the Democratic Party. But could Democrats achieve this ambitious aim without breaking the Union (and their party) over a renewed question of slavery expansion? And then, too, they would face deteriorating relations with Mexico, which regarded Texas as *theirs* and the American annexation an act of territorial aggression.[40]

Choosing the more vulnerable foe, Polk made war against Mexico (which by edict in 1829 had outlawed slavery) and negotiated for Oregon with the British, both choices proving successful. But not before a Pennsylvania Democratic congressman, David Wilmot, claimed lasting fame as the avatar of New York's James Tallmadge. On August 8, 1846, only three months into the Mexican-American War, Wilmot proposed an antislavery rider to a $2 million appropriations bill providing funding for the conflict and the negotiations to end it. This now-famous "Proviso" asked that "as an express and fundamental condition to the acquisition of any territory from the Republic of Mexico by the United States . . . neither slavery nor involuntary servitude shall ever exist in any part of said territory except for a crime, whereof the party shall first be duly convicted." The main point, simply, was to prevent the war from achieving any gains for proslavery forces, but Wilmot charged straight into a political minefield of sectional conflict that would threaten to split both parties right down the middle, slave states against free. To the alarm of Democratic and Whig leaders alike, the Proviso passed the House, the vote betokening exactly the kind of sectional split the two parties had striven to prevent: Northern Democrats and Whigs in favor, southern congressmen of both parties against. Like Tallmadge's proviso, Wilmot's died in the Senate, where the South still held enough influence to block it. Reintroduced in February 1847, again in 1848 as part of the Treaty of Guadalupe-Hidalgo, and several more times before the so-called Compromise of 1850, the result always proved the same, nevertheless heightening sectional anxieties.[41]

While some northerners opposed slavery expansion just to keep blacks out of the West, many more, like Wilmot's northeastern Pennsylvania constituents, pinned their children's economic future on free-labor farming and fresh western lands. Southern influence in national politics, which antislavery northerners increasingly called "the Slave Power," threatened again to smash that hope. Wilmot forced an antislavery gloss on the territorial clause without any compensatory concession to the South. This time, he demanded, there must be no "give" on the antislavery side, as there had when restrictionist northerners yielded on Arkansas and Missouri. The Wilmot Proviso controversy also highlighted a recent advance of antislavery constitutionalism, spearheaded by the Liberty Party in the early 1840s. That set of principles contended that the *Somerset v. Stewart* case in 1772, the Declaration of Independence, the framers' refraining from use of the words "slavery" or "slaves" in the Constitution, the Northwest Ordinance, the 1808 banning of the slave import trade, and the 36°30' restriction in the Missouri Compromise—taken all together—provided enough weight of precedent to undercut the stance of proslavery jurists. Supreme Court justice John McLean, a free-soil Whig from southwestern Ohio, argued that Wilmot's position interpreted the Constitution correctly. The fundamental law mandated freedom nationally, McLean believed, whereas only local law could maintain slavery. Alternatively, President Polk favored a simple extension of the 36°30' line to the Pacific, dividing the expected spoils of war between rival sections.[42]

Answering both Wilmot and Polk, John C. Calhoun in the Senate voiced the most aggressive proslavery argument of the pre–Civil War period, short of southern secession. In a set of resolutions presented in 1847, Calhoun contended that the Fifth Amendment protection of property rights extended to slave owners the right to take their slaves into any territories belonging to the United States, regardless of prior congressional provision—in other words, into any area of the country whatsoever except where state law already forbade the holding of human chattels. If northern migrants could translocate *their* personal property—their livestock, furniture, farm implements, and so on—then how could Congress prohibit southerners from taking slaves they owned? Here, symbolism mattered almost more than substance. To submit to such northern bullying was to strip southern white men and women of their self-respect as well as their prized belongings. It would degrade them, affront their honor, enslave them politically to an aggressive Yankee majority. Neither House would pass the Calhoun resolutions, but the boldness of them rallied southern spirits all the same.[43]

As Calhoun reflected on the sectional changes that had occurred since the Missouri Compromise, his conclusions seemed to echo those of many from the Lower South in the late 1840s. The North had changed, he told an overflowing and restive crowd in Charleston on August 19, 1848: "As they have grown in power they have increased in their exactions, and at last have boldly avowed their determination to arrest the further progress of the Slave States, by excluding them unconditionally hereafter from all the Territories of the Union." Northerners like Wilmot, he charged, had now repudiated the 1820 settlement, even though that agreement "was proposed by the North, who urged it on Congress, and sacrificed every Northern man who voted against it." Calhoun elaborated further in a January 22, 1849, "Address of Southern Delegates in Congress, to their Constituents," written on behalf of the southern caucus in Washington, signed by forty-eight congressman and senators from the slave states, and widely published in the newspapers. In this account, the South had little "cause to complain" prior to 1819, but that year marked the start of a slow deterioration, bringing "many, and great, and fatal disasters, on the country and its institutions." Southerners who then withstood antislavery voices had "rested their opposition on the high grounds of the right of self-government." Many hailed the 36°30' compromise "as a permanent and final adjustment that would prevent the recurrence of similar conflicts." Now, said Calhoun, the North "no longer respects the Missouri compromise line, although adopted by their almost unanimous vote." That, he thought, left the South with no choice but to deny any right of the federal government "to distinguish between the domestic institutions of one State, or section, and another, in order to favor the one and discourage the other."[44]

By 1850, the fear of northern aggression had prompted some southern writers to even further extremes. For William and Mary College professor Thomas Dew, slavery had been "entailed" on southerners through "no fault" of their own, forcing them to strengthen in "the principle of benevolence and humanity." The South could not discard the institution "without producing greater injury to both the masters and slaves," nor could a northern employer "shake hands" as "familiarly" with his workers as the plantation owner could with his bondsmen. Virginia's George Fitzhugh in *Slavery Justified* (1850) would argue that free competition offered no more than a zero-sum game, a struggle only "to better one's condition, to pull others down or supplant them," whereas the southern plantation constituted the "beau ideal" of harmonious society. In the South, nature compelled "master and slave to be friends," while in the North, "employers and free laborers [became] enemies." Fitzhugh's later, more extensive works, *Sociology for the South* (1854) and *Cannibals All!* (1856), carried the fiction of paternalistic slaveholders beyond the absurd, declaring enslaved men and women to be the "happiest, and, in some sense, the freest people in the world," in contrast to the mistreated working class of the manufacturing states.[45]

Because Calhoun made himself both a symbol of southern rights and a lightning rod for attacks, his private correspondence reflected the range of opinion on the Wilmot Proviso controversy. On the expansion of slavery, "I hold that it is not a question upon which Congress can constitutionally legislate," opined Laurel Summers of Scott Country, Iowa, to Calhoun in October 1848. Therefore, "Congress should not only *frown* down the *Wilmot Proviso*, but the *Missouri Compromise* line also; for if they have power to pass the one they have power to pass the other also." A month later, by contrast, a New England "FRIEND OF THE UNION" scolded Calhoun for acting as "the Guide & champion of the South" in his encouragement of public meetings in "S. Carolina & elsewhere." Did he wish "to be placed in the predicament" he had "occupied in 1832"?[46]

But mostly Calhoun heard from sympathetic fellow southerners. In late November, Z. L. Nabers wrote from Carrolton, Alabama, "that our country is rapidly approaching a crisis, when the rights of the South & South West are to be disregarded, or our glorious confederacy dissolved." He applauded

Calhoun's support for a Southern Convention "to adopt such measures as will protect our rights." A few days later, Nathan Gaither of Columbia, Kentucky, "disappointed" with Zachary Taylor's election as president, expressed his fear for the future: "I see our fate clearly if the free soil doctrine is pressed to consummation. The Union is gone beyond redemption." And in January 1849, from Wilson Lumpkin in Athens, Georgia: "The people of the slave holding States, must submit to degradation, inequality & and most flagrant injustice: or resist, as best they may, the arrogant strides of an unconstitutional & despotic majority."[47] Reaction in the slave states to the Wilmot Proviso featured three important elements: It replicated parts of their answer to the Tallmadge Amendment in 1819; it reflected Calhoun's "southern rights" extremism; and, most interesting, it elevated the Missouri Compromise from the level of mere legislation to that of sacred text. Looking at proslavery provisions in the U.S. Constitution, the Virginia legislature in February 1849 reminded that "without the compromises then solemnly entered into, the union of the States never could have been formed." The Proviso, by contrast, expressed "palpable disregard" for those compromises, making "still further aggressions upon the rights of the southern States." For Congress to "disregard alike . . . the spirit and principles of . . . the Missouri Compromise"— along with "every consideration of justice, of constitutional right, and of fraternal feeling"—in favor of the Wilmot Proviso, would force Virginians to choose between "submission to aggression and outrage on the one hand, or determined resistance on the other, at all hazards to the last extremity."[48]

Farther west, Missouri legislators in December 1847 insisted that "the peace, permanency, and welfare of our national Union" depended on "strict adherence to the letter and spirit" of the March 1820 law that enabled their state's admission. Again in 1849, they emphasized that preservation of the Union depended on applying "the principles of the 'Missouri Compromise'" to the recent territorial acquisitions—"if by such concession future aggressions upon the equal rights of the States may be arrested, and the spirit of antislavery fanaticism be extinguished." If necessary, Missouri would stand "in hearty co-operation" with its sister slave states for their "mutual protection" against northern "encroachments." But also, with an audacity consistent with its past actions, the assembly asserted that the "right to prohibit slavery in any Territory belongs exclusively to the people thereof, and can only be exercised by them in forming their constitution for a State government, or in their sovereign capacity as an independent state." So much for the 36°30' line.[49]

Faced with sectional crisis within their own ranks and Polk's decision not to seek reelection, the Democrats had nominated Lewis Cass of Michigan for the presidency in 1848. As Cass interpreted the territorial clause of the Constitution, Congress held very minimal power over slavery expansion; it could neither adopt the Wilmot Proviso nor extend the 36°30' division. Missouri's 1849 statement echoed that. By his logic, the Missouri Compromise had exceeded federal powers by limiting slavery expansion at all, and the Confederation Congress, too, had trampled the liberties of territorial inhabitants when it instituted the Northwest Ordinance. Instead, the only proper method had to be rooted in the sovereignty of the people—or "popular sovereignty," in the Democrats' new catch-phrase—whereby only the voters in each federal territory would determine the issue for themselves, *prior* to statehood. Congress, then, would have to accept a decision rooted thus in the ancient tradition of local self-government. As the Missouri legislature implied, this would be carrying forward the Missouri part of the 1820 compromise—whereby that state had entered the Union according to the popular will of voters there—and eliminating the rest.[50]

Historically, of course, the refusal of the federal government to take prescriptive action had de facto established slavery. In theory, antislavery forces that in 1848 had regrouped as the Free Soil Party might prevail, too, under "popular sovereignty," or so Cass and other Democratic candidates argued before northern audiences. In the South the Democrats promised the opposite result: that an absence of federal action guaranteed a bright future for slavery in the West. Cunning politically, though disingenuous and operationally unclear, "popular sovereignty" appealed widely as a new basis for sectional agreement—an "improved" alternative to the Missouri Compromise—even though Cass, losing the presidential election of 1848 to the Whig Taylor, would gain no benefit for himself.[51]

As for the Mexican Cession, the largest part of the territory added in the 1848 Treaty of Guadalupe-Hidalgo, geography and prior governance discouraged slavery expansion. The arid climate and dry soil held little promise for plantation-style agriculture. Mexico had banned slavery there long before the treaty, a sanction that would stand unless congressional action (or regional development) determined otherwise. Meanwhile, the 1849 discovery of gold in California lured away gold-seekers of all descriptions, swelling the population of California almost overnight. The large majority of these new settlers wanted California, annexed by the United States in 1846, admitted to the

Union as a free state. At a convention held in Monterey in October 1849, California delegates agreed on a constitution that prohibited slavery. Voters ratified the document a month later. That satisfied President Taylor, who imagined that quickly admitting California as a free state would circumvent another ugly confrontation between North and South over slavery in the territories.[52]

Instead, the crisis that unfolded in 1850 proved to be as threatening to the Union as that of 1820, the sectional divide wider than ever, with little chance of another Missouri-like solution to settle the matter. In potential, it amounted to as much a secession crisis as the Missouri one might have become if not for the compromise. To the South, the right to participate equally in the destiny of the territories now meant as much as the independent sovereignty of new states had in 1820. Georgia congressman Robert Toombs, a former Whig and more moderate than some southerners, echoed that reality when he told northern representatives: "Deprive us of this right and appropriate this common property to yourselves, it is then your government, not mine." With the prospect of both California and New Mexico as free states, likely to be followed by Oregon, Minnesota, and Utah, southern congressmen and senators reacted with horror at the likelihood of northern majorities in both houses, bent on destroying slavery everywhere, along with everything else that depended on it.[53]

"Compromise" Redux, 1850

Returning now to the Senate, Henry Clay, the historic leader of the Whig Party, quickly found himself at odds with President Taylor, its official head. By urging quick admission of California and New Mexico as free states, bypassing the territorial stages, Taylor appeared to favor the Wilmot Proviso in principle. Clay took a different tack, hoping to resolve a crisis but also to spite Taylor, who had ignored the ego-sensitive Whig patriarch. The Kentucky senator's plan, like Taylor's, proposed California's admission as a free state, but it also would cut the Mexican Cession into two separate parts (New Mexico and Utah)—without "restriction or condition" on slavery. Leaving the slavery expansion question open meant that passing Clay's compromise would indirectly repudiate the Wilmot Proviso, soothe southern feelings, and mitigate the danger of disunion. Proslavery parts aside, however, southern senators performed a constitutional about-face from their 1819–1820 stance by recoiling from Clay's initiative and refusing to sacrifice all of California no matter what people living there preferred. Mississippi senator Jefferson Davis, who favored extension of the 36°30' line, thought southern California might accommodate cotton planting and feature enough room for several new slave states. For southerners, the issue had transformed into sectional self-protection, or even survival, against an increasingly hostile, antislavery North. That meant they would now accept whatever it took constitutionally to gain an outcome that would safeguard their vital interests.[54]

Then, fate intervened. Under the blazing Washington heat of July 4, 1850, after an outdoor holiday celebration, the president slaked his thirst with large quantities of iced water, chilled milk, and cherries. The result was intense gastroenteritis coupled with horrific diarrhea, carrying the seriously dehydrated sixty-three-year-old to his grave within a few days. The new chief executive, Millard Fillmore, proved more amenable than Taylor to Clay's compromise, but other opponents contrived to keep this so-called omnibus bill sidetracked. The key point of conflict remained the extent of congressional power over westward expansion, along with the all-important Texas boundary question on which hinged the possibility of several future slave states. Frustrated and physically ailing, the seventy-three-year-old Clay now repaired to the Rhode Island shore for much-needed rest, leaving compromise negotiations to a Democrat, Stephen A. Douglas of Illinois.[55]

Favoring the elements of Clay's package but lacking a majority for the "omnibus" as a whole, Douglas tried an alternative approach: splitting the bill into parts and pushing those through Congress piecemeal. That worked. The so-called Compromise of 1850 became law in September, with Fillmore's signature on not one but several bills, all passing along sectional lines, a different Senate or House coalition behind each. California entered the Union as a free state, the fate of New Mexico and Utah left to the ambiguous workings of "popular sovereignty." Apart from territorial issues, the settlement of 1850, really more a sectional truce than a true compromise, fixed the boundary between Texas and New Mexico (greatly reducing the area of Texas), pledged the federal government to assume the Texas debt, ended the public slave trade in the District of Columbia, and included the Fugitive Slave Act of 1850, prescribing harsh penalties for anyone who sheltered runaways. Over the next several years, both the New Mexico and Utah territorial legislatures passed laws protecting slavery, even though neither had much to protect; the 1860 census would reveal only twenty-nine slaves residing in Utah territory and zero in New Mexico. In this far Southwest, geography, soil quality, and climate did more than political action to slow the expansion of slavery.[56]

Had no further question of slavery in the West arisen, the Republican Party might never have formed, Abraham Lincoln might never have been elected, and a civil war between North and South might not have started, at least not in 1861. Would the Missouri Compromise, along with the 1850 modifications in western policy, hold the Union together after all? Ironically, it would be Douglas, deserving so much credit, or blame, for the 1850 settlement, who would answer that question and, in doing so, pave the road leading to Fort Sumter and ending at Appomattox.

Kansas-Nebraska and Beyond

As of 1854, the Missouri Compromise had for thirty-four years taken care of the question of slavery north of latitude 36°30' in the extensive area of the Louisiana Purchase. The Kansas-Nebraska Act of 1854 now would end all that by erasing the line that had geographically divided North from South and engineered sectional peace. No single event more ensured disunion by 1861. Devastating the Democratic Party and heralding the Whigs' ruin as well, this key measure would also constitute the final blow to the Second Party System that had kept sectional conflict at bay. As a direct consequence, a new, strictly northern, Republican Party, an antislavery and anti-southern political coalition of groups united in opposing the expansion of slavery, organized and spread quickly throughout the North. The bi-sectional Know-Nothing party of the 1850s, appealing to anti-immigrant and anti-Catholic fears, would fall short of impeding the Republicans' advance.[57]

Douglas, who wrote the legislation, acted on complex motivations, not least his own political ambition. At first, he tried to circumvent rather than destroy the Missouri Compromise by simply declaring that territorial inhabitants were to have full control over their domestic institutions, which obviously included slavery. But some southern Democrats insisted on more. With President Franklin Pierce busy dispensing patronage favors to northern free-soil Democrats to keep them in the party, southerners wanted a litmus test of northern Democratic support for their interests too. A revision of Douglas's bill became that test—in the form of an unequivocal repeal of the 1820 compromise. Douglas, a northern Democrat who pursued the presidency as hotly as Clay had, needed heavy support in both North and South to win in 1856 or

1860. Pushing for repeal of the 36°30' restriction might give the Illinois senator the kind of credibility he needed in the slave states. Aside from national
politics, Douglas sought for Illinois a western railroad from Chicago through
the northern part of the Louisiana Territory, still heavily populated by native
tribes—the Blackfeet and Sioux—and until this time off-limits to legal white
migration, as well as slavery. That policy of non-settlement, an unintended
result of the Missouri Compromise, seemed to Douglas and many fellow Illinoisans a barrier to economic progress. At the same time, southerners, eager
to prevent a further multiplication of free states, had stood against opening
the region. As long as the northern plains remained closed to both lawful
settlement and transportation advances, neither Chicago nor St. Louis could
grow to its potential as a great urban emporium of western commerce, stunt-
ing development of both northern and southern parts of Illinois.[58]

At this point, northern antislavery opinion formed exactly opposite from
the southern reaction to the Wilmot Proviso—but with equal reverence for
the 1820 settlement. Opponents of slavery expansion now emphasized the
36°30' line as fundamental law, unalterable by congressional action. James O.
Putnam, in an influential speech delivered in the New York state senate,
printed in Albany, and widely circulated through the country, asserted not
only that the Missouri Compromise had ascended to holy writ but also that
a "political North" had rallied around it. Putnam, a Yale-educated Buffalo attorney who a few years later would gravitate to the Republican Party via the
Know-Nothings, had been elected to the New York Senate in 1853. He had
no sympathy, he said, for "northern antislavery fanaticism," but it appalled
him that southerners in Washington now saw the 1820 statute as holding
no greater force than any other law, subject the same to repeal. That was its
"mere legal relation," Putnam asserted. Beyond that, the compromise had
gained substantive meaning and political weight comparable to "a treaty, or a
compact, or a constitutional provision." In "spirit" and "of right," he insisted,
"it has *the binding force of them all.*" Other northerners, Putnam noted, had
said the same almost from the time the Thomas Amendment passed. One example, indeed, had been Hezekiah Niles, the economic-nationalist Baltimore
editor of *Niles' Weekly Register*, who had declared on March 11, 1820, that
while it was "true the Compromise is supported only by the letter of a law,
repealable by the authority which enacted it," the circumstances of the case
had given "this law a moral force, equal to that of a positive provision of the
Constitution." If destroying the 36°30' line seemed, for Putnam, like tearing

down the Parthenon, he proffered further counsel in that vein for the South: "Beware of Greeks bearing gifts."[59]

The New York legislature, following Putnam's lead, resolved in February 1854 that repealing the line would be "a gross violation of plighted faith," an "outrage and indignity upon the free States," who had assented to the admission of Missouri and Arkansas." More than just a "compromise," the 1820 law had assumed the status of "a solemn compact," carrying "binding force." Altering that could only prove "destructive of that confidence and regard which should attach to the enactments of the federal legislature." Connecticut's legislature followed, in May and June 1854, with similar sets of resolutions, adding that "the attempt to extend slavery over a vast region, from which it has been by law excluded with the consent of the slaveholding States, ought to awaken the people of Connecticut to the aggressive character of slavery as a political power, and to unite them in determined hostility to its extension." However much the Constitution had fortified slavery, it also obligated the federal government to protect life and liberty, as well as property, giving it "no more power to establish slavery than to establish a monarchy." Thus, slavery, like the rule of tyrannical kings, now connoted the *antithesis* of republicanism.[60]

The 36°30' line, of course, *had* to be repealed for popular sovereignty to gain credence as a national policy. In that sense, the territorial parts of the Compromise of 1850 already had made the line politically obsolete. But for southerners on Douglas's side, an official annulling of 36°30' meant a lot more. Some rearticulated the conviction that any kind of federally imposed line of restriction undercut the equality of the states, treating those with slavery as second-class members of the republic. As Henry Breckinridge wrote in April 1854, "if in passing bills to organize Nebraska and Kansas, Congress should refuse to abrogate or repeal [the line,] . . . the people of the South will feel with twofold keenness the mark of inferiority put on them in 1820." Others in both North and South, like Douglas himself, saw the Nebraska bill as a long overdue reassertion of the right of local self-government, an acknowledgment that white people in the territories remained sovereign where they lived, not a federal government many hundreds of miles away. Douglas's populist rhetoric could resonate perhaps more with other latter-day Jacksonian Democrats in the North than it did in the South. It emphasized westward movement, a continuously expanding yeoman-farmer frontier, as essential for the reinvigoration of individual freedom. That replication of democratic practices in the distant West, free from a possibly ill-informed and potentially arbitrary central power, was, Douglas claimed, what "popular sovereignty" really meant.[61]

"Black Republicans"

It embodied exactly what Whig and Democratic operatives had tried to prevent for a quarter of a century: a new, strictly sectional political party, committed to facing the slavery issue head on, with support enough in the North to win control of the federal government. Even the most level-headed southerners, mixing political disdain and genuine fear for their future, called them "Black Republicans."

In the 1850s, the Republican Party always claimed to be moderate in its intentions. Most of its leaders said they wanted not to disturb slavery in the southern states but to end the westward expansion of slaveholding and thus set the institution on course for "ultimate extinction." Some of the more conservative Republicans resembled "Old Line" Whigs in the tradition of Daniel Webster and Henry Clay. This contingent included men like R. M. Corwine and Thomas Ewing in Ohio and David Davis of Massachusetts, strongly anti-abolitionist and amenable just to having the Missouri Compromise line restored. But to southern ears, already alarmed by the increasingly shrill attacks of abolitionists, the Republican creed of "free soil, free labor, free men" denoted something far more sinister. To them, it meant what the Wilmot Proviso had symbolized: tyranny, subjection, and humiliation; the terror of slave uprisings; the demise of property rights and the cotton kingdom; an upending of southern self-government; and the traumatic loss of a traditional, delicately structured social system. For southerners, white slaveholders and nonslaveholders alike—especially after the shock of John Brown's raid in 1859—the "death knell of the Union" that Jefferson thought he heard in the Missouri debate had amplified to a cacophony of deadly intentions signaling near-certain destruction. Disunion and, if necessary, civil war, would appear their only salvation.[62]

This new Republican Party actually combined several political groups unified by *their* common fear of a voracious "Slave Power." They drew in former Liberty Party men and Free Soilers, antislavery Democrats and Conscience Whigs, along with nativists from the Know-Nothing Party who had come to regard aggressive slaveholders as an even greater menace to the republic

than the massive influx of German and Irish Catholics. Although they offi-
cially disavowed connection with the radical abolitionists, these Republicans
identified themselves as anti-*southern* as much as antislavery, incorporating
much of the abolitionist image of slaveholding culture as arrogant, slothful,
sexually depraved, and contemptuous of honest workingmen. Their newspapers characterized the political economy of the South as stunted by slavery: inefficient, underdeveloped, and discouraging not only to free labor but
also to modern capitalistic enterprise—in all, the opposite of the culture,
society, and economy that most northerners now envisioned for the West
and America's future. Southern spokesmen, meanwhile, pointed to the cotton boom of the 1850s as evidence of how much their rural plantations contributed to the nation's economy, making them the most important producers of *real* wealth, in contrast with greedy merchants, Wall Street bankers,
and other leech-like "middlemen" of the urban Northeast. One southern-
sympathizing Philadelphian, writing privately in December 1848, believed
northern cities generated most of the "pernicious sentiments" directed toward the South, yet those urban places "and indeed all the flourishing manufacturing towns, . . . owe all their prosperity and wealth, to the profits realized from customers and consumers in the slave holding States."[63]

Republicans, like Liberty Men and Free Soilers before them, advanced
an antislavery interpretation of the Constitution and tended to view the
Missouri Compromise with ambivalence. Two-time Liberty Party standard-
bearer James G. Birney, himself a former Kentucky slave owner, regarded
Missouri as the real starting point of "Slave Power" ascendancy. Ohio governor Salmon P. Chase, a former Jacksonian Democrat turned Free Soiler,
and now a Republican, referred farther back in time. He believed slaveholders had steadily tightened their illegitimate grip on federal power since the
earliest years of the Republic. The acceptance of land cessions from southern states with stipulations that slavery would be allowed, the fugitive slave
law of 1793, the Louisiana Purchase and the acquisition of Florida without
prohibition of slavery, and then the 1820 compromise permitting slavery in
Missouri and protecting slaveholders' rights in the southern part of the trans-
Mississippi region—all of these, plus Texas, the Mexican-American War, the
1850 settlement, and finally Kansas-Nebraska, pointed to the immoral grip of
slaveholders on federal policy making.[64]

Still, the repeal of the 36°30' line more than anything else alerted Republicans to an immediate "Slave Power" threat. Chase and former Whig

Charles Sumner, bidding for support from disenchanted northern antislavery Democrats, had condemned the repeal "as a gross violation of a sacred pledge" and "a criminal betrayal of previous rights[,] . . . part and parcel of an atrocious plot to exclude from a vast unoccupied region immigrants from the Old World and free laborers from our own States, and convert it into a dreary region of despotism, inhabited by masters and slaves." Abraham Lincoln, still speaking as a moderate antislavery Whig at a meeting of that party in Scott Country, Illinois, assailed the extension of slavery into free territory as a "great wrong and injustice."[65]

The Supreme Court's Dred Scott decision of 1857 further galvanized the belief that a conniving proslavery minority had instilled its unsavory influence at the highest echelons of the federal government. The key issue was whether Congress in fact held the constitutional power to prohibit slavery in a territory of the United States, as it had in the Missouri Compromise— or, for that matter, whether it could delegate to the territories themselves power to decide that question, as Douglas's "popular sovereignty" alternative had contended. Southern justices who dominated the court saw the case as a chance to resolve the sectional slavery-expansion question that had bedeviled lawmakers in Washington and the whole country for nearly four decades. The outcome was precisely the opposite.[66]

Scott was a Missouri slave who, with the help of antislavery northern benefactors, had sued for his freedom on grounds that he had lived for several years with his master, an army physician, in the free state of Illinois and in the Wisconsin Territory, where slavery had been prohibited by the 36°30' line. At first, the court addressed the narrower question of whether the Constitution could be interpreted to regard blacks as citizens with the right to seek legal recourse in a federal court. If not, then Scott's fate rested exclusively on the proslavery laws of Missouri. The Fugitive Slave Act of 1850, moreover, had denied escaped slaves any kind of legal protection. Further, if Congress had overextended its powers in 1820 by outlawing slavery north of 36°30', then Scott's claim, especially without benefit of citizenship, could go nowhere, leaving him enslaved.[67]

In the end, seven of the nine justices voted against Scott's appeal. All nine wrote opinions, but Chief Justice Roger B. Taney's spoke for the majority. Blacks "had no rights which the white man was bound to respect," he announced. At the writing of the Constitution, the African race had been regarded as "beings of an inferior order," lawfully and justly consigned to slavery as much for their own benefit as for that of whites. Even though some states had later granted them citizenship, nothing in either the Declaration of Independence or in the Constitution had conferred on them rights and privileges equal to whites'. Legal rights for slaves had been no part of the founders' vision. Scott, therefore, held no standing in federal court.[68]

That left the more substantive issue of congressional power. The question of Scott's temporary residence in Illinois posed no problem for Taney. The court had said in earlier decisions that a slave's status when taken—or escaping—into a free state remained unchanged, resting with the slave state to which he or she had to be returned. As for a slave's living in territory north of 36°30', the same held true: Under the Fifth Amendment, a citizen's enslaved property remained as secure in a federal territory as in a slave state. Further, the 36°30' agreement had been unconstitutional; Congress had no power to overrule the property rights of slaveholders by banning them from any federal territory, nor could it convey to a territory an authority denied to the federal government in the first place. Only a state, under its sovereignty after admission to the Union, owned that kind of power over slavery. Theoretically, then, Taney's pronouncement undercut both Douglas's "popular sovereignty" and the position of the Republican Party on the expansion of slavery westward. The Calhounite doctrine had prevailed. Beyond that, nothing really had been settled. The high court had ruled, but would the country go along?[69]

Antislavery people took encouragement from the dissenting opinions of justices Benjamin Curtis and John McLean. Republican editors in the North scorned the ruling as carrying no moral force they felt bound to honor. Douglas scrambled to rescue "popular sovereignty" and, with it, his own political hopes. Before antislavery audiences, he insisted that the right to hold slaves in the territories still meant nothing without the enforcement power of "police regulations and local legislation" that a community hostile to slavery would refuse to provide. That remained his position in his 1858 debates in Illinois against Lincoln who, in turn, assailed Douglas's moral indifference, condemned the Kansas-Nebraska Act, and told sympathetic listeners that the Supreme Court, someday in the hands of Republicans, would reverse its mistaken decisions. As in his famous "House Divided" speech, Lincoln often invoked the same arguments that northern restrictionists had introduced in the Missouri debate, trusting that the true inertia of republicanism promised ultimate freedom for all.[70]

In years to come, the "House" that Lincoln and his party would "save" was, of course, not the *old* Union at all. The "new birth of freedom" he promised in 1863 went far beyond the prewar structure of compromises, accommodations, and concessions for slaveholders in the South. By that point, little choice remained but to complete the long-dreaded endgame. Northern military might, in the name of freedom nationally, would at last settle things. Looking back, the antislavery "Quaker Poet," John Greenleaf Whittier, had composed in 1848 perhaps the most fitting epitaph for the old republic: "The fates are just; they give us but our own; Nemesis ripens what our hands have sown."[71]

epilogue

Willard's Hotel

"THE GHOST of this murdered republic rises everywhere, and meets everyone," twenty-three-year-old Henry Brooks Adams, correspondent for the *Boston Daily Advertiser*, grimly informed anxious readers on the evening of New Year's Day, 1861. Grandson of one president, great-grandson of another, Adams would live to observe the Washington scene for more than half a century and become one of the greatest historians America would ever produce. For all the obligatory calls, the artificial pleasantries, the servings of cake, eggnog, and apple toddy, the strained efforts of gentlemen "toiling to be amusing" and "avoid politics," an unshakable pall still hung over the capital. Except perhaps for this one day, everyone spoke of the dreaded possibility of civil war, of streets drenched in blood, assassinations, buildings in flames. Horrifying rumors circulated everywhere. Merchants despaired for lack of customers. Some residents had already closed their houses; others stuffed belongings into carpetbags and prepared to flee the city.[1]

So far, nothing had come of desperate efforts for yet another sectional agreement to lift the bleakness of this "great secession winter." South Carolina, making good on its threat to leave the Union if Lincoln were elected, had seceded on December 20, while the six other states of the Lower South prepared to do the same. In the Senate just two days earlier, seventy-four-year-old John J. Crittenden of Kentucky, using the very desk Henry Clay once occupied, had presented an extensive compromise plan including six constitutional amendments intended to mollify the South and forestall a wholesale loss of the slave states. The idea was to make slavery so impervious to political action that no one, especially not the incoming Republican administration, could touch it. The Crittenden package offered protection of slavery in all federal installations located in the slave states, guaranteed the right to hold slaves in the District of Columbia, proscribed Congress from interfering with the interstate slave trade, promised federal compensation for unrecovered fugitive slaves, and pledged to make the changes beyond power of repeal. That pledge would extend also for the three-fifths and fugitive-slave clauses. In addition, Congress would be expressly forbidden from meddling with slavery in the states. The key provision, however, would apply the old Missouri settlement to any territories "now held or hereafter acquired" by the United States: a redrawing of the 36°30' line to the Pacific.[2]

It was too late. Neither house of Congress would support all this. From the Republican perspective, of course, Crittenden's proposals betokened not a "compromise" at all, but just another surrender to the South, with slavery more entrenched than ever. Republicans would have to repudiate not only their core beliefs but practically everything they promised voters who had just elected Lincoln. Besides, events since the early days of the republic had shown that federal willingness to protect slavery had led only to southern efforts to expand it. Unlike so many northern politicians before him, Lincoln would not buckle under disunionist threats. As he privately instructed William Kellogg of Illinois, his Republican confidant in the House of Representatives: "Entertain no proposition for a compromise in regard to the *extension* of slavery. The instant you do, they have us under again; all our labor is lost, and sooner or later must be done over. . . . The tug has to come and better now than later."[3]

During the Missouri debate, too, everything lay at stake, the factors of timing and geography proving critical. Also in play, both culturally and politically, were two competing concepts of union—an old one of sovereign states, by then traditional, being reasserted; a new one, more modern and nation-centered, germinating. The old carried the day in 1820, with the Missouri Compromise; the new in 1863, with Lincoln's Emancipation Proclamation and its consequences. The old perspective regarded the Union as less than perpetual, contingent on the safeguarding of essential liberties in North and South alike; the new one insisted on conformity with free-labor ideals and looked to national power to dictate and enforce those ideals. Both the rhetoric and the habit of sectional compromise had lost their force—and thus the old Union, its sustainability.[4]

By 1860, North and South had evolved beyond the remedy of bargain making. Most of the so-called compromises on slavery had only been postponements anyway, a playing for time. The only one that really bought much time was Missouri, and its efficacy had ended with the Mexican-American War, largely an unjust and immoral conflict, as its opponents often said. The sins of those war makers, like those of the iniquitous Biblical fathers, would visit future generations. In the early decades of the Republic, even slaveholders often conceded that slavery should be ended. Since then, they had come to regard their institution not only as necessary economically but also interwoven with their sectional pride, sense of honor, and even self-government. In retrospect, one might see the rallying of southern sectional consciousness during the Missouri debate as no less a launching point for the idea of a southern nation than the South Carolina tariff controversy of the early 1830s. Much of the North, meanwhile, had grown to see the ending of slavery as a test whether freedom in America, as Lincoln's Republicans now conceived it, could actually survive. Each side now considered the other a despotic, conspiratorial foe, determined to undercut cherished values, just as each had perceived the British back in Revolutionary times. And each knew the futility of bargaining with that kind of enemy.[5]

It must have been tempting in 1860, as it is today, to blame earlier politicians for their failure to prohibit slavery expansion. But for them to do that would have required a powerful nation-state capable of compelling the obedience of anti-federal southerners and, later, anti-national westerners. Barring all other contingencies, that kind of modern state *might* have emerged in America within two decades after 1820 if restrictionists had been able to hold their ground in the Missouri fight and a dominant northern free-soil party developed as a result. In that event, some of the slave states might have seceded *then*, giving up their share of the trans-Mississippi West, instead of waiting until 1860–1861. Some northerners would have welcomed that departure instead of fighting to save a dysfunctional union. Afterward, under intensifying demographic and foreign pressure to end slavery, southern states might finally have done so and, perhaps in time, have rejoined the United States. But devotion to that old, internally flawed union proved strong in 1820, as it would in years to come, hence the pro-southern compromise of that year and others to follow, until the coping mechanisms that held rival sections together for so long had finally worn away.

One last-ditch effort, a peace conference held at Virginia's request, took place in February 1861, at Willard's Hotel in Washington. Located two blocks from the White House, Willard's specialized in providing two things: first, elaborate meals followed all day long by whiskey and cigars; second, a venue for behind-the-scenes political deals. One writer has suggested that congressmen and senators on any given morning settled more business in Willard's dining room, as they breakfasted lavishly on roasted pigeons, oysters, fresh river herring, and pigs' feet, than they did on Capitol Hill. A landmark even in its early days, the hotel had welcomed prominent guests since its opening in 1818. Back then, the "Great Compromiser" himself, Henry Clay, had ordered many a mint julep at Willard's celebrated bar.[6]

Former president John Tyler presided over the conference at Willard's, and twenty-one states sent delegates, only to find it would take far more than luxurious furnishings and plenty of liquor to resolve the problem they now faced. Their main idea for compromise was similar to the one Crittenden had proposed two months earlier: recognition of slavery in the territories south of 36°30', along with guarantees to protect slavery in states where it already existed. The only part that did pass in Congress, just barely, was a proposed constitutional amendment guaranteeing slavery in the slave states, which even many Republicans, including Lincoln, could have supported at that time. This would have been the Thirteenth Amendment, the first explicit protection of "slavery"—and the first use of that word—to appear in the Constitution. The states, of course, never approved the revision. Only after the bloodiest war in American history did the *real* Thirteenth Amendment, the one we know today, make the momentous question raised by Missouri a moot point at last.

Notes

Prologue: Knell of the Union?

1. Clay, Adams, and Calhoun, quoted in Robert Pierce Forbes, *The Missouri Compromise and Its Aftermath: Slavery and the Meaning of America* (Chapel Hill, NC, 2007), 94.
2. *Annals of Congress*, House, 16th Cong., 1st sess., 1584.
3. See especially Gordon S. Wood, *Empire of Liberty: A History of the Early Republic, 1789–1815* (New York, 2009), and the essays in *What Did the Constitution Mean to Early Americans?* ed. Edward Countryman (New York, 1999).
4. On the South, see William W. Freehling, *The Road to Disunion*, vol. 1: *Secessionists at Bay, 1776–1854* (New York, 1990) and vol. 2: *Secessionist Triumphant, 1854–1861* (New York, 2007), and Lacy K. Ford, *Deliver Us from Evil: The Slavery Question in the Old South* (New York, 2009).
5. See generally Matthew Mason, *Slavery and Politics in the Early American Republic* (Chapel Hill, NC, 2006). On the concept of the "public sphere," see John L. Brooke, "Reason and Passion in the Public Sphere: Habermas and the Cultural Historians," *Journal of Interdisciplinary History* 29 (summer 1998): 43–67, and "Consent, Civil Society, and the Public Sphere in the Age of Revolution and the Early American Republic," in *Beyond the Founders: New Approaches to the Political History of the Early American Republic*, ed. Jeffrey L. Pasley, Andrew W. Robertson, and David Waldstreicher (Chapel Hill, NC, 2004), 207–50. For market change affecting social and economic relations around the country in the pre–Civil War period, see Charles G. Sellers, *The Market Revolution: Jacksonian America, 1815–1846* (New York, 1992); Daniel W. Howe, *What Hath God Wrought: The Transformation of America, 1815–1848* (New York, 2007); and John L. Larson, *The Market Revolution in America: Liberty, Ambition, and the Eclipse of the Common Good* (Cambridge, UK, 2009).
6. Michael E. Woods, "What Twenty-First-Century Historians Have Said about the Causes of Disunion: A Civil War Sesquicentennial Review of the Recent Literature," *Journal of American History* 99 (Sept. 2012): 415–39. On the slavery question pre-1819, see Mason, *Slavery and Politics*. On the problems of nation building in the early republic, see especially Max M. Edling, *A Revolution in Favor of Government: Origins of the U. S. Constitution and the Making of the American State* (New York, 2003).
7. Southern regional distinctions are relevant in analyzing the 36°30' compromise vote as well as later sectional questions. For that framework, I have borrowed

from Don E. Fehrenbacher, *The South and Three Sectional Crises* (Baton Rouge, LA, 1980), 5–6, 69.

CHAPTER ONE: Origins

1. Winthrop Jordan, *White over Black: American Attitudes toward the Negro, 1550–1812* (Chapel Hill, NC, 1968), 44–100; George M. Frederickson, *The Black Image in the White Mind: The Debate on Afro-American Character and Destiny, 1817–1914* (New York, 1971), 43–70, esp. 61, 64, 66, 68.

2. Byrd and Reid, quoted in Rhys Isaac, *The Transformation of Virginia, 1740–1790* (New York, 1982), 39–40, 118; Bertram Wyatt-Brown, *Southern Honor: Ethics and Behavior in the Old South* (New York, 1982), 66.

3. Among many works on American Revolutionary ideology, see especially Bernard Bailyn, *The Ideological Origins of the American Revolution* (Cambridge, MA, 1967); Gordon S. Wood, *The Creation of the American Republic, 1776–1787* (Chapel Hill, NC, 1969) and *The Radicalism of the American Revolution* (New York, 1991); and, more recently, Jack P. Greene, *The Constitutional Origins of the American Revolution* (Cambridge, UK, 2011). On the *Somerset* decision, see George William Van Cleve, *A Slaveholders' Union: Slavery, Politics, and the Constitution in the Early American Republic* (Chicago, 2010), 31–40; also, David Waldstreicher, *Slavery's Constitution: From Revolution to Ratification* (New York 2009), 39–42.

4. For reinforcement of this view, see Kenneth S. Greenberg, *Masters and Statesmen: The Political Culture of American Slavery* (Baltimore, MD, 1985).

5. Gary J. Kornblith, *Slavery and Sectional Strife in the Early American Republic, 1776–1821* (Lanham, MD, 2010), 24–27.

6. Don E. Fehrenbacher, *The Slaveholding Republic: An Account of the United States Government's Relations to Slavery* (New York, 2001), 26–28; Kornblith, *Slavery and Sectional Strife*, 30–31.

7. Richard Henry Lee to George Washington, July 15, 1787, in *Letters of Delegates to Congress, 1774–1789*, ed. Paul H. Smith et al., 26 vols. (Washington, DC, 1976–2000), 24:356–57. See also Lee to William Lee, July 30, 1787, ibid., 381–82.

8. See Paul Finkelman, "Slavery and the Northwest Ordinance: A Study in Ambiguity," *Journal of the Early Republic* 6 (winter 1986): 343–70.

9. Fehrenbacher, *Slaveholding Republic*, 28–33, esp. 33; Kornblith, *Slavery and Sectional Strife*, 33–34; Leonard L. Richards, *The Slave Power: The Free North and Southern Domination, 1780–1860* (Baton Rouge, LA, 2000), chap. 2.

10. Fehrenbacher, *Slaveholding Republic*, 31–33. On southern elitist notions of republicanism, see Harold A. Ohline, "Republicanism and Slavery: Origins of the Three-Fifths Clause in the United States Constitution," *William and Mary Quarterly*, 3rd ser., 28 (Oct. 1971): 563–84; also, Freehling, *Secessionists at Bay*, 146–47.

11. Fehrenbacher, *Slaveholding Republic*, 32–33; Richards, *Slave Power*, 31–34.

12. Fehrenbacher, *Slaveholding Republic*, 33–37.

13. Ibid., 35–36. On anti-black racism in the early Northwest, see Eugene H. Berwanger, *The Frontier against Slavery: Western Anti-Negro Prejudice and the Slavery Extension Controversy* (Urbana, IL, 1967), chaps. 1–2.

14. On differences in racism between the North and South, see Frederickson, *Black Image in the White Mind*, chaps. 2–4. For southern perspectives on the Constitution, see Don E. Fehrenbacher, *Constitutions and Constitutionalism in the Slaveholding South* (Athens, GA, 1989) and *The Dred Scott Case: Its Significance in Law and Politics* (New York, 1978), chaps. 1–2.

15. Smith, quoted in Kornblith, *Slavery and Sectional Strife*, 38. See also Mason, *Slavery and Politics*, chaps. 1–2.

16. For a record of the debate on Hillhouse's initiative, see William Plumer, *Memorandum of Proceedings in the United States Senate, 1803–1807*, ed. Everett Somerville Brown (New York, 1923), 113–16; also, James M. Banner Jr., "James Hillhouse" in *American National Biography*, ed. John A. Garraty and Mark C. Carnes, 24 vols. (New York, 1999), 10:813–14.

17. Jackson, Smith, and Franklin, quoted in Plumer, *Memorandum*, 115–17, 120.

18. Kornblith, *Slavery and Sectional Strife*, 46–47.

19. Hammond and Rudd, quoted in George Dangerfield, *The Awakening of American Nationalism, 1815–1828* (New York, 1965), 108.

20. *New-York Columbian* (New York City), Apr. 26, 1819; Yoshawnda L. Trotter, "James Tallmadge," in Garraty and Carnes, *American National Biography*, 21:280–81; Richards, *Slave Power*, 53–54, 62–68, 121–24. See also David N. Gellman, *Emancipating New York: The Politics of Slavery and Freedom, 1777–1827* (Baton Rouge, LA, 2006), chaps. 7–9.

21. Forbes, *Missouri Compromise and Its Aftermath*, 34; Kornblith, *Slavery and Sectional Strife*, 56.

22. Jay to Daniel Raymond, Dec. 21, 1819, from *The Correspondence and Public Papers of John Jay*, ed. Henry P. Johnson, http://oll.libertyfund.org/title/2330/220826 (accessed Dec. 13, 2011); Roger G. Kennedy, *Burr, Hamilton, and Jefferson: A Study in Character* (New York, 2000), 92.

23. Miller, quoted in Gellman, *Emancipating New York*, 156.

24. Ibid., chap. 8.

25. Tompkins, quoted in ibid., 206; *Albany Advertiser*, Jan. 25, 1817.

26. *Albany Gazette*, Apr. 3, 1817; Donald J. Ratcliffe, "The Decline of Antislavery Politics, 1815–1840," in *Contesting Slavery: The Politics of Bondage and Freedom in the New American Nation*, ed. John Craig Hammond and Matthew Mason (Charlottesville, VA, 2011), 267–90, esp. 269; Freehling, *Secessionists at Bay*, 144–45.

27. From the *Commercial Advertiser* (New York, NY), reprinted in the *Albany Gazette*, July 9, 1817.

28. *New-York Columbian*, Apr. 22, 1819; Dangerfield, *Awakening*, 108.

29. Charles D. Lowery, "James Barbour" and "Philip Pendleton Barbour" in Garraty and Carnes, *American National Biography*, 2:141–44.

30. Charles D. Lowery, *James Barbour: A Jeffersonian Republican* (Tuscaloosa, AL, 1984), 85–86, 84–107, 90, 97, 101, 132.

31. Susan Dunn, *Dominion of Memories: Jefferson, Madison, and the Decline of Virginia* (New York, 2007), 7–12, quotation on 12.

32. For the struggle of great Tidewater planters with economic change, see Timothy H. Breen, *Tobacco Culture: The Mentality of the Great Tidewater Planters on the Eve of Revolution* (Princeton, NJ, 1985), 160–210. On the impact of the Panic of 1819 on Virginia and the Southeast, see John McCardell, *The Idea of a Southern Nation: Southern Nationalists and Southern Nationalism, 1830–1860* (New York, 1979), 20–24.

33. Dunn, *Dominion of Memories*, 9–10, 42, 45; McCardell, *Idea of a Southern Nation*, 23, 25, 339–40. A good study of the massive migration out of Virginia is David Hackett Fischer and James C. Kelly, *Bound Away: Virginia and the Westward Movement* (Charlottesville, VA, 2000).

34. Madison to Francis Corbin, Nov. 26, 1820, in *The Papers of James Madison: Retirement Series*, ed. David B. Mattern, 2 vols. to date (Charlottesville, VA, 2009–), 2:160–61; Lowery, *James Barbour*, 12. On Madison's experience in Virginia's ailing economy, see Drew R. McCoy, *The Last of the Fathers: James Madison and the Republican Legacy* (Cambridge, UK, 1989), 173–92.

35. On the "War Hawks," see Donald R. Hickey, *The War of 1812: A Forgotten Conflict* (Urbana, IL, 1989), 29–30; J. C. A. Stagg, *The War of 1812: Conflict for a Continent* (Cambridge, UK, 2012), 5, 41; and Alan Taylor, *The Civil War of 1812: American Citizens, British Subjects, Irish Rebels, and Indian Allies* (New York, 2010), 128. On the "Old Republicans," see Lance Banning, *The Jeffersonian Persuasion: Evolution of a Party Ideology* (Ithaca, NY, 1978), 284, 290; also, Norman K. Risjord, *The Old Republicans: Southern Conservatism in the Age of Jefferson* (New York, 1965).

36. Randolph, quoted in Edling, *Revolution in Favor of Government*, 145.

37. For Clay's role in the American Colonization Society, see Merrill D. Peterson, *The Great Triumvirate: Webster, Clay, and Calhoun* (New York 1987), 65, 284–86. On the ACS generally, see Eric Burin, *Slavery and the Peculiar Solution: A History of the American Colonization Society* (Gainesville, FL, 2005), and P. J. Staudenraus, *The African Colonization Movement, 1816–1865* (New York, 1961).

38. "Speech at Organization of American Colonization Society," Dec. 21, 1816, in *The Papers of Henry Clay*, ed. James F. Hopkins et al., 10 vols. (Lexington, KY, 1959–1992), 2:263–64; Peterson, *Great Triumvirate*, 10, 51, 123, 236. On the fear that free blacks would become a permanent and disruptive underclass, see Douglas R. Egerton, "'Its Origin is Not a Little Curious': A New Look at the American Colonization Society," *Journal of the Early Republic* 5 (winter 1985): 463–80.

39. Peterson, *Great Triumvirate*, 12–13.

40. Kenneth S. Greenberg, *Honor and Slavery* (Princeton, NJ, 1996), 53–54, 55–62. On Clay as a War Hawk, see Peterson, *Great Triumvirate*, 4, 18, 39–42. On dueling in the pre–Civil War South, see also Wyatt-Brown, *Southern Honor*, 57, 166–67, 328, 349–61, 400.

41. "Gradual Abolition of Slavery . . . ," reprinted in Poulson's *American Daily Advertiser* (Philadelphia, PA), July 7, 1818, 181.

42. *Charleston City Gazette*, quoted in the *City of Washington (DC) Gazette*, Dec. 19, 1817; "ABOLITION OF SLAVERY," *Milledgeville (GA) Reflector*, quoted in the *Christian Messenger* (Middlebury, VT), Nov. 11, 1818.

43. Harper, quoted in Ford, *Deliver Us from Evil*, 71.

44. To Gentlemen of the Colonization Society of Kentucky, Dec. 17, 1829, in Hopkins et al., *Papers of Henry Clay*, 8:138–58, esp. 151; Forbes, *Missouri Compromise and Its Aftermath*, 28–32.

45. James Monroe, "Special Message," Dec. 17, 1819, in *Messages and Papers of the Presidents*, comp. James D. Richardson, 10 vols. (Washington, DC, 1896), 2:63–65. On Monroe's commitment to colonization, see Forbes, *Missouri Compromise and Its Aftermath*, chap. 1.

46. In New York, for example, see Gellman, *Emancipating New York*, 206–13. For the abolitionist response to the colonization idea, see Frederickson, *Black Image in the White Mind*, chap. 1.

CHAPTER TWO: The West

1. John Craig Hammond, "Slavery, Settlement, and Empire: The Expansion and Growth of Slavery in the Interior of the North American Continent, 1770–1820," *Journal of the Early Republic* 32 (summer 2012): 175–206. See also Hammond, *Slavery, Freedom, and Expansion in the Early American West* (Charlottesville, VA, 2007).

2. On the distinction between "slave societies" and "societies with slaves," see Ira Berlin, *Many Thousands Gone: The First Two Centuries of Slavery in North America* (Cambridge, MA, 1998), 8–9, 7–13, 22, 98, 105–8.

3. Paul C. Nagel, *Missouri: A History* (Lawrence, KS), 30–32.

4. For the importance of westward expansion in the Jeffersonian economic vision, see especially Drew R. McCoy, *The Elusive Republic: Political Economy in Jeffersonian America* (Chapel Hill, NC, 1980), 196–208.

5. Stephen Aron, *American Confluence: The Missouri Frontier from Borderland to Border State* (Bloomington, IN, 2006), 151–52.

6. On the limited knowledge of the trans-Mississippi Northwest during early decades of the republic, see Peter J. Kastor, *William Clark's World: Describing America in an Age of Unknowns* (New Haven, CT, 2011).

7. King, quoted in Dangerfield, *Awakening*, 116.

8. Nagel, *Missouri*, 36–48; John Craig Hammond, "'Uncontrollable Necessity': The Local Politics, Geopolitics, and Sectional Politics of Slavery Expansion," in Hammond and Mason, *Contesting Slavery*, 138–60, esp. 142–43.

9. Aron, *American Confluence*, 98–100.

10. Ibid., 154–55, 159, 172–73; Hammond, "Uncontrollable Necessity," 142–43.

11. Hammond, "Uncontrollable Necessity," 140–48.

12. Ford, *Deliver Us from Evil*, 74–5; McCoy, *Last of the Fathers*, 265, 267–74, 280; Peterson, *Great Triumvirate*, 60–61.

13. Ford, *Deliver Us from Evil*, 76.

14. Freehling, *Secessionists at Bay*, 151–52. For statistics on slave population growth, see Songho Ha, *The Rise and Fall of the American System* (London, 2009), 58.

15. Nicholas and Giles, quoted in Ford, *Deliver Us from Evil*, 73.

16. Breckinridge, quoted in ibid., 73–74.

17. *Alexandria (VA) Gazette*, Feb. 19, 1819.

18. See www.loc.gov/rr/program/bib/ourdocs/northwest.html for the text of the Northwest Ordinance.

19. Richard Henry Lee to Francis Lightfoot Lee, July 14, 1787, in Smith et al., *Letters of Delegates*, 24:353–55, esp. 354. On Cutler, see Andrew R. L. Cayton, "'A Quiet Independence': The Western Vision of the Ohio Company," *Ohio History* 90 (winter 1981): 5–32, and *Frontier Republic: Ideology and Politics in the Ohio Country, 1780–1825* (Kent, OH, 1986), 14, 17, 21, 24, 28–30, 111, 153.

20. Dane to King, July 16, 1787, in Smith et al., *Letters of Delegates*, 24:357–59, quotation on 358.

21. Grayson to Monroe, Aug. 8, 1787, ibid., 393–96, esp. 393–94.

22. See Finkelman, "Slavery and the Northwest Ordinance," 347–48.

23. Paul Finkelman, "Evading the Ordinance: The Persistence of Bondage in Indiana and Illinois," *Journal of the Early Republic* 9 (spring 1989): 21–51; Hammond, "Uncontrollable Necessity," 142.

24. Tardiveau, quoted in Finkelman, "Slavery and the Northwest Ordinance," 363.

25. Ibid., 369.

26. "Freeborn Sons," quoted in John Craig Hammond, *Slavery, Freedom, and Expansion in the Early American West* (Charlottesville, VA, 2007), 78; see also 76–95.

27. Ibid., chaps. 5–6.

28. See Nicole Etcheson, *The Emerging Midwest: Upland Southerners and the Political Culture of the Old Northwest, 1787–1861* (Bloomington, IN, 1996). Also, Jeremy Adelman and Stephen Aron, "From Borderlands to Borders: Empires, Nation-States, and the Peoples in Between in North American History," *American Historical Review* 104 (June 1999): 814–23.

29. Hammond, *Slavery, Freedom, and Expansion*, chap. 6; Adam Rothman, *Slave Country: American Expansion and the Origins of the Deep South* (Cambridge, MA, 2005), chap. 7.

30. Several northeastern newspapers noted the closeness of the Illinois vote. See, for example, "Illinois," *Spirit of the Times & Carlisle (PA) Gazette*, Oct. 12, 1818.

31. "[Illinois; Slavery; after Slavery]," *Essex Register* (Salem, MA), Oct. 3, 1818; *National Advocate* (New York City), Sept. 30, 1818; *New-York Daily Advertiser*, Nov. 17, 1818.

32. *National Messenger* (Georgetown, DC), Nov. 25, 1818; *New-York Daily Advertiser*, Nov. 28, 1818.

33. For the Illinois debate, see *Annals of Congress*, House, 15th Cong., 2nd sess., 296–98, 305–11. Also, the report from the *New York Commercial Advertiser*, Nov. 27, 1818, and the *National Intelligencer*, reprinted in the *Spectator* (New York City), Dec. 1, 1818.

34. *Annals of Congress*, House, 15th Cong., 2nd sess., 306–7, 310–11.

35. "NEW STATE OF ILLINOIS SLAVERY," *Times* (Hartford, CT), Dec. 8, 1818.

36. For the Illinois vote, see *Annals of Congress*, House, 15th Cong., 2nd sess., 311.

37. Hammond, *Slavery, Freedom, and Expansion*, 57; Drew R. McCoy, "James Madison and Visions of American Nationality in the Confederation Period: A Regional Perspective," in *Beyond the Confederation: Origins of the Constitution and American National Identity*, ed. Richard Beeman, Stephen Botein, and Edward C. Carter II (Chapel Hill, NC, 1987), 226–58.

38. Robert V. Remini, *Andrew Jackson and the Course of American Empire, 1767–1821* (New York, 1977), 293–94.

39. See Robert V. Remini, *The Battle of New Orleans: Andrew Jackson and America's First Military Victory* (New York, 1999).

40. Jackson, quoted in Rothman, *Slave Country*, 139.

41. Ibid., 170–71. On capitalistic forces in the shaping of slavery and the South, see especially Gavin Wright, *Slavery and American Economic Development* (Baton Rouge, LA, 2006), and Walter Johnson, *River of Dark Dreams: Slavery and Empire in the Cotton Kingdom* (Cambridge, MA, 2013).

42. Christopher Clark, *Social Change in America: From the Revolution to the Civil War* (Chicago, 2006), 123–27, esp. 125; Rothman, *Slave Country*, 177.

43. *Louisiana Gazette*, quoted in Rothman, *Slave Country*, 83.

44. For slaveholders' "paternalism," see generally Eugene D. Genovese, *Roll, Jordan, Roll: The World the Slaves Made* (New York, 1972); for more recent insights, see Ford, *Deliver Us from Evil*, 148–51, 200–203, and Jeffrey R. Young, *Domesticating Slavery: The Master Class in Georgia and South Carolina, 1670–1837* (Chapel Hill, NC, 1999), esp. 6–10, 45, 78, 152–53, 241.

45. "Soldiers' Bounty Lands," from the *Nashville (TN) Whig*, reprinted in the *New Hampshire Patriot* (Concord), Apr. 15, 1817.

46. Aron, *American Confluence*, 153–54.

47. Boon's Lick inhabitants, quoted in ibid., 153.

48. Ibid., 157–58, 158–60, 172.

49. Schoolcraft, quoted in ibid., 160. See Diane Mutti Burke, *On Slavery's Border: Missouri's Small-Slaveholding Households, 1815–1865* (Athens, GA, 2010), chap. 1.

50. Aron, *American Confluence*, 162–63, 164, 172–73.

51. "The 4th July, 1817," *Missouri Gazette and Public Advertiser* (St. Louis), July 12, 1817; David Waldstreicher, *In the Midst of Perpetual Fetes: The Making of American Nationalism, 1776–1820* (Chapel Hill, NC, 1997), 269–93, esp. 270–71.

52. Aron, *American Confluence*, 166–70, Darby quoted on 170.

53. Ibid., 164–65, 173–74, 175–77. See generally David Brion Davis, *Inhuman Bondage: The Rise and Fall of Slavery in the New World* (New York, 2006), esp. chaps.

9–10; also, Walter Johnson, *Soul by Soul: Life Inside the Antebellum Slave Market* (Cambridge, MA, 1999), 58, 117–34.

54. "A VOICE IN THE WILDERNESS," from the *Missouri Gazette*, reprinted in the *Weekly Aurora* (Philadelphia, PA), Feb. 8, 1819; Clark, *Social Change*, 135–36.

55. Silby and Post, quoted in Hammond, *Slavery Freedom, and Expansion*, 59, 61; "The true Ambition of an honest Mind," *Missouri Gazette and Public Advertiser* (St. Louis), Nov. 16, 1808; Burke, *On Slavery's Border*, chap. 1.

56. "BLACK COLONY," *Missouri Gazette and Public Advertiser*, Mar. 22, 1817; Aron, *American Confluence*, 174–77.

57. Hammond, "Uncontrollable Necessity," 148–55.

CHAPTER THREE: Impasse

1. "NEXT CONGRESS," *Cabinet* (Schenectady, NY), Nov. 11, 1818; George Rogers Howell and John H. Munsell, *History of the County of Schenectady, N.Y., from 1662 to 1886* (New York, 1886), 138.

2. William C. Allen, *History of the United States Capitol: A Chronicle of Design, Construction, and Politics* (Washington, DC, 2001), chap. 3. On political life in the early national capital, see James Sterling Young, *The Washington Community, 1800–1828* (New York, 1966).

3. For a clear delineation of strains within the Jeffersonian party, see Richard E. Ellis, "The Market Revolution and the Transformation of American Politics, 1801–1837," in *The Market Revolution in America: Social, Political, and Religious Expressions, 1800–1880*, ed. Melvyn Stokes and Stephen Conway (Charlottesville, VA, 1996), 149–76, esp. 150–53.

4. The 1816 tariff passed with the help of 17 of 50 southern votes in House and 7 of 10 in the Senate, the Bank bill of 1816 with 34 of 51 southern House yeas and 9 of 11 in the Senate (see Ha, *Rise and Fall of the American System*, 49, 53).

5. "SLAVERY," *Albany (NY) Gazette*, Sept. 1, 1817; Bourne, quoted in Glover Moore, *The Missouri Controversy, 1819–1821* (Lexington, KY, 1953), 28; Ratcliffe, "Decline of Antislavery Politics," 269–73, 270; "HORRORS OF SLAVERY," *Columbian Centinel* (Boston, MA), Nov. 12, 1817. On Kendrick, see Richard S. Newman, *The Transformation of American Abolitionism: Fighting Slavery in the Early Republic* (Chapel Hill, NC, 2002), 108–9.

6. See "Remarks of Mr. Cobb, of Georgia," *City of Washington (DC) Gazette*, Mar. 27, 1819.

7. On the "unmasking" of a southern gentleman, see Kenneth S. Greenberg, *Honor and Slavery* (Princeton, NJ, 1996), 25–27.

8. See the report on the Tallmadge Amendment in the *New York Commercial Advertiser*, Feb. 16, 1819. On the concept of "aggressive nationalism," see Richard E. Ellis, *Aggressive Nationalism: McCulloch v. Maryland and the Foundation of Federal Authority in the Young Republic* (New York, 2007).

9. *National Intelligencer,* quoted in the *Mercantile Advertiser* (New York City), Feb. 19, 1819.

10. Hammond, "Uncontrollable Necessity," 147–48.

11. Freehling, *Secessionists at Bay,* 146–48; Richards, *Slave Power,* 44–46.

12. Richards, *Slave Power,* 44–46; Peter B. Knupfer, *The Union as It Is: Constitutional Unionism and Sectional Compromise, 1787–1861* (Chapel Hill, NC, 1991), 96. See Barbour's speech of Feb. 10, 1820, *Annals of Congress,* House, 16th Cong., 1st sess., 1218–42, esp. 1231–32. On earlier Federalist dissatisfaction, see James M. Banner Jr., *To the Hartford Convention: The Federalists and the Origins of Party Politics in Massachusetts, 1789–1815* (New York, 1970).

13. "Missouri—Slaves," *Washington Whig* (Bridgeton, NJ), Feb. 23, 1819; "STATE OF MISSOURI," *Richmond (VA) Enquirer,* Feb. 25, 1819; *City Gazette* (Charleston, SC), Feb. 26, 1819; Philip P. Barbour, *Annals of Congress,* House, 16th Cong., 1st sess., 1391.

14. On the persistence of cross-sectional pre–Civil War reverence for the Union, see, for example, Paul C. Nagel, *One Nation Indivisible: The Union in American Thought, 1776–1861* (New York, 1964), and Knupfer, *Union as It Is.*

15. On Tallmadge's free-soil intentions, see the *New York Commercial Advertiser,* Feb. 16, 1819. See also Woods, "What Twenty-First Century Historians Have Said about the Causes of Disunion," 426–28; Larry Gara, "Slavery and the Slave Power: A Crucial Distinction," *Civil War History* 15 (Mar. 1969): 5–18; and Susan-Mary Grant, *North Over South: Northern Nationalism and American Identity in the Antebellum Era* (Lawrence, KS, 2000).

16. Wyatt-Brown, *Southern Honor,* 19; "PORTRAITURE OF SLAVERY," from the *American Monthly Magazine and Critical Review,* reprinted in the *Albany Argus* (Albany, NY), July 11, 1817; "THOUGHTS ON SLAVERY," *American Watchman* (Wilmington, DE), July, 23, 1817; *Alexandria (VA) Gazette,* Feb. 19, 1819.

17. *Poulson's American Daily Advertiser* (Philadelphia, PA), Nov. 26, 1819; "Slavery and the Missouri Question," *North American Review* (Jan. 1820), quoted in Joshua Michael Zeitz, "The Missouri Compromise Reconsidered: Antislavery Rhetoric and the Emergence of the Free Labor Synthesis," *Journal of the Early Republic* 20 (Fall 2000): 447–85, quotation on 471–72.

18. Clark, *Social Change,* 16, 158, 138–41, 152, 173–74, 227–28.

19. Larson, *Market Revolution in America,* 42–43.

20. "Statesmen and Politicians, Political Economy—No. I," *Niles' Weekly Register,* June 7, 1817. On Niles, see also Knupfer, *The Union as It Is,* 97–98.

21. [Mathew Carey], *Considerations on the Impropriety and Inexpedience of Renewing the Missouri Question* (Philadelphia, 1820), 6–7, 39–40, 69; Matthew Mason, "The Maine and Missouri Crisis: Competing Priorities and Northern Slavery Politics in the Early Republic," *Journal of the Early Republic* 33 (winter 2013): 675–700, esp. 699. See also David M. Potter, *The Impending Crisis, 1848–1861,* ed. Don E. Fehrenbacher (New York, 1976), 43–45. On Carey's antislavery views, see

Beverly C. Tomek, *Colonization and Its Discontents: Emancipation, Emigration, and Antislavery in Antebellum Pennsylvania* (New York, 2011), 63–92.

22. "Remarks on Tallmadge Amendment," Feb. 15, 1819, in Hopkins et al., *Papers of Henry Clay*, 2:670. On the possible compatibility of slavery and the "American System," see Andrew Shankman, "Neither Infinite Wretchedness nor Positive Good: Mathew Carey and Henry Clay on Political Economy and Slavery during the Long 1820s," in Hammond and Mason, *Contesting Slavery*, 247–66. James Madison, following the controversy from retirement at Montpellier, agreed with Clay's view: "[T]he Missouri question, as a constitutional one, amounts to the question, whether the condition proposed to be annexed to the admission of Missouri would or would not be void in itself, or become void the moment the territory should enter as a State within the pale of the Constitution." And as an issue of "expediency & humanity," he continued, reflecting his acceptance of the "diffusion" theory, "it depends essentially on the probable influence of such restrictions on the quantity & duration of slavery, and on the general condition of slaves in the U.S." See Madison to Robert Walsh Jr., Nov. 27, 1819, in Mattern et al., *Papers of James Madison: Retirement Series*, 1:553–58, quotation on 557.

23. For Taylor's speech, see *Annals of Congress*, House, 15th Cong., 2nd sess., 1170–79, esp. 1170, 1174. For Fuller's speech, see ibid., 1179–84. On Taylor, see Richards, *Slave Power*, 70, 75–81, 89, 95, 122.

24. *Annals of Congress*, House, 15th Cong., 2nd sess., 1191–93 (esp. 1193), 1205.

25. For Barbour's speech, ibid., 1184–91.

26. *Annals of Congress*, House, 15th Cong., 2nd sess., 1188.

27. Ibid., 1195–1203, 1204.

28. For Tallmadge's speech and Cobb's reply, see ibid., 1203–14, 1214; Greenberg, *Honor and Slavery*, 25. On southern threats of secession during the Missouri crisis, see Elizabeth R. Varon, *Disunion! The Coming of the American Civil War, 1789–1859* (Chapel Hill, NC, 2008), 39–53. On the importance to slaveholding southerners of being regarded as true Americans, see William J. Cooper Jr., *Liberty and Slavery: Southern Politics to 1860* (New York, 1983), 142.

29. *Alexandria (VA) Gazette*, Feb. 17, 1819. For the vote, see *Annals of Congress*, House, 15th Cong., 2nd sess., 1214–15, and Senate, 273.

30. Whitman, quoted in Forbes, *Missouri Compromise and Its Aftermath*, 46. See *Annals of Congress*, House, 15th Cong., 2nd sess., 1272–82, and Senate, 272–73. Also, Freehling, *Secessionists at Bay*, 149–50, and Moore, *Missouri Controversy*, 59–64.

31. Letter to the editor, *St. Louis Enquirer*, Mar. 31, 1819.

32. *New-York Daily Advertiser*, Feb. 19 and 20, 1819; Resolutions of the New York Manumission Society, in the *Spectator* (New York City), Mar. 9, 1819.

33. *New-Hampshire Sentinel* (Keene), June 5, 1819; Hammond, "Uncontrollable Necessity," 138–39. For an opposing view, see Moore, *Missouri Controversy*, 65, 170, 342.

34. Freehling, *Secessionists at Bay*, 150–52; Varon, *Disunion*, 33–34; Mason, *Slavery and Politics*, 188–91.

35. "Amphictyon" [William Brockenbrough], *Richmond Enquirer*, Mar. 30–Apr. 2,

1819, reprinted in *John Marshall's Defense of McCulloch v. Maryland*, ed. Gerald Gunther (Stanford, CA, 1969), 71; Fehrenbacher, *South and Three Sectional Crises*, 19–20.

36. "Hampden," quoted in John L. Larson, *Internal Improvement: National Public Works and the Promise of Popular Government in the Early United States* (Chapel Hill, NC, 2000), 132–33.

37. *Preamble and Resolutions offered by Mr. Baldwin, to the House of Delegates, on the Missouri Question* (Richmond, 1819); *Richmond Enquirer*, quoted in the *Edwardsville (IL) Spectator*, June 26, 1819.

38. *St. Louis Enquirer*, May 19, 1819.

39. "MOB AT BOON'S LICK," *Edwardsville (IL) Spectator*, Aug. 28, 1819, reprinted in the *Alexandria (VA) Herald*, Oct. 7, 1819; "Early Journalism in Missouri," Missouri Digital Newspaper Project, the State Historical Society of Missouri, http://shs.nm system.edu/newspaper/mdnp/earlyjournalism.shtml (accessed Aug. 15, 2012).

40. "St. Louis, Missouri," in the *Cherry-Valley (NY) Gazette*, June 27, 1820; from the *Missouri Gazette*, June 23, 1819, reprinted in the *Edwardsville (IL) Spectator*, June 16, 1819. Resident of Franklin, MO, quoted in Hammond, *Slavery, Freedom, and Expansion*, 55. See also, Thomas Hart Benton, *Thirty Years' View; or, A History of the Working of the American Government for Thirty Years, from 1820 to 1850*, 2 vols. (New York, 1879), 1:5.

41. Robert J. Brugger, *Beverley Tucker: Heart over Head in the Old South* (Baltimore, MD, 1978), 45–65, esp. 52–53.

42. Ibid., 53–57.

43. Meeting in St. Louis, reported in the *Political Intelligencer* (Fredericktown, MD), June 26, 1819.

44. See Jefferson to John Breckinridge, Aug. 12, 1803, in *The Portable Thomas Jefferson*, ed. Merrill D. Peterson (New York, 1975), 494–97, esp. 496; James Madison, "Federalist, No. 10," in *The Federalist*, ed. Jacob E. Cooke (New York, 1961), 56–65.

45. [Carey], *Considerations*, 35, 65, 66–67, 68–69.

46. "Remarks on the Missouri Compromise," July 26, 1848, in *The Papers of John C. Calhoun*, ed. Robert L. Meriwether et al., 28 vols. (Columbia, SC, 1959–2003), 25:630–33, quotation on 632.

47. Daniel Raymond, *The Missouri Question* (Baltimore, 1819), 4, 9, 18–19, 20.

48. Ibid., 21, 33, 36.

49. "SLAVERY DEPRECATED," *Berkshire Star* (Stockbridge, MA), Apr. 1, 1819; *New-York Daily Advertiser*, Mar. 29, 1819; "THE MEETING AT NEW-YORK," *Daily National Intelligencer* (Washington, DC), Nov. 22, 1819.

50. [Joseph Blunt], *An Examination of the Expediency and Constitutionality of Prohibiting Slavery in the State of Missouri* (New York, 1819), 3, 5–6, 7–10.

51. Ibid., 8, 9–10, 12, 13. For Jefferson's conclusions about blacks, see "Notes on the State of Virginia," in Peterson, *Portable Thomas Jefferson*, 192–93.

52. For Peters's antislavery perspective and his involvement in the colonization movement, see the *Constitution of the Hartford Auxiliary Colonization Society* (Hartford, 1819) in Special Collections and University Archives, University of Mas-

sachusetts, Amherst (online at www.library.umass.edu/spcoll/digital/antislavery/154 .pdf).

53. "Prohibition of Slavery in Missouri," Jan. 18, 1820, in *American State Papers* 038, *Miscellaneous*, vol. 2, report no. 481.

54. "Prohibition of Slavery in Missouri," Jan. 12, 1820, ibid., report no. 479.

55. Matthew Mason, "Necessary but Not Sufficient: Revolutionary Ideology and Antislavery Action in the Early Republic," in Hammond and Mason, *Contesting Slavery*, 11–31.

CHAPTER FOUR: Compromises

1. "Letter from Dr. Floyd," from the *Lexington (VA) News-Letter*, reprinted in the *St. Louis Enquirer*, May 6, 1820.

2. "AN ELEGY ON SLAVERY," *Herald of the Times* (Fincastle, VA), April 16, 1821.

3. See Charles D. Lowery, "John Floyd," in Garraty and Carnes, *American National Biography*, 8:147–48. On Floyd's politics in later years, see William J. Cooper Jr., *The South and the Politics of Slavery, 1828–1856* (Baton Rouge, LA, 1978), 12, 16–17, 45.

4. "Letter from Dr. Floyd."

5. For recent perspectives on Nat Turner's rebellion, see *Nat Turner: A Slave Rebellion in History and Memory*, ed. Kenneth S. Greenberg (New York, 2003).

6. "Speech on the Admission of Maine," Dec. 30, 1819, in Hopkins et al., *Papers of Henry Clay*, 2:740–48, esp. 742. For a shrewd analysis of Clay as a strategist of sectional compromise, see Knupfer, *Union as It Is*, 21–22, 119–57.

7. On Clay's American System, see Peterson, *Great Triumvirate*, 68–84, and Maurice G. Baxter, *Henry Clay and the American System* (Lexington, KY, 1995).

8. David S. Heidler and Jeanne T. Heidler, *Henry Clay: The Essential American* (New York, 2010), 145–46; Peterson, *Great Triumvirate*, 56–9.

9. Heidler and Heidler, *Henry Clay*, 144; Forbes, *Missouri Compromise and Its Aftermath*, 36, 121.

10. "Remarks on Bill for Missouri Statehood," Feb. 13, 1819, and "Remarks on Tallmadge Amendment," Feb. 15, 1819, in Hopkins et al., *Papers of Henry Clay*, 2:669–70; Peterson, *Great Triumvirate*, 60.

11. Peterson, *Great Triumvirate*, 59–62.

12. For expression of Clay's economic worries, see Clay to Langdon Cheves, Apr. 19, 1819, in Hopkins et al., *Papers of Henry Clay*, 2:687–8.

13. "Toast and Speech at New Orleans," May 19, 1819; "Toasts and Speech at Hopkinsville Dinner," July 3, 1819, ibid., 692–93, 697; Aron, *American Confluence*, 187–92, 194, 198–99.

14. "Response to Resolution of Thanks," Mar. 3, 1819, in Hopkins et al., *Papers of Henry Clay*, 2:680.

15. "Speech on the Admission of Maine," Dec. 30, 1819, ibid., 2:740, 742.

16. Clay to Kendall, Jan. 8, 1820; Clay to Beatty, Jan. 22, 1820; Clay to Combs, Feb. 15, 1820; Clay to Holley, Feb. 17, 1820, ibid., 752–53, 766–67, 780, 780–81.

17. Robert Walsh to Madison, Jan. 2, 1820, in Mattern et al., *Papers of James Madison: Retirement Series*, 1:580–81, quotation on 581; James Barbour to Madison, Feb. 10, 1820; ibid., 2:8–9 (for Madison's response, see ibid., 10–11); Moore, *Missouri Controversy*, 92–93, 97–98.

18. *St. Louis Enquirer*, Mar. 25, 1820, reprinted from the *Richmond Enquirer*, Feb. 17, 1820; *New-Hampshire Sentinel* (Keene), Apr. 22, 1820; *Gazette* (Portland, ME), Feb. 22, 1820.

19. *New-York Daily Advertiser*, Feb. 24, 1819. For the Senate vote on the Thomas Amendment, see *Annals of Congress*, Senate, 16th Cong., 1st sess., 428. Also, Forbes, *Missouri Compromise and Its Aftermath*, 46–47. For clues to Thomas's Illinois strategy, see "A REPUBLICAN," *Edwardsville (IL) Spectator*, Oct. 3, 1820, and Mar. 27, 1821. Also, Joseph E. Suppiger, "Amity to Enmity: Ninian Edwards and Jesse B. Thomas," *Journal of the Illinois State Historical Society* 67 (Apr. 1974): 201–11.

20. *New-York Evening Post*, Feb. 12, 1820; *Annals of Congress*, House, 16th Cong., 1st sess., 1201; Forbes, *Missouri Compromise and Its Aftermath*, chap. 3.

21. For analysis of the House vote, see Moore, *Missouri Controversy*, 107–11, and Fehrenbacher *Three Sectional Crises*, 18–19, 69.

22. Ritchie, quoted in Richard H. Brown, "The Missouri Crisis, Slavery, and the Politics of Jacksonianism," *South Atlantic Quarterly* 65 (winter 1966): 55–72, quotation on 60–61.

23. Ibid., 56.

24. See Ha, *Rise and Fall of the American System*, 63, 67, 72, 75, 92, 104, 120.

25. Fullerton, reported in the *American Advocate* (Hallowell, ME), Apr. 8, 1820. See also Mason, "Maine and Missouri Crisis," 676–78.

26. *Rhode Island American*, quoted in the *Hallowell (ME) Gazette*, June 14, 1820; *New Hampshire Sentinel*, quoted in ibid., Sept. 6, 1820.

27. On the "doughfaces," see Moore, *Missouri Controversy*, 103–6, 201–3, 209–17, and Richards, *Slave Power*, chap. 4.

28. "The Missouri Question," *Niles' Weekly Register* (Baltimore, MD), Nov. 20, 1819.

29. "The Late Election," *Centinel of Freedom* (Newark, NJ), Feb. 15, 1820; "PATERSON MEETING," ibid., Oct. 3, 1820; "To the persons who may compose the next Republican State Convention," ibid., Sept. 19, 1820.

30. *Annals of Congress*, House, 16th Cong., 1st sess, 1578–83, esp. 1578–80, 1582.

31. "To the Freeman of New-Jersey," *Centinel of Freedom* (Newark, NJ), Aug. 8, 1820.

32. "To the persons who may compose the next Republican State Convention," ibid., Sept. 19, 1820.

33. *Annals of Congress*, House, 16th Cong., 1st sess., 1583–86.

34. "THE ADVOCATES OF SLAVERY in the State of New-York, EXPOSED," *Northern Whig* (Hudson, NY), Apr. 11, 1820.

35. Vassalboro meeting, reported in the *Hallowell (ME) Gazette*, Feb. 9, 1820; Henry Putnam, "Maine Not to Be Coupled with the Missouri Question," broadsheet

(Brunswick, ME, 1820). On the earlier conflict between residents of the District of Maine and propertied Bostonians, leading to the momentum for separation, see Alan Taylor, *Liberty Men and Great Proprietors: The Revolutionary Settlement on the Maine Frontier, 1790–1820* (Chapel Hill, NC, 1990).

36. "The Missouri Question," *Weekly Eastern Argus* (Portland, ME), Jan. 18, 1820; "ADMISSION OF MAINE," *Hallowell Gazette*, Jan. 19, 1820; "MAINE AND MISSOURI," from the *American Advocate* (Hallowell, ME), reprinted in the *Eastport (ME) Sentinel*, Feb. 19 and 26, 1820; Mason, "Maine and Missouri Crisis," 682–83.

37. *Weekly Eastern Argus*, Apr. 11 and 25, 1820; "MR. HOLMES' CERTIFICATES," *Gazette* (Portland, ME), May 16, 1820; *American Advocate* (Hallowell, ME), May 13, 1820.

38. Holmes to King, Mar. 29, 1820, quoted in Ronald F. Banks, *Maine Becomes a State: The Movement to Separate Maine from Massachusetts, 1785–1820* (Portland, ME, 1973), 197, see also 184, 187–88, 196, 199–201, 244–45n.

39. Mark Langdon Hill, "Fellow Citizens of the State of Maine," *Bangor (ME) Weekly Register*, Apr. 27, 1820.

40. Hill to King, Jan. 28, 1820, quoted in Banks, *Maine Becomes a State*, 192; Madison to Hill, April [post-17], 1820, in Mattern et al., *Papers of James Madison: Retirement Series*, 2:56–57. On Holmes, Hill, and the eventual political success of "doughfaces" in Maine, see Mason, "Maine and Missouri Crisis," 687–98.

41. See Monroe to Andrew Jackson, Mar. 1, 1817, in *The Writings of James Monroe*, 7 vols., ed. Stanislaus Murray Hamilton (New York, 1902), 6:4–6.

42. Monroe to Thomas Jefferson, July 27, 1817, ibid., 4–6, quotation on 5; 26–29, quotation on 27; "First Annual Message," in Richardson, *Messages and Papers of the Presidents*, 2:11–20, esp. 12; "Second Annual Message," ibid., 39–47, quotation on 46.

43. Monroe to Thomas Jefferson, Feb. 7, 1820, in Hamilton, *Writings of James Monroe*, 6:113–15, quotation on 114.

44. William Plumer Jr. to William Plumer Sr., Feb. 12 and 20, 1820, in William Plumer Jr., *The Missouri Compromises and Presidential Politics, 1820–1825*, ed. Everett Somerville Brown (St. Louis, MO, 1926), 8–12, quotation on 10. On Monroe's skillful behind-the-scenes politics, see esp. Forbes, *Missouri Compromise and Its Aftermath*, chap. 3.

45. Monroe to Thomas Jefferson, Feb. 19, 1820, in Hamilton, *Writings of James Monroe*, 115–16, esp. 116; Monroe to Jefferson, May 1820, ibid., 119–23, esp. 123; Monroe to Andrew Jackson, May 23, 1820, ibid., 126–30, esp. 128; Monroe to Albert Gallatin, May 26, 1820, ibid., 130–34, esp. 131–32.

46. Calhoun to Andrew Jackson, June 1, 1820, in Meriwether et al., *Papers of John C. Calhoun*, 5:164–65, quotation on 164; Calhoun to Virgil Maxcy, Aug. 12, 1820, ibid., 327–28, quotation on 327; Calhoun to Charles Tait, Oct. 26, 1820, ibid., 412–14, quotation on 413.

47. John Quincy Adams, *Memoirs of John Quincy Adams, Comprising Portions of His Diary from 1795 to 1848*, ed. Charles Francis Adams, 12 vols. (Philadelphia, 1874–1877), 5:3–14, quotations on 4, 12.

48. Monroe to James Madison, May 10, 1822, in Hamilton, *Writings of James Monroe*, 284–91, quotations on 289, 291.

49. Jefferson to John Holmes, Apr. 22, 1820, in Peterson, *Portable Thomas Jefferson*, 567–69; Stuart Leibiger, "Thomas Jefferson and the Missouri Crisis: An Alternative Interpretation," *Journal of the Early Republic* 17 (spring 1997): 121–30; Hammond, "Uncontrollable Necessity," 138.

50. See Jefferson, "Notes on the State of Virginia," in Peterson, *Portable Jefferson*, 185–93.

51. Leibiger, "Thomas Jefferson and the Missouri Crisis," 123; Mason, "Maine and Missouri Crisis," 691–92. On Jefferson's devotion to the Union, see Peter S. Onuf, *Jefferson's Empire: The Language of American Nationhood* (Charlottesville, VA, 2000), 8–10, 109–46.

52. Jefferson to Holmes, Apr. 22, 1820, in *The Writings of Thomas Jefferson*, ed. Paul Leicester Ford, 10 vols. (New York, 1892–1899) 10:159. (Ford wrongly transcribed "ear" as "ears." See www.monticello.org/site/jefferson/wolf-ears. For the Library of Congress polygraph copy, see http://memory.loc.gov/master/mss/mtj/mtj1/051/1200/1238.jpg.) According to the Roman biographer Suetonius, the expression "wolf by the ears" may have originated with Emperor Tiberius. "The cause of his hesitation was fear of the dangers which threatened him on every hand, and often led him to say that he was 'holding a wolf by the ears,'" Suetonius remarked in his *Lives of the Twelve Caesars*. Jefferson's library at Monticello contained a 1718 edition of Suetonius's works. Some modern scholars, however, have credited the expression to an ancient Greek proverb.

53. Article 3, section 26, of the Missouri Constitution authorized the state legislature "as soon as may be, to pass such laws as may be necessary, First, to prevent free negroes and mulattoes from coming to, and settling in this state, under any pretext whatsoever." See Forbes, *Missouri Compromise and Its Aftermath*, 108, 110.

54. *Weekly Eastern Argus* (Portland, ME), Jan. 2, 1821.

55. "MISSOURI QUESTION," *St. Louis Enquirer*, Mar. 4, 1820.

56. "MISSOURI QUESTION," *Genius of Liberty* (Leesburg, VA), Feb. 8, 1820; "PUBLIC MEETING AT BOSTON," *Boston Patriot*, Mar. 15, 1820, reprinted in the *American Beacon* (Norfolk, VA), Mar. 27, 1820; "MISSOURI," *Baltimore American*, reprinted in *American Beacon*, Nov. 23, 1820.

57. Dangerfield, *Awakening*, 130–32; Forbes, *Missouri Compromise and Its Aftermath*, 8, 119, 272, 283, 311–12. On Illinois's black code, see Elmer Gertz, "The Black Laws of Illinois," *Journal of the Illinois State Historical Society* (autumn 1963): 454–73, esp. 463–45.

58. *Annals of Congress*, 16th Cong., 1st sess., 228; Gene Allen Smith, *The Slaves' Gamble: Choosing Sides in the War of 1812* (New York, 2013), 210–11.

59. Madison to Monroe, Nov. 19, 1820, in Mattern et al., *Papers of James Madison: Retirement Series*, 2:151–53, quotation on 151; Dangerfield, *Awakening*, 132–36.

60. Monroe to Madison, Nov. 16, 1820, in Mattern et al., *Papers of James Madison: Retirement Series*, 2:149–50; Dangerfield, *Awakening*, 133–34.

61. Peterson, *Great Triumvirate*, 62–65; Forbes, *Missouri Compromise and Its Aftermath*, 10, 112–19, 125, 207.

62. Dangerfield, *Awakening*, 135–36, 136n; Forbes, *Missouri Compromise and Its Aftermath*, 118–19, 311–12.

CHAPTER FIVE: Aftermath

1. On Higbee's Tavern, see John E. Wright, *Lexington: Heart of the Bluegrass* (Lexington, KY, 1982), 7–8, and Charles R. Staples, *The History of Pioneer Lexington, 1779–1806* (Lexington, KY, 1939), 34–35.

2. Benton, *Thirty Year's View*, 1:5.

3. "Toast and Response at Public Dinner," May 19, 1821, in Hopkins et al., *Papers of Henry Clay*, 3:79–82, esp. 81–82; Robert V. Remini, *Henry Clay: Statesman for the Union* (New York, 1991), 197. On linkage of the Baldwin tariff vote to the Missouri crisis, see Ha, *Rise and Fall of the American System*, 66–67, and Moore, *Missouri Controversy*, 321–30.

4. See Lewis Tappan to Clay, June 22 and July 20, 1835, in Hopkins et al., *Papers of Henry Clay*, 8:773–74, 793; Clay to Frederick Freeman, Sept. 27, 1837, ibid., 9:80–81; "Speech in Senate," Feb. 7, 1839, ibid., 278–83.

5. Ritchie, introduction to John Taylor, *Constructions Construed and Constitutions Vindicated* (Richmond, VA, 1820), i; ibid., 291; Larson, *Internal Improvement*, 123–26, 135–6.

6. Aron, *American Confluence*, 187–92.

7. Robert Baird, *View of the Valley of the Mississippi; or, The Emigrant's and Traveler's Guide to the West* (Philadelphia, PA, 1832), 89, 232–33.

8. On Vesey, see especially Douglas R. Egerton, *He Shall Go Out Free: The Lives of Denmark Vesey* (Lanham, MD, 2004). For "Atlantic creoles," see Berlin, *Many Thousands Gone*, 17–28, 39–45.

9. For Charleston on the eve of the Vesey plot, see William W. Freehling, *Prelude to Civil War: The Nullification Controversy in South Carolina, 1816–1836* (New York, 1965), chap. 1, and Ford, *Deliver Us from Evil*, chap. 7.

10. Genovese, *Roll, Jordan, Roll*, 244–45; Alan Taylor, *The Internal Enemy: Slavery and War in Virginia, 1772–1832* (New York, 2013), 349.

11. McCardell, *Idea of a Southern Nation*, 340; Wyatt-Brown, *Southern Honor*, 404–6.

12. According to the early South Carolina historian W. G. Sims, Vesey "had been a spectator of the insurrection on that island [of Saint-Domingue], and brought with him a taste for its horrors to Carolina." See Sims, *The History of South Carolina* (Charleston, SC, 1840), app., 328.

13. On the revolution in Saint-Domingue, see Laurent Dubois and and John D. Garrigus, *Slave Revolution in the Caribbean, 1789–1804: A Brief History with Documents* (New York, 2006). For the reaction in America to revolutionary violence abroad,

see Rachel Hope Cleves, *The Reign of Terror in America: Visions of Violence from Anti-Jacobinism to Antislavery* (Cambridge, UK, 2009), chap. 2.

14. Kornblith, *Slavery and Sectional Strife*, 40–44, Tucker quoted on 43; Gellman, *Emancipating New York*, 103–4, 108–24. For Gabriel's Plot, see Douglas R. Egerton, *Gabriel's Rebellion: The Virginia Slave Conspiracies of 1800 and 1802* (Chapel Hill, NC, 1993), and James Sidbury, *Ploughshares into Swords: Race, Rebellion, and Identity in Gabriel's Virginia, 1730–1810* (Cambridge, UK, 1997).

15. On the Stono Rebellion, see Peter Charles Hoffer, *Cry Liberty: The Great Stono River Slave Rebellion of 1739* (New York, 2010).

16. For Charleston in the 1820s, see Freehling, *Prelude to Civil War*, chap. 1.

17. Wyatt-Brown, *Southern Honor*, 408, 415; Egerton, *He Shall Go Out Free*, 124–25, 130–31. On slaves' perceptions of their masters, see Genovese, *Roll, Jordan, Roll*, 123–49. For an interpretation that casts doubt on the reliability of the *Official Report*, and therefore the reality of the whole conspiracy, but not on the authenticity of whites' reaction and their tendency to blame the Missouri debate, see Michael P. Johnson, "Denmark Vesey and His Co-Conspirators," *William and Mary Quarterly*, 3rd Ser., 58 (Oct. 2001): 915–76.

18. Ford, *Deliver Us from Evil*, 230–31.

19. Ibid., 207–8, 214, 234–35.

20. Ibid., 208–9.

21. *Charleston Courier*, July 10, 1822; Governor Bennett's statement, reprinted in *The Daily Georgian*, Aug. 27, 1822; Wyatt-Brown, *Southern Honor*, 425.

22. "Account of the Negro Plot at Charleston, S.C.," *Baltimore Patriot*, Aug. 30, 1822, and "Negro Plot at Charleston," *Alexandria Gazette*, Sept. 5, 1822; "An Appeal to the People of the United States," *Daily Georgian*, Aug. 13, 1825; Poinsett to James Monroe, Aug. 22, 1822, quoted in Ford, *Deliver Us from Evil*, 239. Harby and Moultrie, quoted in Egerton, *He Shall Go Out Free*, 210, 167. For insight into Bennett's reaction, see Wyatt-Brown, *Southern Honor*, 419–21.

23. *Edwardsville (IL) Spectator*, Oct. 5, 1822; Tallmadge, quoted in Rothman, *Slave Country*, 211; "Remarks of Mr. Walsh, in the *National Gazette*," reprinted in *Salem Gazette*, Sept. 10, 1822.

24. For the aftermath of the Vesey scare, see Ford, *Deliver Us from Evil*, chaps. 8–9.

25. On the Negro-Seaman Act controversy, see Freehling, *Prelude to Civil War*, 111–16.

26. On the Gibbons case, see Thomas H. Cox, *Gibbons v. Ogden: Law, and Society in the Early Republic* (Athens, OH, 2009).

27. Michael F. Holt, *The Political Crisis of the 1850s* (New York, 1978), 6–8.

28. Harry L. Watson, *Liberty and Power: The Politics of Jacksonian America* (New York, 1990), chaps. 2–3; and Robert V. Remini, *Andrew Jackson: The Course of American Freedom, 1822–1832* (New York, 1981), chaps. 2–5.

29. See Brown, "Missouri Crisis, Slavery, and the Politics of Jacksonianism," 58–72; Knupfer, *Union As It Is*, 92.

30. On the election of 1824, see Sean Wilentz, *The Rise of American Democracy: Jefferson to Lincoln* (New York, 2005), 240–53, and Howe, *What Hath God Wrought*, 203–11.

31. On Jackson's campaign, see Remini, *Andrew Jackson: The Course of American Freedom*, chaps. 4–5.

32. For a brief introduction to the "corruption" theme in early-republic politics, see Watson, *Liberty and Power*, 10, 12, 46, 93.

33. Regarding the so-called corrupt bargain, see Remini, *Andrew Jackson: The Course American Freedom*, 89–99, 103–5, and Peterson, *Great Triumvirate*, 128–31.

34. Van Buren to Ritchie, Jan. 13, 1827, quoted in Holt, *Political Crisis of the 1850s*, 20–21.

35. See generally Ratcliffe, "Decline of Antislavery Politics."

36. McCardell, *Idea of a Southern Nation*, 24–26, quotation on 25.

37. Jeremiah Gloucester, from "An Oration on the Abolition of the Slave Trade," 1823; James Forten, from "An Address Delivered before the Ladies' Anti-Slavery Society of Philadelphia," 1836, both in *American Antislavery Writings: Colonial Beginnings to Emancipation*, ed. James G. Basker (New York, 2012), 232–36, quotation on 236; 331–35, quotation on 333. On Forten, see also Tomek, *Colonization and Its Discontents*, 132–62.

38. Gerrit Smith to Henry Clay, 1839, and James Russell Lowell, "Compromise," 1850, both in Basker, *American Antislavery Writings*, 376–78, quotation on 377, 546–49, quotation on 547. William Lloyd Garrison to Friends of the Anti-Slavery Movement, Apr. 18, 1836; Garrison to Henry Clay, Mar. 16, 1849; Garrison to Nathan R. Johnston, Oct. 15, 1860, in *The Letters of William Lloyd Garrison*, ed. Walter M. Merrill and Louis Ruchames, 6 vols. (Cambridge, MA, 1971–1981), 2:84–85; 3:608–13, quotation on 609–10; 4:696–67.

39. Michael F. Holt, *The Fate of their Country: Politicians, Slavery Extension, and the Coming of the Civil War* (New York, 2004), 12–14.

40. On Polk's foreign policy, see Charles G. Sellers Jr., *James K. Polk, Continentalist, 1843–1846* (Princeton, NJ, 1966); David M. Pletcher, *The Diplomacy of Annexation: Texas, Oregon, and the Mexican War* (Columbia, MO, 1973); and Paul H. Bergeron, *The Presidency of James K. Polk* (Lawrence, KS, 1987).

41. Holt, *Fate of Their Country*, 19–49. For the Mexican-American War, see Amy S. Greenberg, *A Wicked War: Polk, Clay, Lincoln, and the 1846 U.S. Invasion of Mexico* (New York, 2012). On the Wilmot Proviso, see additionally Chaplain W. Morrison, *Democratic Politics and Sectionalism: The Wilmot Proviso Controversy* (Chapel Hill, NC, 1967), and Eric Foner, "The Wilmot Proviso Revisited," *Journal of American History* 56 (Sept. 1969): 262–79.

42. Holt, *Fate of Their Country*, 27–28, 29–33; Knupfer, *Union as It Is*, 161–67, esp. 162.

43. Holt, *Fate of Their Country*, 30–36.

44. "Remarks at a Public Meeting in Charleston," Aug. 19, 1848, in Meriwether et al., *Papers of John C. Calhoun*, 26:15–19, esp. 17; "The Address of Southern Delegates

in Congress, to their Constituents," adopted Jan. 22, 1849, ibid., 225–44, esp. 227, 232–33, 234. See also Holt, *Fate of Their Country*, 32–33.

45. Thomas R. Dew, in *The Pro-slavery Argument: As Maintained by the Most Distinguished Writers of the Southern States*, . . . (Charleston, 1852), 451–62, esp. 451, 453, 457, 461–62; Larson, *Market Revolution in America*, 159, 150–51.

46. Laurel Summers to Calhoun, Oct. 21, 1848, in Meriwether et al., *Papers of John C. Calhoun*, 26:100–101; "A FRIEND OF THE UNION" to Calhoun, Nov. 18, 1848, ibid., 134–36, esp. 134–35.

47. Z. L. Nabers to Calhoun, Nov. 29, 1848, ibid., 144–45; Nathan Gaither to Calhoun, Dec. 2, 1848, ibid., 145–46; Wilson Lumpkin to Calhoun, Jan. 3, 1849, ibid., 199–200.

48. "Resolutions of the Legislature of Virginia in Relation to Slavery," Feb. 5, 1849, S. Misc. Doc., 48, 30th Cong., 2nd sess. (serial no. 533), 1–2.

49. "Resolutions of the General Assembly of Missouri, on the Subject of Slavery in the Territories, District of Columbia, and States," Dec. 31, 1849, H. Misc. doc., 5, 31st Cong., 1st sess. (serial no. 581), 1–2.

50. See Christopher Childers, "Interpreting Popular Sovereignty: A Historiographical Essay," *Civil War History* 57 (March 2011): 48–70, and *The Failure of Popular Sovereignty: Slavery, Manifest Destiny, and the Radicalization of Southern Politics* (Lawrence, KS, 2012).

51. On the election of 1848 and events following, see Joseph G. Rayback, *Free Soil: The Election of 1848* (Lexington, KY, 1970); Frederick J. Blue, *The Free Soilers: Third Party Politics, 1848–1854* (Urbana, IL, 1973); and Jonathan H. Earle, *Jacksonian Antislavery and the Politics of Free Soil, 1824–1854* (Chapel Hill, NC, 2004).

52. For the Whig Party and President Taylor's handling of the post-1848 sectional dispute, see especially Michael F. Holt, *The Rise and Fall of the American Whig Party: Jacksonian Politics and the Onset of the Civil War* (New York, 1999).

53. Toombs, quoted in Fehrenbacher, *Three Sectional Crises*, 25.

54. On the Compromise of 1850, see Mark J. Stegmaier, *Texas, New Mexico, and the Compromise of 1850: Boundary Dispute and Sectional Crisis* (Kent, OH, 1996).

55. Holt, *Rise and Fall of the American Whig Party*, chaps. 15–16.

56. For the view that the political settlement of 1850 represented more of an "armistice" than a compromise, see Potter, *Impending Crisis*, 90–120. Peter Knupfer likewise calls the 1850 compromise "a transition event" (see Knupfer, *Union as It Is*, 20).

57. Holt, *Fate of their Country*, 6, 109–12.

58. On Douglas and his responsibility for the Kansas-Nebraska Act, see Robert W. Johannsen, *Stephen A. Douglas* (New York, 1973), chap. 17, and Michael A. Morrison, *Slavery and the American West: The Eclipse of Manifest Destiny and the Coming of the Civil War* (Chapel Hill, NC, 1997), chap. 5

59. James Osborne Putnam, *The Missouri Compromise. Sketch of the Remarks of James O. Putnam, upon the Nebraska Resolutions, February 3, 1854* (Albany, NY, 1854). See also "The Slave Question," *Niles' Weekly Register*, Mar. 11, 1820, esp. 26.

60. "Resolutions of the Legislature of New York . . . ," S. Misc. Doc. 22, 33rd Cong., 1st sess. (serial no. 705), 1–2; "Resolutions of the Legislature of Connecticut . . . ," S. Misc. Doc., 62, 33rd Cong., 1st sess. (serial no. 705), 1; "Resolutions of the General Assembly of the State of Connecticut . . . ," H. Misc. Doc. 96, 33rd Cong., 1st sess. (serial no. 741), 1.

61. Breckinridge, quoted in Morrison, *Slavery and the American West*, 146.

62. Eric Foner, *Free Soil, Free Labor, Free Men: The Ideology of the Republican Party before the Civil War* (New York, 1970), chaps. 1–3.

63. John B. Jones to John C. Calhoun, Dec. 14, 1848, in Meriwether et al., *Papers of John C. Calhoun*, 26:169–71, esp. 170.

64. Foner, *Free Soil, Free Labor, Free Men*, 92, 87–89.

65. David Herbert Donald, *Lincoln* (London, 1995), 168, 170.

66. On the Dred Scott decision, see Potter, *Impending Crisis*, chap. 11, and Don E. Fehrenbacher, *The Dred Scott Case*, and Austin Allen, *Origins of the Dred Scott Case: Jacksonian Jurisprudence and the Supreme Court, 1837–1857* (Athens, GA, 2006).

67. Potter, *Impending Crisis*, 267–70.

68. Ibid., 275–76.

69. Ibid., 286–93; Fehrenbacher, *Slaveholding Republic*, 80, 281.

70. Foner, *Free Soil, Free Labor, Free Men*, 84, 97, 100–101, 181, 290, 292–93; Johannsen, *Douglas*, 568–75; Donald, *Lincoln*, 206–9.

71. John Greenleaf Whittier, "To a Southern Statesman" [probably Calhoun], in *The National Era*, Jan. 27, 1848.

Epilogue: Willard's Hotel

1. Letter from Washington, Jan. 1, 1861, in *Henry Adams in the Secession Crisis: Dispatches to the Boston Daily Advertiser, December 1860–March 1861*, ed. Mark J. Stegmaier (Baton Rouge, LA, 2012), 64.

2. Potter, *Impending Crisis*, 530–32. On Crittenden, see Damon R. Eubank, *In the Shadow of the Patriarch: The John J. Crittenden Family in War and Peace* (Macon, GA, 2009).

3. Lincoln to Kellogg, Dec. 11, 1860, in *The Collected Works of Abraham Lincoln*, ed. Roy P. Basler, 8 vols. (New Brunswick, NJ, 1953), 4:150.

4. Knupfer, *Union as It Is*, 206–11.

5. On the origins of southern nationalism, see McCardell, *Idea of a Southern Nation*, esp. 3–4, 11–48.

6. Adam Goodheart, *1861: The Civil War Awakening* (New York, 2011), 85, 396n63. See also Robert Gray Gunderson, *Old Gentlemen's Convention: The Washington Peace Conference of 1861* (Madison, WI, 1961).

Essay on Sources

The following brief discussion hardly exhausts the massive literature on slavery and sectionalism in the politics of the early-republic and antebellum periods, a body of scholarship well refreshed by recent studies. Many of the selected titles below include extensive bibliographies, furnishing readers far more comprehensive guides to this material than space permits here.

Many younger writers have become attuned to cultural forces—at national, regional, and local levels—in the shaping of political decisions, and this book contends that the Missouri crisis is best approached in such fashion. The "market revolution" of the pre–Civil War period also has received considerable attention since the 1990s, but only a little of that new light has been directed on the Missouri struggle. With the governance of the early republic still so much an experimental work in progress at that time, leaders (top down) and constituents (bottom up) both thought they could affect policy making in fateful ways. The voices and perceptions of ordinary people, more accessible today than ever because of online digital collections of newspapers, pamphlets, rare books, and other once-obscure publications, provide for a richer story of the Missouri crisis, its antecedents, and its long-term reverberations than historians have been able to tell before.

Among secondary works, the classic monograph remains Glover Moore, *The Missouri Controversy, 1819–1821* (Lexington, KY, 1953), even though more recent studies have discredited some of its basic conclusions. Robert P. Forbes, *The Missouri Compromise and Its Aftermath: Slavery and the Meaning of America* (Chapel Hill, NC, 2007), stands as the most comprehensive revisionist study, especially strong in telling the Washington-insider political story of the compromise. Some writers overstate the pervasiveness of the slavery issue, seeing it as operating everywhere in the politics of the early republic, not only where it did but also where it did not. For well-balanced perspectives, see Michael A. Morrison, *Slavery and the American West: The Eclipse of Manifest Destiny and the Coming of the Civil War* (Chapel Hill, NC, 1997); John Craig Hammond, *Slavery, Freedom, and Expansion in the Early American West* (Charlottesville, VA, 2007); Peter B. Knupfer, *The Union as It Is: Constitutional Unionism and Sectional Compromise, 1787–1861* (Chapel Hill, NC, 1991); and Matthew Mason, *Slavery and Politics in the Early Republic* (Chapel Hill, NC, 2006). Knupfer and Mason also fill in the rich backstory of the slavery issue, compromises in national politics, and changing civic culture prior to 1819. Gary J. Kornblith's brief *Slavery and Sectional Strife in the Early American Republic, 1776–1821* (Lanham, MD, 2010) also traces a host of Missouri-related issues back to the beginning of the nation. George Dangerfield's *The Awakening of American Nationalism, 1815–1828* (New York, 1965), following up his prize-winning *The Era of Good Feelings* (New York, 1952), addresses the Missouri Compromise(s) within the framework of a wider struggle between "economic" and "democratic" types of nationalism. A pair of key essay collections demands attention: *Congress and the Emergence of Sectionalism: From the Missouri Compromise to the Age of Jackson*, ed. Paul Finkelman and Donald R. Kennon (Athens, OH, 2008), and *Contesting Slavery: The Politics of Bondage and Freedom in the New American Nation*, ed. John Craig Hammond and Matthew Mason (Charlottesville, VA, 2011). See also three especially perceptive articles: Richard H. Brown, "The Missouri Crisis, Slavery, and the Politics of Jacksonianism," *South Atlantic Quarterly* 65 (winter 1966): 55–72; Joshua M. Zeitz, "The Missouri Compromise Reconsidered: Rhetoric and the Emergence of the Free Labor Synthesis," *Journal of the Early Republic* 20 (fall 2000): 447–85; and Sean Wilentz, "Jeffersonian Democracy and the Origins of Political Antislavery in the United States: The Missouri Controversy Revisited," *Journal of the Historical Society* 4 (fall 2004): 375–401.

Among many studies of the slavery issue in American politics, see Don E. Fehrenbacher, *The South and Three Sectional Crises* (Baton Rouge, LA, 1980) and *The Slaveholding Republic: An Account of the United States Government's Relations to Slavery* (New York, 2001), along with William J. Cooper Jr., *The South and the Politics of Slavery, 1828–1856* (Baton Rouge, LA, 1980). William W. Freehling's massive *The Road to Disunion*, vol 1: *Secessionists at Bay, 1776–1854* (New York, 1990) and vol. 2: *Secessionists Triumphant, 1854–1861* (New York, 2007), emphasize contingency, the importance of individual decision making, and the fear among both southerners and northerners that the other side stood determined to undercut their essential liberties. Among older works, Donald Robinson, *Slavery in the Structure of American Politics, 1765–1820* (New York, 1971), and John Chester Miller, *The Wolf by the Ears: Thomas Jefferson and Slavery* (New York, 1977), still merit attention. David F. Ericson, *Slavery in the American Republic: Developing the Federal Government, 1791–1861* (Lawrence, KS, 2011) argues that slavery contributed positively to American state development by obligating the federal government to create the policy infrastructure needed to protect and maintain the institution.

For pre–Civil War politics and belief more generally, David M. Potter, *The Impending Crisis, 1848–1861* (New York, 1976), remains essential reading. Sean Wilentz's *The Rise of American Democracy: Jefferson to Lincoln* (New York, 2005) and Daniel Walker Howe's *What Hath God Wrought: The Transformation of America, 1815–1848* (New York, 2007) both offer the most up-to-date comprehensive treatments of the early republic period generally. Morrison's *Slavery and the American West* shows how opposing concepts of the meaning of the American Revolution eventually drove a philosophical wedge between North and South, as both sections looked westward. Elizabeth Varon's *Disunion! The Coming of the American Civil War, 1789–1859* (Chapel Hill, NC, 2010) traces, among other themes, the often subtle ways that political leaders used the threat to dissolve the republic in pursuing various partisan and sectional ends.

Michael F. Holt's extensive work, especially but not limited to *The Political Crisis of the 1850s* (New York, 1978), *The Rise and Fall of the American Whig Party: Jacksonian Politics and the Onset of the Civil War* (New York, 1999), and *The Fate of Their Country: Politicians, Slavery Extension, and the Coming of the Civil War* (New York, 2004), provides the most expert understanding of pre–Civil War party politics at both national and state levels. For the Wilmot Proviso, see Chaplain W. Morrison, *Democratic Politics and Sectionalism: The Wilmot Proviso Controversy* (Chapel Hill, NC, 1967). On the problems of nation building in the early republic, see Max M. Edling, *A Revolution in Favor of Government: Origins of the U.S. Constitution and the Making of the American State* (New York, 2003), and Brian Balogh, *A Government Out of Sight: The Mystery of National Authority in Nineteenth-Century America* (Cambridge, UK, 2009). Regarding the rise of the Republican Party, see Eric Foner, *Free Soil, Free Labor, Free Men: The Ideology of the Republican Party before the Civil War* (New York, 1970), and William E. Gienapp, *The Origins of the Republican Party, 1852–1856* (New York, 1987).

Regarding the vast literature on the institution of slavery in America and the white attitudes that sustained it, some excellent places to start include Winthrop Jordan, *White over Black: American Attitudes toward the Negro, 1550–1812* (Chapel Hill, NC, 1968); George M. Frederickson, *The Black Image in the White Mind: The Debate on Afro-American Character and Destiny, 1817–1914* (New York, 1971); Edmund S. Morgan, *American Slavery, American Freedom: The Ordeal of Colonial Virginia* (New York, 1975); Ira Berlin, *Many Thousands Gone: The First Two Centuries of Slavery in North America* (Cambridge, MA, 2000); Walter Johnson, *Soul by Soul: Life Inside the Antebellum Slave Market* (Cambridge, MA, 2000); and Peter Kolchin, *American Slavery, 1619–1877* (New York, 1993). Also, the extensive scholarship of Eugene D. Genovese, including but not limited to *The Political Economy of Slavery: Studies in the Economy and Society of the Slave South* (New York, 1961), *Roll, Jordan, Roll: The World the Slaves Made* (New York, 1974), *Slavery in Black and White: Class and Race in the Southern Slaveholders' New World Order* (Cambridge, UK, 2008), and, with Elizabeth Fox Genovese, *Fatal Self-Deception: Slaveholding Paternalism in the Old South* (Cambridge, UK, 2011), has transformed the landscape of slavery studies over the past half century. Two important works challenging the idea that southern slavery was essentially noncapitalistic and pre-"modern" are Gavin Wright, *Slavery and American Economic Development* (Baton Rouge, LA, 2006), and Walter Johnson, *River of Dark Dreams: Slavery and Empire in the Cotton Kingdom* (Cambridge, MA, 2013). Most of the information historians have on Denmark Vesey is derived from white sources collected during investigation of the Vesey plot. See especially Douglas R. Egerton, *He Shall Go Out Free: The Lives of Denmark Vesey* (Madison, WI, 1999), and John Lofton, *Insurrection in South Carolina: The Turbulent World of Denmark Vesey* (Yellow Springs, OH, 1964).

It is tempting for modern writers (and, certainly, for popular filmmakers) to interject their own moral judgment in favor of antislavery northerners and to depict southern slaveholders as flattened, almost one-dimensional characters. Among the more carefully calibrated works on the antebellum South and slaveholders, see Lacy

K. Ford, *Deliver Us from Evil: The Slavery Question in the Old South* (New York, 2009); Bertram Wyatt-Brown, *Southern Honor: Ethics and Behavior in the Old South* (New York, 1982); and Robert J. Brugger, *Beverley Tucker: Heart over Head in the Old South* (Baltimore, 1978). Michael O'Brien's *Conjectures of Order: Intellectual Life in the American South, 1810–1860,* 2 vols. (Chapel Hill, NC, 2004) places the development of antebellum southern thought, including proslavery belief, in a transatlantic framework.

From the enormous body of work on the antislavery movement, see especially, David Brion Davis, *The Problem of Slavery in the Age of Revolution, 1770–1823* (Ithaca, NY, 1975) and *Inhuman Bondage: The Rise and Fall of Slavery in the New World* (New York, 2006). Richard S. Newman's *The Transformation of American Abolitionism: Fighting Slavery in the Early Republic* (Chapel Hill, NC, 2002) pushes the origins of the radical abolitionist movement back to the earliest years of the republic. James Brewer Stewart, in his *Abolitionist Politics and the Coming of the Civil War* (Amherst, MA, 2008), shows the steady agency of small numbers of abolitionist agitators in bringing about the final reckoning with slavery. On gradual emancipation in the northern states, see Arthur Zilversmit, *The First Emancipation: The Abolition of Slavery in the North* (Chicago, 1967), and Joanne Pope Melish, *Disowning Slavery: Gradual Emancipation and "Race" in New England, 1780–1860* (Ithaca, NY, 1998).

On constitutionalism and law as relating to slavery, see William M. Wiecek, *The Sources of Antislavery Constitutionalism in America, 1760–1848* (Ithaca, NY, 1977); George William Van Cleve, *A Slaveholders' Union: Slavery, Politics, and the Constitution in the Early American Republic* (Chicago, 2010); David Waldstreicher, *Slavery's Constitution: From Revolution to Ratification* (New York, 2009); Austin Allen, *Origins of the Dred Scott Case: Jacksonian Jurisprudence and the Supreme Court, 1837–1857* (Athens, GA, 2006); Don E. Fehrenbacher, *Sectional Crisis and Southern Constitutionalism* (Baton Rouge, LA, 1995) and *Slavery, Law, and Politics: The Dred Scott Case in Historical Perspective* (New York, 1981); and Peter B. Knupfer, *The Union as It Is: Constitutional Unionism and Sectional Compromise, 1787–1861* (Chapel Hill, NC, 1991).

Leading works on the market revolution and social transformation include Christopher Clark, *Social Change in America: From the Revolution through the Civil War* (Chicago, 2006); John L. Larson, *Internal Improvement: National Public Works and the Promise of Popular Government in America* (Chapel Hill, NC, 2000) and *The Market Revolution in America: Liberty, Ambition, and the Eclipse of the Common Good* (Cambridge, UK, 2009); Charles G. Sellers, *The Market Revolution: Jacksonian America, 1815–1846* (New York, 1991); and Howe, *What Hath God Wrought.* John Ashworth's two major volumes, *Slavery, Capitalism, and Politics in the Antebellum Republic,* vol. 1: *Commerce and Compromise, 1820–1850* (Cambridge, UK., 1995) and vol. 2: *The Coming of the Civil War, 1850–1861* (Cambridge, UK, 2007), offer a Marxist perspective, emphasizing not individual agency but labor systems and class conflict. On political economy in America from the Revolution to the Jacksonian period, the work of Drew R. McCoy, *The Elusive Republic: Political Economy in Jeffersonian America* (Chapel Hill, NC, 1980) and *The Last of the Fathers: James Madison and the Republican*

Legacy (Cambridge, UK, 1989), remains indispensable. For an excellent collection of essays on this material, see especially *The Market Revolution in America: Social, Political, and Religious Expressions, 1800–1880*, ed. Melvyn Stokes and Stephen Conway (Charlottesville, VA, 1996).

On the cultural importance of early American newspapers and magazines in this period, see Jeffrey L. Pasley, *"The Tyranny of the Printers": Newspaper Politics in the Early Republic* (Charlottesville, VA, 2001), and Richard R. John, *Spreading the News: The Postal System from Franklin to Morse* (Cambridge, MA, 1995). On the concept of the "public sphere" as applied to the early republic, see John L. Brooke, "Consent, Civil Society, and the Public Sphere in the Age of Revolution and the Early American Republic," in *Beyond the Founders: New Approaches to the Political History of the Early American Republic*, ed. Jeffrey L. Pasley, Andrew W. Robertson, and David Waldstreicher (Chapel Hill, NC, 2004), 207–50, and David Waldstreicher, *In the Midst of Perpetual Fetes: The Making of American Nationalism, 1776–1820* (Chapel Hill, NC, 1997).

On cultural change in the North, see David N. Gellman, *Emancipating New York: The Politics of Slavery and Freedom, 1777–1827* (Baton Rouge, LA, 2006); Beverly C. Tomek, *Colonization and Its Discontents: Emancipation, Emigration, and Antislavery in Antebellum Pennsylvania* (New York, 2011); and, more generally, Leonard L. Richards, *The Slave Power: The Free North and Southern Domination, 1780–1860* (Baton Rouge, 2000). Susan-Mary Grant's *North over South: Northern Nationalism and American Identity in the Antebellum Era* (Lawrence, KS, 2000) concentrates on how northern nationalists by the 1840s increasingly defined themselves by negative reference to the southerners and their culture. Marc Egnal, in *Clash of Extremes: The Economic Origins of the Civil War* (New York, 2009), contends that economic development, especially in the Northeast and Northwest, provided the essential discontinuity between sections that led to civil war.

For the West, Adam Rothman, in *Slave Country: American Expansion and the Origins of the Deep South* (Cambridge, MA, 2005), provides an indispensable study of slavery expansion into the Southwest in decades following the American Revolution. Hammond's *Slavery, Freedom, and Expansion* is masterly in showing not only the extent of federal governmental weakness in the West but also how federal policymakers often bowed to local practices and preferences regarding slavery. See also Hammond's "Slavery, Settlement, and Empire: The Expansion and Growth of Slavery in the Interior of the North American Continent, 1770–1820," *Journal of the Early Republic* 32 (summer 2012). By contrast, William H. Bergmann, in *The American Nation State and the Early West* (Cambridge, UK, 2012), views federal state-building efforts in the Northwest before 1815 as being much more effective than many other historians have supposed. Also for the Northwest, see Nicole Etcheson, *The Emerging Midwest: Upland Southerners and the Political Culture of the Old Northwest, 1787–1861* (Bloomington, IN, 1996), and Andrew R. L. Cayton, *The Frontier Republic: Ideology and Politics in the Ohio Country, 1780–1825* (Kent, OH, 1986). For the Northwest Ordinance and its antecedents, see Peter S. Onuf, *The Origins of the Federal Republic:*

Jurisdictional Controversies in the United States, 1775–1787 (Philadelphia, PA, 1983). On anti-black racism in the Northwest, see Eugene H. Berwanger, *The Frontier against Slavery: Western Anti-Negro Prejudice and the Slavery Extension Controversy* (Urbana, IL, 1967), and Dana Elizabeth Weiner, *Race and Rights: Fighting Slavery and Prejudice in the Old Northwest, 1830–1870* (DeKalb, IL, 2013). On the Louisiana Purchase, see Jon Kukla, *A Wilderness So Immense: The Louisiana Purchase and the Destiny of America* (New York, 2003), and Peter J. Kastor, *The Nation's Crucible: The Louisiana Purchase and the Creation of America* (New Haven, CT, 2004).

For general background on Missouri, see Stephen Aron, *American Confluence: The Missouri Frontier from Borderland to Border State* (Bloomington, IN, 2006), and Paul C. Nagel, *Missouri: A History* (New York, 1977). Diane Mutti Burke's *On Slavery's Borders: Missouri's Small-Slaveholding Households, 1815–1865* (Athens, GA, 2010) argues that various geographical and economic influences kept slavery in the Mississippi and Missouri River counties on a smaller scale, milder, and more intimate between whites and blacks than in the Deep South. Alternatively, Jeffrey C. Stone, in *Slavery, Southern Culture, and Education in Little Dixie: Missouri, 1820–1860* (New York, 2006), examines slaveholders' paternalistic practices in the central region of the state, "Little Dixie," where the ratio of slaves to whites did approach those of areas farther south.

INDEX

Sumner, Charles, 70

Supreme Court, U.S., 135, 156; *Dred Scott* case, 155–56; *McCulloch v. Maryland*, 3, 79, 83, 112. *See also individual court cases*

Tait, Charles, 113

Tallmadge, James, 1, 4, 16–20, 29, 45–47, 64, 66–67, 68, 74, 76, 77–78, 133, 142; opposition to three-fifths clause, 75

Tallmadge Amendment, 1, 40, 74, 115, 135; broader implications of, 4, 65; and diffusion, 67; enacting gradual emancipation, 19, 27, 63, 70, 82; House vote on, 75–76; opposed by Clay, 24, 93, 94; opposition to, 82, 94, 103, 108, 110, 137; reflecting antislavery passions, 49, 63–64, 78; seen as threat to republicanism, 75, 80, 82; Senate vote on, 75–76; similarities with Wilmot Proviso, 143, 146; support for, 15, 16, 76, 78, 83, 111, 136

Taney, Roger B., 155, 156

Tappan, Lewis, 124

Tardiveau, Barthelemi, 41

tariffs, 58, 135, 160; of 1816, 62, 120; of 1820, 123; of 1828 and 1832, 134; opposition to, 3, 23, 64, 74; as part of Clay's "American System," 93, 101; support for, 25, 28, 72, 73, 83, 95, 137

Taylor, John, of Caroline, 20, 21

Taylor, John W., 94, 98, 119–20

Taylor, Zachary, 146, 147, 148, 149

Tazewell, Littleton, 91

Tecumseh, 48

Télémaque (free black), 126. *See also* Vesey, Denmark

Tennessee, 5, 47, 48, 117; admission to Union, 31; manumission society in, 27; migrants from, 34, 43, 44; slavery in, 37, 39, 125

Texas, 5, 49, 142; annexation of, 33, 101, 112, 115, 141–42; boundary question regarding, 149, 154

Thatcher, George, 37

36°30' line, 4, 33, 106, 112, 115, 141, 144, 146, 156, 161; defining trans-Mississippi frontier, 33; and *Dred Scott* case, 155, 156; and free-labor expansion, 4, 101; possible extension of, to Pacific, 105, 143, 147, 149, 159; repeal of, 151, 152, 154; as restriction on slavery,

2, 98, 99, 110, 143, 150, 155, 161; in Thomas Amendment, 98, 99

Thomas, Jesse B., 44, 47, 91, 76, 103; and Thomas Amendment, 2, 98

Thomas, Mary Pendleton, 20

Thomas Amendment, 2, 33, 98, 112, 117, 151

three-fifths clause, 12, 13, 14, 66, 67, 75, 78, 88, 97, 159

Tiffin, Edward, 42

Tompkins, Caleb, 106

Tompkins, Daniel D., 18

Toombs, Robert, 148

treaties, 34, 47, 49

Treaty of Paris (1763), 34, 40

Treaty of Paris (1783), 7–8

Treaty of San Lorenzo, 34

Troup, George M., 23

Troup, Robert, 17

Tucker, Nathaniel Beverley, 82–83

Tucker, St. George, 23, 82, 129

Turner, Nat, 92

Tyler, John, 142, 161

Tyranny Unmasked (Taylor), 124

United States: devotion to Union among citizens, 71, 78, 112; territorial limits, 3; threats of disunion, 75, 79, 96–97, 99, 148, 153, 159. *See also* North; South; West; West, trans-Mississippi

Upper South, 5, 11, 26, 36, 39, 43, 50, 62, 82. *See also* Arkansas; North Carolina; Tennessee; Virginia

Utah, 148, 149

Van Buren, Martin, 138

Vermont, 8, 19, 43, 59

Vesey, Denmark, 126–28, 129–33

Vesey, Joseph, 126

Virginia, 138, 139, 146, 161; cession of western land claims to U.S., 8, 45; economy of, in post-Revolution period, 21–22

"Virginia Dynasty," 67

"Virginia Resolutions" (Madison), 124

Walsh, Robert, Jr., 97

Ware, Ashur, 108

War Hawks, 23, 24, 25, 73, 120